T0328563

Transition from Slavery in Zanzibar and Mauritius

This book is a product of CODESRIA Comparative Research Network with the Zanzibar Indian Ocean Research Institute (ZIORI) and the University of Mauritius.

Transition from Slavery in Zanzibar and Mauritius

A Comparative History

Abdul Sheriff
Vijayalakshmi Teelock
Saada Omar Wahab
Satyendra Peerthum

CODESRIA

Council for the Development of Social Science Research in Africa
DAKAR

© CODESRIA 2016

Council for the Development of Social Science Research in Africa
Avenue Cheikh Anta Diop, Angle Canal IV
BP 3304 Dakar, 18524, Senegal
Website : www.codesria.org

ISBN : 978-2-86978-680-6

All rights reserved. No part of this publication may be reproduced or transmitted in any form or by any means, electronic or mechanical, including photocopy, recording or any information storage or retrieval system without prior permission from CODESRIA.

Typesetting: Alpha Ousmane Dia
Cover Design: Ibrahima Fofana

Distributed in Africa by CODESRIA
Distributed elsewhere by African Books Collective, Oxford, UK
Website: www.africanbookscollective.com

The Council for the Development of Social Science Research in Africa (CODESRIA) is an independent organisation whose principal objectives are to facilitate research, promote research-based publishing and create multiple forums geared towards the exchange of views and information among African researchers. All these are aimed at reducing the fragmentation of research in the continent through the creation of thematic research networks that cut across linguistic and regional boundaries.

CODESRIA publishes *Africa Development*, the longest standing Africa based social science journal; *Afrika Zamani*, a journal of history; the *African Sociological Review*; the *African Journal of International Affairs*; *Africa Review of Books* and the *Journal of Higher Education in Africa*. The Council also co-publishes the *Africa Media Review*; *Identity, Culture and Politics: An Afro-Asian Dialogue*; *The African Anthropologist, Journal of African Tranformation, Method(e)s: African Review of Social Sciences Methodology*, and the *Afro-Arab Selections for Social Sciences*. The results of its research and other activities are also disseminated through its Working Paper Series, Green Book Series, Monograph Series, Book Series, Policy Briefs and the CODESRIA Bulletin. Select CODESRIA publications are also accessible online at www.codesria.org.

CODESRIA would like to express its gratitude to the Swedish International Development Cooperation Agency (SIDA), the International Development Research Centre (IDRC), the Ford Foundation, the Carnegie Corporation of New York (CCNY), the Norwegian Agency for Development Cooperation (NORAD), the Danish Agency for International Development (DANIDA), the Netherlands Ministry of Foreign Affairs, the Rockefeller Foundation, the Open Society Foundations (OSFs), TrustAfrica, UNESCO, UN Women, the African Capacity Building Foundation (ACBF) and the Government of Senegal for supporting its research, training and publication programmes.

Contents

Preface

Abdul Sheriff

The coincidence of two islands in the western Indian Ocean of a similar size in terms of area and population, but with different histories of human habitation, and more particularly, with a contrasting experience of slavery, provided a unique case for comparative history of transition from slavery in Zanzibar and Mauritius. While the former is close to the East African coast, and has been settled by humans for perhaps as long as thirty centuries, the latter in the middle of the Indian Ocean was uninhabited when discovered by the Europeans in the sixteenth century. The Europeans came with a system of slavery that was an extension from the familiar Atlantic system, although slaves came from a broader range of sources, including Asia, Madagascar and Africa. Zanzibar, on the other hand, had been involved in intimate commercial, social and cultural interactions across the Indian Ocean for at least two millennia, including slave trade and slavery that was tinged by an older slavery tradition influenced by Islam. In the nineteenth century, dependent slave systems developed on the islands; but while Zanzibar represented a variant of an Indian Ocean slave system, Mauritius represented a variant of the Atlantic system – yet both flourished when the world was already under the hegemony of the global capitalist mode of production.

The opportunity was therefore taken by two directors of the Zanzibar Indian Ocean Research Institute (ZIORI), Professors Abdul Sheriff and Vijayalakshmi Teelock, to initiate a research project on a comparative history of slavery and its transition to free labour in the two islands. The research was undertaken primarily by two young scholars, Mrs Saada Wahab and Mr Satyendra Peerthum, who conducted intensive research in their respective countries, and was coordinated by the two directors. The project was kindly funded by the Council for the Development of Social Science Research in Africa (CODESRIA). We are very grateful to the Executive Secretary of CODESRIA, Dr Ebrima Sall, for encouraging us to undertake such a study; to Abdon Kouassivi Sofonnou, for following up on our progress with many helpful suggestions; and, finally, to Tesfaye Tafesse, for his very pertinent comments which helped us finalise our report. The CODESRIA grant enabled us to organise three workshops – the inaugural and final workshops in Zanzibar in December 2011 and April 2012, and the mid-term workshop in Mauritius in January 2012, which allowed us to work more closely to bring out the comparative aspect of our programme.

We hope that the comparative study on Mauritius and Zanzibar will prove helpful to those involved in comparing the Atlantic experience with that in the Indian Ocean for the better understanding of both.

List of Tables, Figures and Photographs

Tables

Figures

Photographs

Abbreviations

MNA   Mauritius National Archives
ZNA   Zanzibar National Archives
BPP   British Parliamentary Papers
PRO   Public Record Office (British National Archive)

Glossary

Affranchissement	Manumission of the slave or apprentice through purchase or freed by his or her owner
Arpent	Old French measurement for land. One arpent is equivalent to 1.043 acres (one hectare is equivalent to 2.47 acres or 2.57 arpents)
Bredes	Leafy green vegetables
Camp des Noirs Libres	Suburb of Port Louis, capital of Mauritius, housing freed slaves in the eighteenth century
Edda	The transitional period, after divorce or a husband's death during which a woman cannot remarry
Gens de Couleur	A free Coloured or a legally free non-European, usually of African, Malagasy, European and Asian origin or of mixed ancestry
Harem	Private area of a Muslim household
Kijakazi	Slave girl
Maroonage	The practice of slaves running away from their owners
Matricule Department	The office where government-owned slaves, during the French and early British Period, were housed, clothed, fed and put to work
Metayage	Sharecropping
Metayers	A sharecropper or a land tenant who shares his produce with his landlord in exchange for the use of his land
Mzalia/ Wazalia	Born slave(s), born into the owner's household
Mjinga	Fresh, unskilled slave from interior of Africa
Mjakazi	Female slave who worked as a domestic servant
Non-praedial slaves	Non-agricultural slaves
Pas Géometriques	Crown land or government land located near or on the sea coast
Petit morcellement	The small-scale sub-division of plots of land which took place during the mid-nineteenth century
Praedial slaves	Agricultural slaves
Procureur General	Attorney-General
Sharia	Islamic law dictated either by Qur'an or Sunna (the Prophet's tradition)

Suria	Female slave who cohabitated with the slave master as a secondary wife with certain legal rights and social status
Temps margoze	Expression in Mauritian Creole concerning the bitter days or the days of slavery
Vieux affranchis	Freed slaves or slaves who were freed prior to 1 February 1835, either by purchasing their own freedom or being manumitted by their owner
Wachukuzi	Porters
Wasia	Testament or will

Contributors

Abdul Sheriff was born and educated in Zanzibar. He studied Geography (BA 1964) and African History (MA 1966) at the University of California at Los Angeles, and African History (PhD 1971) at the School of Oriental and African Studies (SOAS), University of London. He taught history at the University of Dar es Salaam (1969-1991); was Chairman and Member of the Presidential Committees on the State University of Zanzibar (1995-2002); Advisor and Principal Curator of the Zanzibar Museums (1993-2005); Executive Director of the Zanzibar Indian Ocean Research Institute (ZIORI 2007-12); and Chairman of the Tanzania Constitutional Forum (2011-15). He has written or edited a number of books, including *Slaves, Spices & Ivory in Zanzibar* (1987), *Zanzibar Under Colonial Rule* (ed. with Ed Ferguson, 1991), *History & Conservation of Zanzibar Stone Town* (1995), *The Dhow Cultures of the Indian Ocean – Cosmopolitanism, Culture & Islam* (2010), and *The Indian Ocean: Oceanic Connections & the Creation of New Societies* (ed. with Engseng Ho, 2014), as well numerous scholarly articles. He was awarded the Prince Claus Award 'in recognition of exceptional achievement in the field of culture and development' in 2005. Professor Sheriff's current research interest is on the history of Zanzibar, the Swahili coast and the Indian Ocean.

Vijayalakshmi Teelock teaches and researches Mauritian and Indian Ocean History at the University of Mauritius. She is Founder and Coordinator of the Centre for Research on Slavery and Indenture at the University of Mauritius; and Member of the UNESCO International Committee of the Slave Route Project. She has published *Bitter Sugar: Slavery and Slavery in 19th century Mauritius* (1998), *Select Guide to Sources of Slavery* (1994) ; edited with Thomas Vernet an Inventory of Sources on Mauritian Slavery from the Col C4, French National Archives (2011) and *Traites, esclavage et Transtition vers l'engagisme* (2015), amongst other publications. Professor Teelock has coordinated numerous projects relating to the history and archaeology of Slavery and Indenture, and Heritage in Mauritius.

Saada Omar Wahab is an Assistant Lecturer teaching and doing research on history at the State University of Zanzibar (SUZA). She studied History (Master of Arts) at the University of Dar es Salaam with a thesis on 'Nationalization and Re-Distribution of Land in Zanzibar: The Case Study of Western District, 1965-2008.' She is currently preparing for PhD studies on the History of Maritime Trade: A Case Study of Indian Traders in Zanzibar, c. 1870s – 1963.

Satyendra Peerthum obtained his B.A (Hons) in History from the University of Cape Town and M.A. from the University of Mauritius. In 2004, he was an awardee of an Outstanding Young Person of the Year by the Young Economic Chamber of Mauritius. He was a Researcher for the Truth and Justice Commission (2009-11), the Nelson Mandela Centre for African Culture, and the National Heritage Fund (2002, 2003, 2010). He was a part-time lecturer in history at the University of Mauritius (2002-2007) and the Charles Telfair Institute (2012-2013). He is now based in the Research Unit of the Aapravasi Ghat World Heritage Site in Port Louis, Mauritius. He coordinated two international indentured labour conferences (in 2011, 2014) and several AGTF publications. His areas of specialisation include the study of slavery, indentured labour system, the Mauritian working class and cultural heritage issues in Mauritius. He has presented academic papers at many conferences, published several academic articles and books, and participated in several TV programmes and documentaries on history. He is currently working on three publications on heritage sites, the Liberated Africans, and the Antoinette Sugar Estate in Mauritius which are due to be published in 2016.

1

Introduction

Abdul Sheriff and Vijayalakshmi Teelock

Comparative Methodologies

Comparative history is a popular theme in historiographical literature, but it is important to determine methodologically what one is comparing or contrasting, and what conclusions can be drawn from that which would be of wider significance than the two or more cases under discussion. At the crudest level, one may compare some unique traits randomly isolated and compared across time and space, and out of context of their different cultures, etc, which may be intriguing but may not prove meaningful. Some scholars may ask if being an island adds an important dimension to the study of comparative slaveries and emancipations. Others argue that some countries can be compared but some may be cases of 'exceptionalism' (e.g. 'American exceptionalism'). A similar argument has been made for Mauritius by some scholars. The nineteenth century philosopher John Stuart Mill tried to explore comparative methodologies using existing work on the natural sciences. For example, in his 'Method of Agreement', one compares two situations which differ in every respect save one, and 'The Method of Difference' in which one compares two situations which are alike except in one respect. This is empiricist and ahistorical, and can hardly be applicable to our study. We are studying similar societies, but similar does not mean identical.

A breakthrough in comparative historical studies can be said to have been made by George Frederickson's comparative study of the USA and South Africa which has relevance to our methodological approach. His approach has allowed us to clarify our proposed methodology and conceptualization of the problems and issues involved in the study of slavery and its aftermath. First, he recommends the comparison of only two countries rather than a multinational study. To him, vast comparative surveys are devoid of meaning because the situations are often not comparable, yet have been compared. Comparing, for example, Roman slavery, Russian serfdom and colonial slavery does not add to any increased knowledge or understanding of colonial slavery. One reason advanced by Frederickson for choosing only two countries is because most scholars start off being specialists in one country, and that of one particular theme in a country. To compare with another country inevitably means the analysis is skewed as knowledge of primary sources may not have been as extensive as in the first country being studied. There is much reliance on secondary sources, and this does not do justice to the second country under consideration.

In the case of the present project, the danger was present, and it was felt that constant interaction between the two groups by email and face-to-face workshops was required. Familiarity with each other's primary sources has been gained, and the younger researchers have benefited from the expertise of scholars in their respective fields in their own countries. Actual visits to the country, combined with lengthy visits to cultural and historical sites, each accompanied by detailed explanations of issues at hand, have combined to give first-hand knowledge of the country, and avoided the pitfall of being a mere academic exercise devoid of relevance to the country and its contemporary issues. The potential weakness identified by Frederickson has thus been somewhat mitigated.

Secondly, a close reading of Frederickson's methodological treatment of issues such as slavery, its legacy and consequences, is very appropriate for our study, and allowed for identification of elements of comparison for considering slavery and post-slavery in Zanzibar and Mauritius. In relation to slavery and emancipation, the topic is unique in terms of its 'globality' and 'totality', factors which we should not ignore. The space involved is huge as, geographically, it spans three continents and oceans; chronologically it extends over a thousand years; the interconnectedness of regions is great; the number and type of institutions that affected all sectors of society - not just economic but land, social, ethnic, cultural, and political issues are vast; and there have been much 'politics' over the study of the theme. In addition, the study of slavery over the years has become interdisciplinary, and the discipline of history has become infused and inspired by the works and methodologies of anthropologists, economists, literary persons and archaeologists, to cite a few.

The issues are not vastly different from the Caribbean, with one major exception: the race or colour factor is not omnipresent in Zanzibar while it is in the Caribbean. In the Caribbean, the analysis and debates have focused on correlation of land, labour, capital, population density, influence of settler communities on the fate of ex-slaves, and the transition to freedom. There has been a heated debate between Bolland and Green on Belize when compared with other sugar-and-slave Caribbean countries. Green argued that we are in the presence of 'similar people performing similar functions under similar circumstances', and it is this 'that renders comparative analysis meaningful'.[1] Bolland criticized Green's analysis in which 'the human agent, namely the planter/slave-owner, is absent from this statement, and we are led to believe that it was simply population density that prevented the slaves from cultivating provision grounds'. Instead, Bolland urged the adoption of sociological comparative analysis to devise an appropriate methodological framework, the adoption of broader rather than narrower comparative analysis for the reasons stated by Andreski:

> The body of ideas which concern the most general problems of social life is some-times called general theory, sometimes comparative sociology, because wide ranging comparisons constitute the only method of testing hypotheses which refer to such problems. Second, I urge that the political dimension of social history, that is, the multiplicity of ways – cultural, economic, military, legal, psychological – by which class authority is formulated, implemented, maintained, and resisted, be placed at the centre of our analysis of post abolition societies in the Caribbean.[2]

With Bolland, we come closer to talking not of traits but sociological theories; yet functional sociology may lack a historical dimension to explain change and evolution of societies over time with which we are concerned in this study.

A comparative history of slavery and the transition from it in Zanzibar and Mauritius necessarily has to be placed within the context of a wider comparative study of the subject in the Atlantic and Indian Ocean worlds. Both countries are islands, with roughly the same size of area and populations, a common colonial history, and both are multicultural societies. However, despite inhabiting and using the same oceanic space, there are differences in experiences and structures which deserve to be explored. This comparison has to be seen in the context of their specific historical conjunctures and the types of slave systems in the overall theoretical conception of modes of production within which they manifested themselves, a concept that has become unfashionable but still essential.

The starting point of many such efforts to compare slave systems has naturally been the much-studied slavery in the Atlantic region which has been used to provide a paradigm with which to study any type of slavery anywhere in the world. However, as Karl Marx[3] has commented, it emerged at a specific historical moment and was a particular manifestation of slavery at the 'rosy dawn of the capitalist mode of production' when some of the forces governing that mode had begun to blossom, and therefore affect the operation of the system of slavery. It was also naturally influenced by the prevailing ideological systems, particularly Christianity, whose origin can be traced to different circumstances and periods, which nevertheless affected it and in turn were affected by it.

However, slavery has been around almost as long as recorded history. Around the Indian Ocean and elsewhere in Africa and Asia, it has taken many different forms at different times of history, influenced by different modes of production prevailing at different times and places, and occasionally emerging as the dominant mode. The Indian Ocean was also a meeting point of a great variety of religions and systems of beliefs which had arisen at different places and under different circumstances, and they naturally influenced the types of slavery that developed, and in turn were inevitably influenced by it. The prevailing system of belief that dominated the western half of the Indian Ocean over the past millennium with which we are concerned has been Islam. While Islam has influenced the different systems of slavery that developed over this large area and long period, it would be a mistake to lump all these manifestations of slavery under a single rubric of 'Islamic slavery', as will be discussed at greater length below.

While the canvas for our discussion on the comparative history of slavery and emancipation is necessarily broad, there is a need for this particular study to focus on a more limited period from the late eighteenth century to the beginning of the twentieth century when the capitalist mode of production had become global. Moreover, and ironically, both islands to be studied are located within the western corner of the Indian Ocean, although in fact, in a nutshell, they represent the two contrasting systems of slavery, the Atlantic and the Indian Ocean, in a single ocean.

Slavery in Zanzibar has been described as 'Islamic slavery'. This is not quite accurate as although many elements were Islamic, especially as regards domestic slavery, plantation slavery in nineteenth century Zanzibar was governed by the forces of the global capitalist system. Mauritian slavery was, however, 100 per cent colonial slavery. There were no indigenous traditional texts or systems as the island had been uninhabited before the arrival of the Europeans who set about establishing a commercial network in the Indian Ocean using Mauritius as their headquarters. Both islands were linked, however, in more ways than one. The bulk of the slaves arriving in Mauritius from the 1770s onwards were shipped from Zanzibar and the East African Coast which was becoming crucial in the transhipment of slaves to colonial islands of the Mascarenes and elsewhere in the Indian Ocean. Both established plantation economies although with different products, Zanzibar with cloves and Mauritius with sugar, and in both cases, the slaves faced a potential conflictual situation between former masters and slaves in the post-emancipation period.

The contrast in how the outcomes evolved is one of the most interesting comparisons made for this project and will be treated in depth in chapters 4 and 5. Accessibility of land, both in terms of price of land and availability for squatting, willingness of owners to allow a certain margin of 'freedom' to ex-slaves to market their produce independent of the plantation, all played their part in influencing outcomes. Also important was the role of the colonial state: in Mauritius, the state played its habitual role as in the Caribbean, aligning itself firmly in the pro-plantation economy lobby, and issuing stringent anti-labour legislation to control movements of slaves around the island, and wishing also to restrict movement of newly arrived immigrants. Cheap wage policy was enforced by bringing down wages so that ex-slaves could no longer market their labour. The situation was different in Zanzibar. Although the British colonial government promoted plantation economics, cheap labour immigration was not attempted because a cheaper source of immigrant labour was to be found on its doorstep in mainland Tanganyika.

One as yet unresearched area of study, even in the Caribbean where studies are far advanced compared to the Indian Ocean, has been on female slaves. There have been no studies focused on female slaves in Mauritius so far. The situation in Zanzibar is only slightly better. It was therefore considered crucial to include this, however preliminary the study on both islands. In both islands, however, the sources dictated the methodology, as sources relating to women of a higher social status were more available than for the female plantation slaves. In Zanzibar, the privileged role of the *suria* whose status was defined by *Sharia* law was explored; and in Mauritius, the manumission of female slaves was explored as they formed the majority among manumitted slaves. Both sets of women, however, resembled each other as 'elites'. Their 'economic futures' as well as that of their children were, however, in sharp contrast from one another: unlike Zanzibari slave-owners who wanted more and more children, whether of slaves or free mothers, in Mauritius, slave owners did not accept their slave or Coloured offspring so easily, and more often than not, refused to acknowledge them.

Emancipation Methodology

Our study is focused especially on transition from slavery in Zanzibar and Mauritius. Therefore a critical examination of emancipation methodology is also very relevant. Eric Foner's work is a classic for comparative studies of emancipation as is Rebecca Scott's.[4] Foner's view of emancipation as a struggle between institutions of slavery and ideological, economic, social and political forces is very relevant to our study. The struggle over land is one of the primary struggles also in Zanzibar and Mauritius with squatting being resorted to in both islands. In Mauritius the plantation economy had just 'taken off' while in Zanzibar, squatting emerged when the plantation system began to break down. However, when the plantation economy became consolidated in Mauritius and land speculation increased, ex-slaves were thrown off the land in large numbers as acres of land made way for sugar cultivation: the numbers of small planters and vegetable growers slumped. In Zanzibar, the situation was different as ex-slaves and others squatted and grew food crops on the owner's plantations. This was possible as in Zanzibar, land between widely spaced clove trees needed to be kept free of weeds, and therefore could be used by squatters for annual food crops; and once planted, clove trees needed to be picked only twice a year when labour was intensive. In nineteenth century Mauritius, all the space on a sugar plantation was used. Land availability, type of crop, and willingness of owners to grant some measure of freedom in labour conditions contributed to the huge contrast between the two islands.

Citizenship rights, much at issue in the USA, were not an issue in Mauritius where ex-slaves were for the most part 'marginalized' in the new economic and demographic configuration. However, in Zanzibar the ex-slaves were able to negotiate contracts with their owners and when the contracts did not satisfy them, they simply left the plantations. In the USA, freedmen's access to land had the potential to reduce their reliance on employment for wages. An ex-slave worker may have had the freedom to hunt, etc., but if the worker depended on his employer's permission to pasture a cow on the estate, was he 'compromised in his ability to challenge working conditions'? Ex-slaves could also negotiate conditions of work: task work was preferred by slaves and the freed because there was more control over the pace of work and how it was accomplished. There is an 'unparalleled degree of control over the pace and length of the work day and the opportunity to acquire significant amounts of property'.[5] Comparing countries, according to Foner, illuminates links between the different bands of evidence, and reveals connections that are not always apparent in studies of single countries.

Comparisons of emancipation in terms of developments in the economies also present similarities and also reveal adjustments that occurred in the economic system as a result of emancipation. In southern USA, small white farmers took over cotton production which remained high. In Haiti, the revolution led to an end of the plantation economy and the rise of small-scale agriculture. In Barbados and Antigua, population density was high, and there was no decline in the economy. In Mauritius, ex-slaves either moved out or were pushed out to make way for cheap contractual labour; in Zanzibar some freed slaves moved to the town while others were persuaded to stay on the land as squatters picking cloves seasonally. By the 1920s, about a half of clove production was on large plantations while the other half was done by small producers, as in Mauritius where indentured labourers and their descendants also produced nearly half of the sugar on the island on smaller plots.

The different 'concepts of freedom' also provide another stimulating field of study and can be viewed as constituting a battleground for ex-slaves and their former owners: What should be the pace of work of ex-slaves? Did the ex-slave only have the right to choose an employer or did these rights or freedom also imply the right not to work?

The role of the state in this period of transition deserves a comparative study. Did it sit on the fence or actively promote one particular type of economic development and one type of social order? In Mauritius opinions (and opinions they remain as no in-depth study has been conducted yet) range from those who believe that ex-slaves were ignored by the British because they were too busy setting up the plantation system, to those who claim they did not care much about ex-slaves' lives because they were no longer working in sugar production. Comparative study of Zanzibar and Mauritius under the British illustrates very great differences. What were these differences due to? Was having local Arab plantation owners different from having local French colonists? What was the geopolitics of the situation that affected British relations with local elites? One must not forget either that Mauritius was a Crown Colony (direct rule) while Zanzibar was a Protectorate (indirect rule).

Finally, what was the fate of these economies in the post-emancipation period? Again, while much has been written about the Caribbean, in-depth studies of Mauritius have shown the restructuring of the economy as a result of sugar expansion and labour immigration, but not in terms of the fate of ex-slaves. How important was the output and economic activities of slave-based economies? Did economies decline or not after emancipation? This did not happen in Mauritius but success of the economy did not translate into success for ex-slaves. There were multiple but similar outcomes in both islands. First, was the fact that indigenous Zanzibaris as well as Arabs owned slaves, and secondly, that land outside the plantation area was communally owned. After emancipation, some ex-slaves entered into sharecropping ventures with former owners of rice farms; others entered, as we have seen, into squatting arrangements with former owners, and the remaining went to live in the towns. This was similar to Mauritius where many ex-slaves for various reasons, shied away from participation in the plantation economy and ended up either in town, entered into sharecropping arrangements, or simply squatted on available land.

Elements of Comparison in Post-emancipation Mauritius and Zanzibar

To explore these similarities as well as differences in the human experience and the economic structures and systems put in place after emancipation, it was felt that a historicist as well as structuralist methodology was required. The focus would be on basic facts for comparative study. The study needed to be framed in the temporal space from late eighteenth century to early twentieth century. The comparative study would not be engaged in 'trait hunting' but would illuminate links between the different bands of evidence and reveal connections that are not always apparent.

A comparison of the origins of slave trade and slavery in Zanzibar and Mauritius was thought to be essential as these were vastly different and would impact on the post-emancipation process. It was necessary also to look not only at slaves but also slave ownership as this too impacted on post-emancipation outcomes in both islands. What were the mechanisms, links (Indian/Arab/European), and routes and networks: ivory/slaves in between this, the actors?

The nature of slavery in both islands needed to be compared: plantation slavery started later in Zanzibar and Mauritius compared to other British colonies. How did slaves fare in the transition to a plantation economy under slavery in both islands? The question of gender naturally arises as in the Caribbean women were not brought into plantation labour, but also in Mauritius. This impacted on the choices and decisions taken by these women after abolition. In Zanzibar, women played very different roles in slavery in the households as well as on the plantations. The issues relating to gender point to another important issue relating to demographics: there was an imbalance in the gender ratio in Mauritius due to importation of young males for work in the Mascarenes, while in Zanzibar this was not the case. Implications for social life in Mauritius led to accusations of 'immoral behaviour' in the colonies. In one aspect Mauritius and Zanzibar resembled each other on the question of gender: in both, some women found opportunities for self-advancement in the relationships they forged with their owners. However, one crucial difference existed: in Zanzibar these were legal relationships, while those in Mauritius were illicit.

Gender differences were one of the many between slaves: there were also the difference of status in Mauritius between locally-born and foreign-born slaves, as locally-born slaves were considered more knowledgeable and experienced at their work and given skilled jobs, and often converted to Christianity. This was also true in Zanzibar between fresh slaves – *wajinga* ('uncivilised') – and *wazalia* (local born). Occupational differences were felt: with domestics, urban and skilled slaves even earning a wage while the worse off were the manual workers and the plantation slaves.

Slavery, emancipation and transition from slavery in the last decades before it was abolished are particularly important as they impact, perhaps more greatly than in earlier periods, on the outcomes after abolition. How did life change for the ex-slave when the slaves became free in Zanzibar and Mauritius? What did 'freedom', 'autonomy', mean for the slaves? Did they want land, for example, and did they obtain it? If not, why? What were other forces at work: economic, social and political, to stop further land ownership? What laws existed to control mobility of ex-slaves? In the Caribbean, there has been no uniformity in the post-emancipation experience. Much has depended on availability of land/labour/capital, on size of the territory, availability of alternative labour and crop being grown, and alternative economic futures.

However, as slavery was primarily a labour system, the type of labour that ex-slaves performed, the terms agreed upon with employers, possibility of bargaining as many had hoped they would, were all thought to be critical issues to be dealt with in this comparative study. If they did have some bargaining power and could be called 'free' labour, how was this affected by massive importation of labour in Mauritius and by migrations from the mainland in Zanzibar? Was their status reduced? What was the impact of the emerging capitalist economy on both islands, how did the populations in each fare under the expanding plantation economy? In Zanzibar the plantation economy shrunk as peasant clove production increased, and as much produced by large landowners as by small peasants a majority of whom were not ex-slaves by the 1920s. In Mauritius the sugar plantation economy continued to reinforce itself and expanding its acreage and labour force. What was the balance of internal pressures and external forces? Were the ex-slaves marginalised? In both islands, it seems, therefore, ex-slaves were quite far removed from the local economy.

'Islamic Slavery' or Slavery in Islamic Societies?

A number of references have been made to the role of Islam in the operation of slavery in Zanzibar, and it is appropriate to consider the role of religion in slavery. For more than a quarter of a century the terms 'Islamic slavery' or 'Arab slavery' have been bandied about in academic literature interchangeably in a way that the Atlantic slavery has not been described as 'Christian slavery' or 'European slavery'; for it is not religion or race as such but the mode of production that can explain the phenomenon, whatever the religious justification that may be used to initiate and perpetuate it ideologically. In the case of both Zanzibar where Islam has been the dominant religion for nearly a millennium, and Mauritius where Christianity was the ideology of the slave-owning class, the origin and fundamental principles of both these religions arose under quite different circumstances, but were adapted to the specific conditions of slavery during the epoch dominated by the capitalist mode of production as a world system.

Slavery existed in Mecca in the seventh century when the society was basically tribal, but it was undergoing a profound commercial revolution as a result of being involved in long-distance caravan trade for which Mecca had developed as a hub between the Yemen, the Byzantine and the Persian empires, and even across the Red Sea to Ethiopia to the west.[6] This was bringing in new wealth and inequalities into the society, and even slaves, about which Islamic reforms were particularly concerned. But slavery was a marginal institution, consisting primarily of captives from inter-tribal warfare, and the society was by no means dominated by a slave mode of production. Islam did not invent slavery, and like other contemporary religions, it did not abolish it either. Judging from references to it in the Qur'an and the Hadiths (Prophet's Traditions), it appears to have been a distasteful institution that was merely tolerated. Many of the injunctions in Islam concentrated on ameliorating the condition of slavery.

According to Bernard Lewis, the Qur'an brought about specific Islamic 'humanitarian reforms' which had revolutionary consequences. The first was the fundamental principle of Islamic jurisprudence that 'the basic condition of the human being was freedom'[7] and slavery was an exceptional condition, sanctioned as punishment for unbelief. The second was the ban on the enslavement of Muslims except in strictly defined circumstances – birth in slavery, or capture in war of non-Muslim prisoners – and later the exemption was extended to cover all 'Peoples of the Book', Jews and Christians. Islam repeatedly asserted the essential equality of believers in the eyes of God regardless of status or race – 'even if he is an Ethiopian bastard'.[8] They were not merely chattel but human beings with social status and certain religious and legal rights and duties, although they were less than those of free people. The Qur'an also recommended marriage between one's male and female slaves, and made it a moral duty of the master to find a spouse for his or her slaves, and to pay their dowry if the female slaves belonged to other owners.[9] In his Farewell Pilgrimage sermon the Prophet exhorted his followers:

> Fear God in the matter of your slaves. Feed them with what you eat and clothe them with what you wear, and do not give them work beyond their capacity. ...Do not cause pain to God's creation. He caused you to own them and had He so wished, He would have caused them to own you.[10]

Islam did not stop at exhortation to kindness, but went on to set up a whole battery of regulations on the treatment of slaves, and the means by which they could move out of servility. For a religion that has been associated with slavery for so long in popular literature, it comes as a great surprise that 10 out of 19 references to slavery in the Qur'an relate to manumission of slaves under all sorts of circumstances.[11] In one of the Hadiths, freeing or ransoming a slave is seen as a way to ascend the steep hill towards righteousness. Manumission was also prescribed as atonement for the accidental killing of a believer, the breaking of an oath, or for perjury, and as a fine before a man could remarry his divorced wife. One of the sayings of the Prophet insisted that he who beats a slave could only expect forgiveness if he set him or her free, and another stated that he who freed a Muslim slave shall be freed from the fires of hell.[12] The Qur'an specifically provided for a slave to earn or buy his or her own freedom in instalment through a formal contract (*mukataba*), and urged the owner to help his or her slave in that effort, even with a portion of the *zakat* (Islamic tax), and it was one of the seven purposes to which public alms (*sadaqa*) could be put. A slave could be manumitted on the death of the owner who expected a rich reward in the afterlife.

Islam thus had a built-in system of manumission that provided for gradual exit from servitude into freedom, and provided for the integration of slaves into the society. There was thus potential for a large class of freedmen as a substantial and regular feature of the Islamic system of slavery with important social consequences. There was a large class of freed slaves all around the shores of the Persian Gulf at the beginning of the twentieth century long before the British began to manumit slaves in the 1920s and 1930s.[13] Already by 1875, there were some slaves in Pemba who had not only been freed by their owners but even given landed property and slaves to work them long before the general emancipation in 1897. When the British abolished slavery in Zanzibar, nearly a third of the slaves were freed by their owners voluntarily. Instead of seeking monetary compensation from the British, they hoped for a better reward in heaven (see chapter 2).

The second institution relates to the integration of captives and slaves in societies. A large majority of the slaves in the time of the Prophet were captives from wars, most of them initially Arabs. Rape and forced cohabitation has been part of the history of man's inhumanity to women. Many societies developed certain regulations and traditions which provided for a transition from the outsider unfree to a member of the society that Miers and Kopytoff discuss for African societies.[14] Other societies developed more exclusivist traditions to keep their societies 'lily white' by marginalizing the result of such inevitable cohabitation to the periphery. For example, we know of forced cohabitation between white slave owners and black female slaves in the American South, but for various religious and racialist reasons, the owners refused to acknowledge the paternity of their children by their slave mistresses. It becomes national news when somebody claims descent from a certain American president. Ali Mazrui described this as 'descending miscegenation' as the offspring inherited the status of their mothers, black and slave, whatever the mix of genes inherited from their biological parents.[15]

Islam faced a similar situation when it began to expand right across the Middle East, and women were taken as part of the booty. However, the Prophet defined the ideal in one of the Traditions when he stated that 'a master of a woman-slave who teaches her good manners and educates her in the best possible way (the religion) and manumits her and then marries her' will receive a double reward in the after-life. This was a straight case of a regular marriage prescribed even for a slave after manumission, but he also recognized the common practice at that time of intercourse with captive and slave women. In ancient Arabian custom, children of free men by their slaves were also slaves unless they were recognised and liberated by their fathers. The Qur'an and the Traditions institutionalised it to provide for the automatic integration of the enslaved mother as well as her offspring. Once a slave woman had conceived by her master, her status changed to that of a *suria* or a 'secondary slave wife'. She became an *umm al-walad* (mother of the child), and she could not thereafter be sold or pawned. However, it must be added that she still remained bound to her master/husband, and was automatically freed only on his death. Moreover, no provision was made for her to inherit from him as his free wives; she had to be sustained by her children or by voluntary bequest by her husband in his will.[16]

Even more remarkable was the status of their offspring. According to many schools of Islam, they were free children of their free fathers with full rights like those of children by free mothers, including inheritance, even to the throne. This soon became the norm and unremarkable in a society where even rulers were often children of slave mothers, such as the Abbasids and the Busaidi dynasty in Zanzibar and Oman. Islam thus provided a window of upward social mobility, that Ali Mazrui described as 'ascending miscegenation', by which both the mother and her offspring were drained out of the slave pool. This had important consequences for the integration of society, although this does not erase the initial tragedy of enslavement of the woman or her forced cohabitation with her owner.[17]

It would be ahistorical to assume that all these Islamic injunctions operated in all Islamic societies that practiced slavery under all circumstances. It is obvious from the tenth century plantation slavery in southern Iraq that even while many of the Abbasid rulers were children of slave mothers, the conditions of slaves on the desiccated flats around Basra were so oppressive and exploitative that they culminated in the Zanj Rebellion. In the case of plantation slavery in Zanzibar in the nineteenth century, which was operating within the world capitalist system, social relations between masters and slaves also had to answer to the capitalist demands of supply and demand. While conditions of slavery were different from those that reigned in the Caribbean or elsewhere due to local circumstances, it would be naive to assume that Muslim owners always adhered to all the Islamic injunctions about slavery.

There was a greater possibility of adherence in the case of domestic slaves where more intimate personal relations could develop between owners and slaves, with a greater probability of manumission and incidence of secondary slave wives and their offspring. The result was a society that was thoroughly mixed racially as to be physically indistinguishable, and linguistically it became entirely Swahili-speaking. In a recent genetic study in Zanzibar, it emerged that while the diagram for genes inherited from fathers shows the familiar racial division of Zanzibar with 35 per cent of the sample showing ancestry from across the sea, the diagram for genes inherited through mothers shows 98 per cent of the inhabitants having had African mothers.[18]

The Atlantic Model and its Extension into the Indian Ocean

The focus of scholarly interest in the Anglo-American academic world has traditionally been the slave trade and slavery on the Atlantic side. Even the French, despite their historic importance in the Indian Ocean, have focussed on ports which traded in the Atlantic. The Indian Ocean trade, and in particular the Mascarenes trade, has been neglected.

Comparing Indian and Atlantic Ocean Slave Trades

The Mascarene Islands (Mauritius and Réunion), situated in the middle of the Indian Ocean to the east of Madagascar, were not previously inhabited. The system of slavery that was introduced from the eighteenth century was in a sense an extension of the Atlantic model involving a massive importation of slaves from India, Madagascar and the African continent to work in economic, domestic and military activities, with the plantation economy emerging only at the end of the eighteenth century, under the overall hegemony of Roman law and Christianity.

While historians of the Indian Ocean have for long known about the specific and special nature of the Indian Ocean world and the ties that bound the littoral states of the Indian Ocean for thousands of years, it is only in recent years that this fact seems to have attracted the attention of Atlantic-based scholars and even

UNESCO. There has also been an attempt to understand Indian Ocean slavery and slave trade using Atlantic models, theories and concepts. Yet the Indian Ocean has been found, time and time again, to have certain specificities, and the study of Mauritius and Zanzibar amply demonstrates this. The Mascarenes trade, in particular, has been neglected. Differences in the two European slave trades include the fact that in the Atlantic, Britain was the largest trading power. In the south-western Indian Ocean, it is the French who dominated the trade. The Mascarenes Islands were crucial in this trade as they were used as bases for the French armateurs to launch slaving missions to Madagascar, Eastern and South Africa, South and South-East Asia and the Caribbean.[19]

Secondly, while for the British the slave trade was the activity of specialists, French traders were more versatile, engaging in a number of maritime activities in addition to the slave trade.

Thirdly, the Atlantic slave trade is seen as a 'triangular trade' while in the Indian Ocean the evidence points to a 'quadrangular trade'.[20] This conclusion has been arrived at by recent scholars after studying the real trajectory of the ships and by paying close attention to the timing of the voyages, their tonnage and the goods that they contained, and country for which they were really destined. It is seen then that ships' official itineraries were not what was carried out in practice. Ships arriving in Mauritius bound for the Indies were in fact diverted: they went on short slave trading voyages to Madagascar and Eastern Africa, before resuming their voyages to India and China. This practice started as early as 1723. These 'short' trips were missed by earlier historians such as Toussaint and Mettas, but recently (2012) a spate of detailed studies have been carried out demonstrating this 'unofficial' diversion of ships.[21] Thus ships leaving France and destined to India and China also contained cargo of 'goods' destined for the Mascarenes where they could be sold easily. Those stopovers should not therefore be viewed 'as simple transit stops, but rather as ones which could yield substantial profits as these goods did not necessarily sell well in India or China'. A *mémoire*, recently analysed by Mcwatters, stated that in India, there was no market for European goods. Those who purchased European goods were the Frenchmen and women living in the Mascarenes.

The differences between the Atlantic and the Indian Ocean experiences of the mid-to-late eighteenth century are quite stark. Two examples: in contrast to the Caribbean where the Haitian revolution and a fall in plantation production decreased long-distance trade for a generation, in Mauritius sugar and plantation production increased. Secondly, the impact of European wars on the slave trade differed in the two oceans. In the Indian Ocean, unlike in the Atlantic, the wars were not necessarily detrimental to the slave trade or trade in general, as corsair activity in particular proved very profitable.

Thus, war changed the way trade investments were conducted, but it did not shut down all opportunities for profitable operations. The Mascarenes, where the bulk of the maritime traffic was centred, also served as a naval base. It was rare to find any voyages specifically destined for the Mascarenes, unless they were small ships with small tonnages. Finally, an as yet unexplored area of study but possibly constituting a major area of difference with the Atlantic is the profits derived from the slave trade which were possibly more consequential in the Indian Ocean.

As far as slavery is concerned, the most important differences between the Caribbean and Indian Ocean appear to be structural and cultural in nature. Within Mauritius, for example, the nature and character slave-ownership rested in stark contrast to the British colonies in the Caribbean: while most slave-owners owning large plantations in the British Caribbean were 'absentee' owners, in Mauritius this was not the case. Most were of French origin and were established in Mauritius.[22] Capital ownership was therefore local, although a large number of creditors were British. These, however, left the island after the crash of 1848.

The local structural differences between the Caribbean and Mauritius are huge. Mauritius has been described in the past as a 'variant' of Caribbean slavery. Today, after further research and comparative work on the Caribbean and Mauritian situations, this is not viewed as being necessarily so. Further studies are required to explore the structural differences between the two.

There are also other differences in terms of the evolution of the sugar economy. First, sugar did not continue to prosper in the Caribbean for many reasons, including unavailability of labour (as ex-slaves did not wish to remain on the plantations), because British subsidies were no longer forthcoming and cheaper sugar was being produced elsewhere. In Mauritius, sugar not only prospered but expanded. Massive importation of indentured labour and export of sugar to India and Australia ensured the continuation of the plantation economy, whereas in the Caribbean, with the loss of a guaranteed British market, sugar could no longer be profitably shipped to Europe. Most importantly, as stated earlier, capital invested in sugar plantations was not British, but local. The compensation money obtained from the British was reinvested in sugar estates and other economic activities whereas in the Caribbean, absentee land and slave owners re-invested in Britain, not in the Caribbean. In this manner, in post-emancipation world economic history, the British Caribbean became a 'scenic sideshow'[23] for the British, while Mauritius developed into a major plantation economy from the 1850s onwards.

In terms of cultural origins and contemporary cultural make-up of society, there are also huge differences. James Walvin starts his chapter in *Black Ivory* stating that there were three quarters of a million slaves who were given their freedom and that all of them shared their roots in Africa. This was not the case for Mauritius. In Mauritius and Reunion islands, as well as in South Africa, a large number of slaves were either Malagasy or of Asian origin.

But there is one very important similarity which is a major theme in this project, and that is the fate of ex-slaves after abolition and emancipation.

Literature Review

The study of the East African slavery and slave trade in the colonial period was preoccupied with the export of slaves from East Africa to Arabia and elsewhere in a thinly veiled attempt to counterbalance the horrendous dimensions of the Atlantic slavery. It was also used by imperial historians like Coupland to justify colonialism by presenting the anti-slavery crusade as a humanitarian movement to free Africans from Arab or Islamic slavery.[24] These historians relied on the widely exaggerated estimates of a British Parliamentary Committee which had argued for the export of 50,000 slaves per annum from East Africa to Arabia. The tendency was continued in the post-colonial period by some American historians who tried to strengthen the argument by a statistical exercise. On the one hand, they systematically downgraded the size of the Atlantic slavery from an estimated total of 17 million to 11.5 million over a couple of centuries, notably the seventeenth and eighteenth centuries.[25] On the other hand, they conjured up the so-called 'Islamic slavery' in a broad arc across the Sahara, the Red Sea and the Indian Ocean, for 12 centuries from the seventh to the nineteenth centuries, arriving not surprisingly at the same 17 million. The problem with this game of numbers is that while the census of the Atlantic slave trade is based on a lot of customs and shipping statistics, such statistics are not available for the East African slave trade except for a few years in the 1860s. Austen carried out a laudable exercise of collecting and collating an enormous amount of historical data, but unfortunately it is very sparse indeed, and most of it is anecdotal. He therefore developed a complicated mathematical formula transforming the predominantly qualitative statements into quantitative series. Although the method was challenged, the total for the so-called 'Islamic slave trade' has proved too attractive for the textbook writers.[26]

In a thoughtful and challenging essay defining an agenda for research on the slave trade in the Indian Ocean, the French historian, Hubert Gerbeau (1979), challenged historians not to reduce the history of the slave trade to a paragraph in commercial history, merely counting bodies and piastres. He urged them to try to introduce a human dimension to it, to give a voice to those transported, to inquire into the life of the people who were leaving and those who had arrived; in short, to study it as part of the 'total history' of civilisations.

As regards the East African coast, Sheriff (1987) began a re-examination of the slave sector, demonstrating its transformation from one based on the export of slaves to a productive sector that employed slave labour within East Africa to produce cloves and food grains for export to the East and the West. Cooper (1977, 1980) extended the analysis to the coast of Kenya and introduced a comparison with varying forms of slavery in the American South, which was perhaps not as illuminating, but he also traced the fate of the freed slaves in the second volume.

A breakthrough in the debate on the comparative history of slave trade and slavery in the Indian Ocean began with a re-examination at the conference in

London of the economics of the Indian Ocean slave trade which was edited by Clarence-Smith (1989). More systematic was a series of conferences at Avignon and McGill initiated by Professor Gwyn Campbell who began a comparative study of slavery systems in the Indian Ocean World (IOW). There was a deliberate attempt to break what was verbally described at the first conference as the 'tyranny of the Atlantic model' which was considered a specific manifestation at the dawn of the capitalist mode of production. In the IOW, on the other hand, slavery has existed for several millennia and in numerous forms of unfree labour crossing boundaries imperceptibly from one form to another. The series began with an examination of the structure of slavery in the IOW (Campbell 2003); slavery, bondage and resistance (Alpers and Salman 2005); abolition and its aftermath (2005) which considered indigenous forces for abolition as well as placing the western crusade in its historical context; women in slavery (Miers and Miller 2008); children in slavery (Miers and Miller 2009); and sex in slavery (Campbell and Elbourne 2014).

The attempt to broaden the debate on slavery was received with considerable hostility on the part of North American scholars at the Goa Conference (Prasad and Angenot 2008), seen as an attempt to decentre the painful experience of African slavery in the West which has hitherto dominated the debate and even the Unesco Slave Routes programme.

Ralph Austen had used the Islamic label as a prop for his quantification exercise without offering any theoretical formulation of the concept; and others have followed with unbridled polemics against Islam (e.g., Gordon 1989). But the question still remains whether there is anything that can legitimately be described as Islamic in relation to slave trade and slavery beyond the fact that some of the participants in the slave trade in this broad arc from the Sahara to East Africa were Muslims, in the same way as many of those involved in the Atlantic were Christians, without justifying the attachment of a religious label to either phenomenon. A careful examination of the fundamental texts and history of Islam shows that it tolerated it but tried to ameliorate the condition of slaves in some very significant ways. Arafat[27] had shown that more than a half of the references to slavery in the Quran relate to emancipation of slaves for all sorts of reasons which was an in-built feature of Islamic slavery throughout its life. Bernard Lewis,[28] in a number of treatises on slavery in Islam, followed by Hunwick,[29] demonstrated remarkable reforms that were far advanced compared to those of other religions of the time. One of the most important was the fact that while intercourse between slave owners and their slaves is a universal feature, offspring born of such intercourse in Islamic *Sharia* were legitimate and free children of the owner from birth, and that the mother also became free on the death of her husband. Islam provided an avenue for social reintegration of some of the slaves and their offspring, which is an issue raised by Gerbeau mentioned above as an important part of the study of slavery.[30]

In the Mascarenes islands, particularly of Mauritius, the study of slavery and slave trade can be said to have started with Karl Noel's *Histoire de l'"Esclavage a l'ile de*

France,[31] which many see today as an apology for slavery as Noel stated that slavery was mild in Mauritius compared to the Caribbean. Use of primary sources was limited in his work however, and it is in the 1980s that a generation of historians began to produce 'history from below' type of histories of slavery, though focussed on personalities such as Ratsitatanina[32] the Malagasy Prince, who was projected as a leader of a slave revolt, and resistance studies.[33] Further studies emerged, such as Muslim Jumeer's[34] PhD thesis on Indian manumitted slaves, which he never published; the proceedings of a Slavery Conference in Mauritius where preliminary studies on slavery and slave trade were presented were published in 1986. In the 1990s, came Teelock's *Bitter Sugar*,[35] focussing on the impact of sugar on slaves' lives; and a host of publications on slave 'resistance' by the Peerthums (father and son),[36] and Amedee Nagapen.[37] British slavery in Mauritius has also been a focus, with few venturing into the French period of slavery in Mauritius. More recently, however, Megan Vaughan has published 'Creating the Creole Island'.[38]

A great number of studies have emerged on the slave trade, each trying to 'finalise' (if that is ever going to be possible) the figures of the slave trade (legal and illicit) to the Mascarenes.[39] Despite a start by the Truth and Justice Commission in Mauritius,[40] the figures for Mauritius have never been disaggregated, and indeed many historians remain sceptical about the fact that it can ever be accomplished. The slave trade database initiated by the Truth and Justice Commission into which scholars are inserting data being collected from archives around the world will hopefully appease this scepticism somewhat. Some of the figures mentioned in earlier works have been revised by historians as they update their work.[41]

The consequences and legacy of slavery have also been the subject of debate but little scholarly writing in Mauritius particularly.[42] There is a distinct tendency to apply and transfer to Mauritius concepts and situations applicable to the Caribbean, and this has led to erroneous assumptions especially where cultural orientations and decisions made by ex-slaves after emancipation are concerned. The current project of comparative perspectives is therefore crucial to understand the differences between Mauritius and the Caribbean with which it has often been compared in debates and to underline the uniqueness of the Mauritian situation.

Linked to the subject of consequences is that of reparations. However, in Mauritius this debate has been restricted to the issue of financial compensation even if few studies have been carried out as to make substantive claims to former colonial slave trading nations. No work on the scale of the 'Legacies of Slave-ownership in Britain' in the United Kingdom has been attempted.[43] A number of articles by Mauritian scholars, such as Jocelyn Chan Low,[44] have appeared but it appears that scholars working out of Mauritius have chosen not to venture any opinion on this issue.

To date, and to our knowledge, there exists no major comparative study focused on Mauritius and any other country. Again the conference proceedings from the 'Esclaves Exclus, Citoyens' focussed on the marginalisation of ex-slaves and their descendants in modern Mauritius. However, some of the scholars today have moved against the positions that they took in the 1990s, and now contest the concept of marginalisation and of reparations for descendants of ex-slaves because, it is argued, few survived into the twentieth century.[45] This view is still hotly contested.

Many scholars have taken to heart what Gerbeau recommended for the study of slavery in the Indian Ocean, and there have been a spate of cultural studies examining links between Madagascar and Mauritius (Pier Larson),[46] the cultural continuum (Edward Alpers),[47] memory and identity studies (Teelock and Alpers, Chan Low),[48] contemporary Creole Culture (Palmyre, Romaine, Carpooran, Police-Michel, Hookoomsingh etc),[49] family history and micro-studies of localities (Teelock, Essoo, Le Chartier). Also exciting have been archaeological studies such as those carried out on the summit of Le Morne, a maroon hide-out, in the abandoned cemetery at the foot of the mountain and related sites around and numerous other archaeological studies. Archaeology in Mauritius has added a new dimension and infused the discipline of history in Mauritius with renewed vigour which had been lacking in recent years.

Data Sources and Methodology

Data Sources

The bulk of sources used emanate from Zanzibari and Mauritian National Archives. Both researchers have ploughed extensively through the collections and covered a fair amount. Access to non-Zanzibari and Non-Mauritian sources, such as documents from the National Archives of the UK, has been limited due to time and travel constraints, but copies of documents available there have been obtained from local archives and from scholars' previous work. The Zanzibar Indian Ocean Research Institute (ZIORI) also had substantial holdings and these were extensively used by the researchers.

The bulk of the archival information consists of official documents such as reports of Magistrates, Surveyors, Collectors of Revenue. However, travellers' writings and personal memoirs provided insightful inside views of the life of slaves. Official correspondences were also used and these were useful for assessing the divergence between metropolitan and local colonial government approaches.

Contemporary newspapers were used to a lesser extent as they tend to portray the views of colonial officials rather than slaves and ex-slaves.

The ZIORI Library, now donated to the Zanzibar State University Library, contained a vast collection which was tapped for secondary sources on slavery in other countries, allowed researchers to engage in comparative study of countries beyond Mauritius and Zanzibar. The most difficult was to extract the slave voices from the primary and secondary sources as direct sources emanating from slaves and ex-slaves are rare for both islands.

Methodology

The archival notes were expanded, organised and systematised. Data obtained were processed and arranged into patterns of information, which could be easily interpreted and analysed. Qualitative and quantitative techniques were used to analyse the data and establish a comparative study of Zanzibar and Mauritius. The results of analysis were presented through extensive discussion between researchers in the several workshops. The comparative analysis was partly undertaken by comparing the 'bands of evidence' available for both Mauritius and Zanzibar: such as characteristics of land ownership, access to capital, structure and statistics of slave ownership, vagrancy and anti-mobility laws and so on.

Assessing the potential for upward mobility of slaves was considered a crucial part of the analysis for both islands as these could explain the actions of ex-slaves after abolition of slavery. However, it was not possible to compare manumission in Mauritius and the *suria* system in Zanzibar as they represented such varied forms of achieving upward mobility.

Conclusion

The two small islands of Mauritius and Zanzibar in the south-western corner of the Indian Ocean, though similar in terms of size and population, and even in their multi-culturality, in fact offer very good case studies for the different traditions of slavery. On the one side was the Atlantic model that had developed at the dawn of the capitalist mode of production, and under the ideological hegemony of Christianity, before it extended into the Indian Ocean during the eighteenth century. On the other hand was the long and varied tradition of slavery in the Indian Ocean that developed in some areas under the influence of Islam with quite specific regulations and injunctions regarding the treatment of slaves, but which had to articulate with the capitalist mode of production when it became a worldwide system. A comparative history of Mauritius in the eighteenth and nineteenth centuries as it developed a slave system to produce sugar, and Zanzibar in the nineteenth century as it developed a plantation system based on slave labour to produce cloves, therefore, offers a fertile field for fruitful comparisons and contrasts between the different models of slavery, and in particular, the role of religious ideologies on the operation of the different slave systems, and the consequent different trajectories of integration of slaves and their offspring in the society.

To what extent these and other circumstances influenced the transition from slavery are issues to be considered comparatively for the two island communities. Emancipation came to the two communities nearly three quarters of a century apart. While both were under the control of the British, Mauritius was a British colony with a powerful French settler lobby, while Zanzibar was a British Protectorate with an Arab sultan who represented the collective interests of the former slave-owning class. When emancipation came, the slave owners in Mauritius demanded financial compensation and the slaves deserted the plantations on a massive scale unless constrained by the apprenticeship system designed to tie them to the land. In Zanzibar, there was considerable ambivalence: although a large number of slaves did desert the plantations for the opportunities of the town, and their masters accepted financial compensation, nearly a third of the owners refused to receive compensation, and some of the slaves, who had limited choices, preferred the security of their old social relationship with their old masters and existence on their plantations as squatters. This was even truer of domestic slaves who put greater faith in the old unequal social relationship with their old masters than in the uncertainties of rootless life when there was little possibility of returning to their original homes in the interior of Africa. This was especially true of the suria who had become part of the slave owner's family, and the owners resented emancipation of the suria the most because they considered it a deliberate break-up of their families, while the suria, unless their domestic situation had become unbearable, were loathe to abandon their relative security and continued relationship with their children who remained with their fathers.

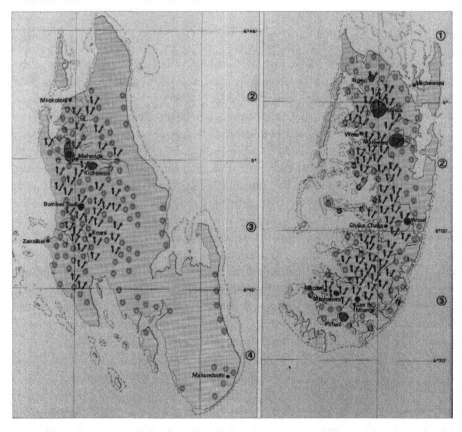

Figure 1.1: Map of Zanzibar showing clove coconut producing areas
Source: Zanzibar National Archives

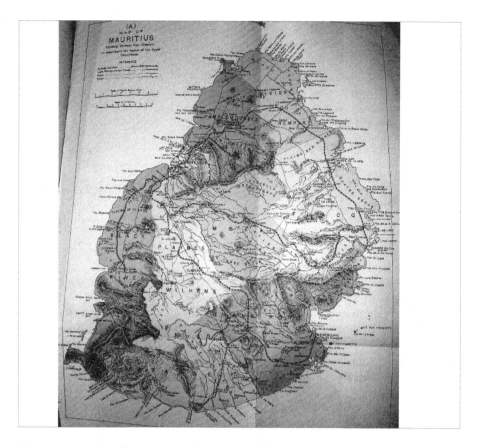

Figure 1.2: Map of Mauritius showing rural districts and agricultural land
Source: Mauritius National Archives

Notes

1. William A. Green, 'The Perils of Comparative History: Belize and the British Sugar Colonies after Slavery', *Comparative Studies in Society and History* Vol. 26, No. 1 (Jan., 1984), pp. 112-119.
2. Andreski is quoted in Nigel Bolland, 'Reply to William Green, The Perils of Comparative History', *Comparative Studies in Society and History* Vol. 26, No. 1 (Jan., 1984), pp.120-125.
3. Karl Marx, *Capital*, Vol. III (Moscow, Progress Publishers, 1971), Ch. XX.
4. See the work of Frederick Cooper, Thomas Holt, and Rebecca J. Scott, *Beyond Slavery: Explorations of Race, Labor, and Citizenship in Post-emancipation Societies,* (Chapel Hill: University of North Carolina Press, 2000), and also Rebecca Scott's 'Comparing Emancipations', *Journal of Social History* 20 (Spring 1987): 565-584 by which the section in this chapter is inspired. See also Eric Foner, *Nothing But Freedom: Emancipation and Its Legacy*, (Louisiana State University Press, 1983), a groundbreaking work attempting to introduce some comparisons with the Indian Ocean world.

5. Foner, *Nothing But Freedom*, p. 575.

6. Although O. Crone, *Mecca Trade and the Rise of Islam*, (Princeton: Princeton University Press. 1986) objects to this interpretation.

7. J. O. Hunwick, 'Black Slaves in the Mediterranean world', in E. Savage, ed., *The Human Commodity*, (London: Cass, 1992), 7, quoting a nineteenth century Moroccan jurist.

8. B. Lewis, *Race & Slavery in the Middle East* (Oxford: OUP, 1990) p.10. 'Abd', in *Encyclopaedia of Islam*-2nd edition 24-40.

9. Qur'an 4.3, 4.25, 24.32, 33.52.

10. Hunwick 1992, p. 7.

11. W. Arafat, 'The attitude of Islam to slavery', *Islamic Quarterly*, 10/1966.

12. Qur'an 2.178, 221; 4.25, 36, 92; 5.89; 9.60; 23.6; 24.33; 32.50; 47.4; 58.3; 70.30; 90.13.24.33. Hunwick 1992: 8.

13. J.G. Lorimer, *Gazeteer of the Persian Gulf, Oman and Central Arabia*, (Calcutta, 1908-15), p.15.

14. S. Miers and I. Kopytoff, eds, *Slavery in Africa: Historical and Anthropological Perspectives*, Madison, (University of Wisconsin, 1977).

15. Ali Mazrui, 'Comparative slavery in Islam, Africa and the West', Paper presented at Istanbul Conference on Islamic Thought, 1997.

16. http://en.wikipedia.org/wiki/Islam_and_slavery. Sayyida Salme / Emily Ruete, *An Arabian Princess Between Two Worlds*, tr. & ed. by E. van Donzel, (Leiden, Brill, 1993).

17. Mazrui, 1997.

18. Personal communication, Himla Soodyall to A. Sheriff, 12.4.2008. See Table 5. .

19. V. Teelock, *Mauritian History: from its Beginnings to Modern Times*, (Port Louis, Mahatma Gandhi Institute, 2nd edition, 2006).

20. See, for example ,works of P. Brest, R. Allen, T. Vernet and M. Guerout.

21. See, for example, Meyer, Guérout, Allen, Filliot Tome II, p. 66. Max Guérout, 'Le navire négrier 'Utile' et la traite Française aux Mascareignes', *Cahiers des Annales de la Mémoire*, no. 9, Nantes 2006.

22. Nicholas Draper, *The Price of Emancipation*, (CUP: 2011).

23. James Walvin, *Black Ivory: Slavery in the British Empire*, (Blackwell Publishers, 2001), p.280.

24. R. Coupland, *East Africa and Its Invaders* (Oxford: Clarendon Press, 1938)

25. P. Curtin, *The Atlantic Slave Trade*: A Census (Madison, Wisconsin: University of Wisconsin Press, 1969)

26. R. A. Austen, 'The Islamic slave trade out of Africa (Red Sea and Indian Ocean): an effort at quantification', Paper presented at the Conference on Islamic Africa: Slavery and related institutions, Princeton, 1977; 'The trans-Saharan slave trade: a tentative census', in H. A. Gemery & J. S. Hogendorn, eds, *The Uncommon Market: Essays in the Economic History of the Atlantic Slave Trade* (New York: Academic Press, 1979); 'The nineteenth century Islamic Slave Trade from East Africa (Swahili and Red Sea Coasts): a tentative census', in Clarence-Smith, ed, *Indian Ocean Slave Trade*, 1989, pp. 21-44. P. Lovejoy, *Transformations in Slavery*, (Cambridge, CUP, 1983).

27. W. Arafat, 'The attitude of Islam to slavery', *Islamic Quarterly* 10/1966.

28. B. Lewis, *Islam*. New York, Harper & Row, 2 vols. 1974; *Race and Slavery, in the Middle East* (Oxford, OUP), 1990.

29. J. O. Hunwick, 'Black Slaves in the Mediterranean world', in E. Savage, ed. *The Human Commodity,* (London, Cass, 1992).
30. A. A. Mazrui, 'Comparative slavery in Islam, Africa and the West', Unpublished paper presented at the Conference on Islamic Thought, (Istanbul, 1997).
31. Karl Noël, *L'esclavage à l'Ile de France pendant l'occupation française, 1715-1810,* Paris, 1953.
32. Asgarally Issa, *L 'Affaire Ratsitatane,* (Ed. Goutte d'eau dans l'océan, 1980).
33. S. Peerthum, 'Resistance against slavery', in U. Bissoondoyal, & SBC Servansing, (eds) *Slavery in South West Indian Ocean,* pp. 124-130.
34. Jumeer, Musleem. 'Les Affranchis et les Indiens libres à l'île de France (1721-1803)'. Thèse de Doctorat de 3ème cycle. Université de Poitiers, 1981.
35. Vijaya Teelock, *Bitter Sugar – Sugar and slavery in nineteenth century Mauritius* (1998).
36. Satyendra Peerthum, 'Forbidden freedom: Prison Life for Captured Maroons in Colonial Mauritius, 1766-1839' in Emmanuel Kofi Agorsah, G. Tucker Childs, eds, *Africa and the African diaspora: cultural adaptation and resistance,* 2005.
37. Amédée Nagapen, *Le marronnage à l'Isle de France-lle Maurice: rêve ou riposte de l'esclave?* (Centre Nelson Mandela pour la Culture Africaine, 1999).
38. M. Vaughan, *Creating The Creole Island: Slavery In Eighteenth-century Mauritius,* (Duke University Press, 2005).
39. From the many scholarly articles, see J.M. Filliot, *La traite des esclaves vers les Mascareignes au XVIIIème siècle.* (Paris, 1974); R.B. Allen, 'Licentious and Unbridled Proceedings: The Illegal Slave Trade to Mauritius and the Seychelles during the early Nineteenth Century.' *Journal of African History,* 42 (2001), 91-116; P.M. Larson, *History and memory in the age of enslavement: Becoming Merina in highland Madagascar, 1770-1822,* (Heinemann, 2000).
40. See, Volume 4 of the Truth and Justice Commission Report, http.www. gov.mu/portal/pmosite.
41. See the changes from R.B. Allen, 'The constant demand of the French : the Mascarene slave trade and the worlds of the Indian Ocean and Atlantic during the eighteenth and nineteenth centuries », *Journal of African History,* 49(1), 2008, pp. 43-72 to the 2010 article: R.B. Allen, 'Satisfying the "Want for Labouring People": European Slave Trading in the Indian Ocean, 1500–1850', *Journal of World History,* vol. 21, no. 1 (2010) M. Guérout, Le navire négrier 'Utile' et la traite Française aux Mascareignes', *Cahiers des Annales de la Mémoire,* no. 9, Nantes, 2006. See also the most recent work by T. Vernet, La première traite française à Zanzibar : le journal de bord du vaisseau l'Espérance, 1774-1775, in Solotiana Nirhy-Lanto Ramamonjisoa; C. Radimilahy, and N. Rajaonarimanana, *et al (dir.), Civilisations des mondes insulaires (Madagascar, canal de Mozambique, Mascareignes, Polynésie, Guyanes),* (Paris, Karthala, 2010).
42. See, for exmaple, the set of papers presented at a Conference in Mauritius published in 2002: J.C. Cangy, J. Chan Low, M. Paroomal, *L'esclavage et ses séquelles: mémoire et vécu d'hier et d'aujourd'hui : actes du colloque international,* Municipalité de Port-Louis, 2002.
43. See the website of the Legacies of British Slave Ownership at http://www.ucl.ac.uk/lbs and proceedings of the Neale Colloquium in British History 2012: Emancipation, Slave-ownership and the Remaking of the British Imperial World, 30-31 March 2012.

44. L.J. Chan Low, 'Les enjeux actuels des débats sur la mémoire et la réparation pour l'esclavage à l'île Maurice', *Cahiers d'études africaines,* 2004/1 n° 173-174, pp. 401-418.

45. See the heated debates surrounding this issue during a ½ day workshop held at the University of Mauritius, 13 April 2012 concerning the TJC report.

46. P.M. Larson, *History and memory in the age of enslavement: becoming Merina in highland Madagascar, 1770-1822,* Heinemann, 2000; *Ratsitatanina's gift: a tale of Malagasy ancestors and language in Mauritius,* Centre for Research on Slavery and Indenture, (University of Mauritius, 2008).

47. E. Alpers, 'Recollecting Africa: Diasporic Memory in the Indian Ocean world', in S. Jayasuriya, and R. Pankhurst, *The African diaspora in the Indian Ocean,* 2003.

48. J. Chan Low, 'Aux origines du malaise créole : Les ex-apprentis dans la société mauricienne (1839-1860)', in E. Maestri (dir.), *Esclavage et abolitions dans l'Océan Indien,* (Paris, L'Harmattan ; Saint-Denis, Université de La Réunion) : 2000, pp. 267-283.

49. Most recent writing include work of anthropologists attached to the Catholic Church: D. Palmyre, *Culture créole et foi chrétienne,* Marye Pike, 2007; A. Romaine, *Religion populaire et pastorale créole à l'île Maurice,* (Karthala Editions, 2003); A. Carpooran, 'Le Creole a l'ecole a Maurice: historique et evolution du debat', (Paris, L'Harmattan, 1978); *Diksioner morisien,* Editions Bartholdi, 2005 and R. Boswell, *Le Malaise Créole: Ethnic Identity in Mauritius* (Berghahn Books, 2006).

2

Slavery and the Slave Trade in the Indian Ocean

Vijayalakshmi Teelock and Abdul Sheriff

The specificities of the Indian Ocean slave trade and slavery have been highlighted in the numerous works of historians of the Indian Ocean such as Ned Alpers, Abdul Sheriff, Richard Allen and Hubert Gerbeau, and are being recognised even by scholars of the Atlantic region. Within the Indian Ocean, however, the specificities of individual countries need to be highlighted and contrasted with each other. Some Indian Ocean countries, such as Zanzibar and Madagascar, were both importers and exporters of slaves, while others without indigenous populations, like Mauritius and Reunion, were solely importers of slave labour. Before embarking on a comparative study of the transition of these slave societies to freedom, it is necessary to have an understanding of the historical context of the establishment of slavery and the peopling of the islands through the slave trade. This is the focus of this chapter.

Mauritius: The Colonial Slave Trade and Slavery

According to latest figures available from Richard Allen and Thomas Vernet, the numbers of slaves exported from the Indian Ocean by Europeans far exceed previous estimates.

Table 2.1: Export of slaves from the Indian Ocean

	1670-1769	1770-1810	1811-1848	Total
Madagascar	35,314-37,931	46,203-53,427	43,808-51,365	125,325-142,723
Eastern Africa	10,677-11,468	99,614-115,189	75,767-88,835	186,058-215,492
India	14,755-15,739		4,994-5,327	6,469-21,066
SE Asia		3,804-4,759		3,804-4,759

Of the total estimated by Allen[1] to date, the French slave trade is still by far the most substantial in the Indian Ocean.

Table 2.2: European slaving nations in the Indian Ocean

British total	10,525 - 12,539 slaves
Portuguese total	41,875 - 83,750 slaves
Dutch total	43,965 - 66,465 slaves
French total	334,936 - 384,040 slaves

Source: Richard Allen, 'Satisfying the "Want for Labouring People": European Slave Trading in the Indian Ocean', Journal of World History, Vol. 21, No.1, 2010, p. 45-73.

It is impossible to calculate the number of slaves who never reached the coast or captivity in the depot, given lack of information. Shell has estimated that another 20 per cent or so should be added to the total of slaves exported during colonial slavery.

It is also not possible, for the time being, to give separate figures of the number arriving in Mauritius alone; figures are given for the Mascarenes as a whole.[2]

Brief history of the slave trade to the Mascarenes in the eighteenth century

The French East India Company was directly involved in the slave trade for many years until it relinquished its rights to private traders. With the proximity of India, Indian textiles were used rather than French textiles, another factor which distinguishes the Atlantic and Indian Ocean slave trades. There were three main destinations for the slaves: Louisiana, St. Domingue and the Mascarenes.

French slave trading in the South West Indian Ocean was started in Madagascar to supply Bourbon Island (Reunion), colonised earlier in 1664. The slaves engaged in agriculture and the women among them married, or cohabited, with French men due to the shortage of French women. Indian prisoners were also landed there. On 20 September 1715, when Guillaume Dufresne D'Arsel took possession of Ile de France (Mauritius) in the name of the King, slavery and the slave trade were already established in neighbouring Bourbon. It started in earnest in Isle de France after the island was ceded to the FEIC on 2 April 1721.[3] Mauritius, until 1735, was subservient to Réunion. From 1721 to 1767, however, although the FEIC controlled the island, the French Government was increasingly present through Royal Commissaries, Directors of the FEIC nominated by the King, and the Syndics chosen by the Assembly of Shareholders. In 1727, Mauritius was given the right to trade directly with Madagascar, without going through Réunion, to build ports, warehouses and houses. With the arrival of Governor Dumas, according to Filliot, trade increased.

The period between 1735 and 1746 is crucial for the establishment of the slave trade, since Governor Labourdonnais chose Mauritius, rather than Réunion, as his base of operations to expand French influence in the Indian Ocean. Vast infrastructural works were envisaged to transform Port Louis into a capital, port, warehousing and commercial centre. Labour from France, Madagascar, Mozambique, West Africa and India was tapped.

Although the focus of historians has been on the French East India Company, the French Government was very much involved, directly and indirectly, in the slave trade from the beginning. In the Indian Ocean, they turned a blind eye to the hostilities occurring between different European powers in Europe. Thus, despite official hostilities between France and Portugal, officials of both countries engaged in an extremely lucrative trade which included slaves in the Indian Ocean. This had been the case since the period of Labourdonnais.

When the Revolutionary Government took over, despite the ban on the slave trade in France, slave trading continued fraudulently in the Indian Ocean. Corsairs were particularly active in continuing this illicit trade and huge profits are believed to have been made, in contrast to the Atlantic Ocean.

The establishment of the Napoleonic regime in 1803 led to the reinforcement of slavery and the resumption of legal slave trade in Mauritius. But even before that, on 20 May 1802, slave trade was permitted again on the grounds that cultivation and prosperity were suffering.[4] On 20 June 1802, the Colonial Assembly (set up under the Revolutionary Government) of Isle de France legalised the slave trade; the same decision was taken by the Colonial Assembly of Bourbon Island on 28 September.[5] This period was marked by a fierce revival of the French slave trade activities in Mozambique. In 1810 when the British took over, the Act suppressing the slave trade was supposed to take effect, but this went unheeded by both the local government and the slave traders. It was not until the 1820s that the slave trade dwindled when planters themselves wished to present a better image of themselves with the British Parliament in order to benefit from better tariffs on sugar, and voluntarily abandoned the slave trade.

Cultural transitions in the slave trade

To understand the cultural background of the slaves and their descendants, it is important to be aware of the different ethnic, linguistic and cultural compositions of slaves arriving in Mauritius. In the eighteenth century, the majority of the slaves came from Guinea and the West African coast; Mozambique which included the whole of the East African coast, Ethiopia, Egypt, from the Cape of Good Hope to Port of Suez; Madagascar and India from the Malabar Coast and east of Cape Cormorin.[6]

The slave registration returns, produced nearly a century later between 1826 and 1835 show roughly the same categorisations being used. However, new categories were included which reflected changes in Mauritian slave society: the category 'Créole', i.e., slaves born locally was added. It is from these registration returns that one can see the multiple ethnicities present in Mauritius during slavery and the cultural 'mix' that had evolved from interaction in the Indian Ocean as a whole.

In the 1826 returns, 'countries of origin' are listed. The most populous group was the 'Créole de Maurice' which by 1826, had been estimated by Shell to constitute roughly a third of the population that was locally born. Next came the 'Mozambique' group as shown earlier encompassing as in 1765, all those from the Eastern Africa coast and the mainland. The third largest group were the 'Malgache', or Malagasy group, comprising all the different groups in Madagascar, including a certain number of Mozambicans exported to Madagascar and re-exported to Mauritius. In much smaller numbers were the 'Créoles' from Rodrigues, Bourbon, Seychelles, Goa, Providence and Six Islands. These were slaves born on these islands and who are also listed in the registration returns as the islands were administered by Mauritius or had been transferred to Mauritius.

A smaller group consisted of Indian slaves from the Malabar Coast and Cochin. From South East Asia could be found a few Malays, some of whom had been introduced illegally into the country after the act of abolition of the Slave Trade had been passed. Finally, from the various islands and African mainland were a very varied group of slaves listed as being from Diégo Garcia, Anjouan, 'Arabs' and 'Arabs' from Mozambique. Little is known about this last group. A few slaves still remained from West Africa known as Guinea and Yoloff slaves, and a suburb of Port Louis, the capital city of Mauritius, still bears the name of Camp Yoloff. One slave was listed as being from Rio de Janeiro.

A rough compilation derived from Richard Allen's work shows the following:

Table 2.3: Country of origin of slaves exported

Year	Country of origin	Percentage (%) of slaves
1670-1769	Madagascar	70
	Mozambique/Swahili coast	19
	South Asia	9
	West Africa	2
1770-1810	Mozambique/Swahili coast	60
	Madagascar	31
	South Asia	9
1811-1848	Mozambique/Swahili coast	59
	Madagascar	38
	Southeast Asia	3

It is clear that, at different times, different sources of slaves were tapped, thus influencing the cultural composition and cultural evolution of the island.

- **'Mozambique'**

Trade with Mozambique started with Réunion Island and continued later with Mauritius. Count Ericeira recommended to the Capitaine-General of Mozambique to provide all facilities for the French slave trade with Mozambique. In 1721, two French ships, the *Duchesse de Noailles* and *L'Indien*, went to Mozambique.

Almost 13 years later, in 1733, the next ship, the *Vierge de Grâce*, went to Mozambique. It took 356 slaves on board, but only 147 arrived alive at Réunion. In 1735, Labourdonnais recommended that a trading station should be established on the west coast of Madagascar to carry out the slave trade with Mozambique and with the Portuguese. After the departure of Labourdonnais, trade slumped somewhat. But by 1753, more and more slaves were required for Mauritius. Negotiations with Portugal were recommended so that trade in Mozambique could take place and establishments were proposed.[7] The definition of what was a Mozambique appears at this time, as "noir Mozambique qui comprendra toute la côte orientale d'Afrique d'Abyssinie d'Égypte, depuis le Cap de Bonne Espérance jusqu'au port Suez".[8]

Although Portuguese laws did not allow foreign ships in Portuguese ports, these laws were circumvented whenever necessary. The Portuguese needed foodstuffs from Mauritius and turned a blind eye, if necessary. The French also went to Ibo (Kerimba Island) which was not under Portuguese administration and also in Inhambane in the south. They traded almost exclusively with the Yao, while later in the nineteenth century, it was the Mataca kingdom that took over the trade.[9]

Due to the fact that much of this was illegal, trading figures are sketchy. It would seem that some 1,300-1,400 slaves a year were brought to the Mascarenes. By 1758, the French controlled the European slave trade of the whole coast from Mombasa to Kilwa, up to Ibo.[10]

- **Swahili coast**

East Africa is considered separately here from 'Mozambique' simply to show that, although the ports were located in what is East Africa today, the actual origins were diverse, as slaves were brought from the hinterland that stretched right into the interior going as far as Malawi and Mozambique. Thus, the journal of the *Espérance*, although marking slaves as coming from Zanzibar, lists one Makonde slave having died of smallpox.[11] When the French Government took over Mauritius in 1766, a new era in the slave trade ensued. Eastern Africa was highly sought after by the French. But until the 1750s, there do not appear to have been many slaves shipped out to the Mascarenes from the Swahili coast, although they had been shipped to Oman before then.

Jean-Vincent Morice can be said to have inaugurated the slave trade with East Africa.[12] He negotiated and signed a 100-year treaty with the sultan of Kilwa, Sultan Hassan bin Ibrahim al-Kilwi al–Shirazi, [13] to supply him with 1,000 slaves a year. The French also wanted to give exclusive rights to the Portuguese to trade in slaves to the Mascarenes, on condition that French traders were given similar rights in Portuguese trading posts such as Kerimba, Mozambique and others.[14]

In 1770, the slave trade with Eastern Africa increased, and five times more slaves were brought from Mozambique than from Madagascar. Between 1785 and 1790, approximately 1,500 slaves left for the Mascarenes each year. In 1793, corsairs raided the Mozambican coast. According to Filliot, the need for new slaves arose because of the increased rate of manumissions. Under French laws, a slave could be manumitted by either self-purchase, by a will or by the owner as a reward. On 4 February 1794, the slave trade was suspended, but corsairs and planters collaborated to circumvent the ban. Early in October 1796, some 100 men, led by French corsairs, attacked the town of Ibo and, two days later, Kerimba Island, and two French ships attacked Lorenzo Marques and burnt the fortress. They expelled the Portuguese from Delagoa Bay and competed with the British and Portuguese for the ivory trade. Napoleonic wars disrupted the trade. An annual average of 9,000 slaves in the late 1780s declined to just over 2,300 in 1794.[15] At the end of the eighteenth century, it was a 'free for all' period with corsairs, Americans and Brazilians competing.

There are similarities with the origins of slaves brought to Zanzibar from the mainland. Amongst these were also slaves brought to Mauritius. There were thirty-two African tribes, such as the Zaramo, Yao, Nyasa, Gindo, Nyema, Nyamwezi, Makua, Mchania, Mrima, Mgogo, Mwera Karani, Manamnji, etc., who provided slaves, of whom the Zaramo, Yao, Nyasa, Gindo, Nyema, and Nyamwezi supplied most slaves to Zanzibar and Mauritius.

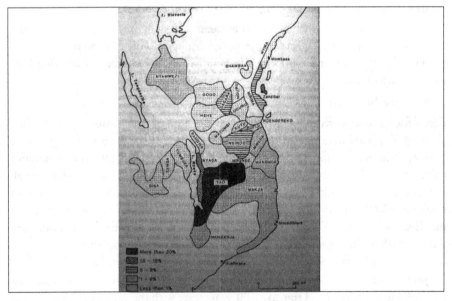

Figure 2.3: Map of Eastern Africa showing proportion of slaves from different tribes freed in Zanzibar in 1860s

Source: W. G. Clarence-Smith, *The Economics of the Indian Ocean Slave Trade*, (London: Cass), 1989, p. 132).

- **'West Africa'**

In contrast to the Atlantic, West African slaves were few in Mauritius due to heavy mortality and higher costs. The FEIC had two main trading posts in West Africa: Ouidah in Benin (formerly Dahomey) and Gorée in Senegal. In Gorée, a fort had been built where French traders, their slaves and goods were 'secure'.[16] In addition to the ships listed by LeLan, the C4 series in the French National Archives mention another ship, the *Fleury*, which was to bring slaves from Senegal.[17] In 1728, the *Méduse* went to Ouidah to purchase some 400 slaves. Several other ships made the voyage to West Africa, among which were: the *Vierge de Grâce*, the *Diane*, the *Duc de Noailles* and the *Badine*. In 1729, two other ships went to Ouidah and Senegal but because of the high death rate, this source of slaves was discontinued. By 1731, the FEIC had a monopoly of the slave trade in Madagascar, and thus banned the trade with India and Senegal. Between 1739 and 1744, under Governor Labourdonnais, some 100 slaves were brought. In 1750, the *Hercule*, the *Chevalier Main*, and B*ristols* brought 789 slaves, out of the 1,090 who embarked from Gorée. This represented a 28% death rate. The last ship to bring in slaves from West Africa was possibly the *Duc de Choiseul*. The location where they lived is found in archival maps of Camp Yoloff and Camp Bambara in Mauritius.

- **'India'**

Indian slaves are not known in the Atlantic Ocean slave trade, and this is another major difference with the Atlantic as it challenges traditional perceptions of 'black' slavery. Chinese slaves from South East Asia were also brought. The year 1728 witnessed the arrival of the first Indian slaves in Mauritius under French rule. The number of Indian slaves increased when private individuals were also permitted to bring in slaves from India. Labourdonnais introduced 70 slaves for his personal use. In 1750, the desire was still there to bring in slaves from India, as well as other areas for the Company.[18] Apart from Pondicherry and Bengal, Goa was also tapped for slaves.[19]

Allen has estimated that between 19,750 and 23,900 slaves arrived from India to the Mascarenes, but for Mauritius alone, the figures are not available.[20] Further research is needed on Asian slaves arriving not only from India, but also from South East Asia. However by the time of the 1847 census, no ex-slave reported having been born in India, thus signifying that there were few if any from the latter part of the eighteenth century.

- **'Madagascar'**

From the French East India Company's point of view, Madagascar was ideal as a source of slaves for the Mascarenes, since it was cheaper than procuring slaves from India or West Africa. It also had the monopoly of trade with Madagascar, except for a brief period between 1742 and 1746, when private traders were allowed to trade. The colonists, for their part, found that proximity with Madagascar tempted Malagasy slaves to maroon more often. It was, therefore, not advisable to send them to work in the port, as they could easily steal vessels and escape to Madagascar.

The closest and safest part of Madagascar to Mauritius was Antongil Bay and later Foulpointe. Their hinterland supplied large numbers of slaves. In 1733, the Company did try to replicate its activities in Senegal by building a permanent trading post in Antongil Bay at Nosy Mangabé, but it failed. From 1750, Foulpointe became more important. Antongil, Tamatave, Fénérive, Mananara, Engontsy and l'île Sainte-Marie were secondary posts. Although Fort Dauphin was the healthiest port, there were few slaves in the hinterland, so the Company used this port more for other trade in rice and salted meat. Many slaves were brought from East Africa originally and resold to French traders on the East coast of Madagascar.

This trade continued right up to 1822. Toussaint's figures of some 20,000 slaves being brought in illegally to the Mascarenes from Madagascar has been revised recently by Larson who estimates a much higher figure of 60,000 slaves. Illegal trade continued also from the Seychelles. For Mauritius alone, it is believed now that from 1800 to 1810, some 3,500 slaves imported is closer to the reality, and from 1810 to 1820, over 6,000 slaves were brought. However, further research is required on this issue.

- **Slavery**

The economic importance of the slave trade and of slavery must be underlined as far as an understanding of the history of the Mauritian economy is concerned and to understand post-emancipation outcomes. Both the slave trade and slavery started as part of the search by the French to find labour for the numerous activities to be undertaken. The slave trade was engaged in the hope of bringing substantial profits. As stated by the Truth and Justice Commission report of November 2011, 'without the establishment of a slave society and economy, there would have been no Isle de France in the eighteenth century and no sugar industry in nineteenth century British Mauritius'. It must be stated, however, that non-slave labour was also sought but not in great numbers. The orphanages of Paris were tapped to bring in young apprentices to be trained in workshops in the Company headquarters located in Port Louis, and free Malagasy and Indian skilled artisans were brought in small numbers also in skilled trades and occupations.

The bulk of labour employed in the revenue-bearing sectors of the economy as well as in domestic homes, however, was supplied by slave labour from 1720s to the 1830s. As also stated by the TJC report, 'the fortunes of many today were built on the prosperity of those who traded and used slave labour in the eighteenth and nineteenth centuries.'

Slavery became established when distinctions appeared between the French and their Malagasy and Indian servants. In 1674, an Ordinance of Jacob de la Haye Article 20 ordered that there would be no marriages between French and *négresses* or between *noirs* and white women. The term 'slave' also appears for the first time in Bourbon.[21] It is there that slavery, as it is understood in Mauritius, became established with maroon hunts, separate Parish Registers and domestic servants being treated as property.[22]

Slave labour was seen as the most reliable source of labour, although a certain amount of free labour was also brought in, in the form of French engagés, and skilled Malagasy and Indian workers and artisans. Labourdonnais personally took charge of acquiring slaves for the island and undertook the massive construction projects in Mauritius: roads, houses, the port, a naval base, the Botanic Gardens etc. The whole infrastructure of Port Louis, the capital, in the eighteenth century could be said to have been built mainly by slaves, but it must be recognised, also by French *engagés* and free skilled people from various parts of the world. The first colonists were not keen on engaging in construction work, and so a large number of slaves were brought from India, Madagascar, West Africa and Mozambique to furnish the labour power required.

But there always seemed to be a chronic shortage of labour. The census of 1766 revealed that of the 67,389 *arpents*[23] (27, 234 ha) of land granted, 3,708 (1,499 ha) were uncultivated due to the absence of slaves.

In addition, the Company also owned slaves who worked in various capacities. When the King took over the island in 1765, the slaves belonging to the Company were ceded to the King. In 1769, out of a total of 1,228 slaves, there were: 162 Malagasies, 436 Guineans, 345 Creoles, 254 Mozambicans, 25 Indians, 2 Creoles from Bourbon, 1 from Pondicherry and 3 from Macao. They were divided into 662 men, 271 women, 139 boys, 126 girls, 21 young male children and 9 female infants.[24]

Despite an increasing amount of interest among researchers on the history of slavery and the slave trade in Mauritius in recent years, no demographic study of the slave population or an assessment of the data available has been carried out. Historians and other researchers have used whatever statistics they could find or were easily at hand, and these have been used indiscriminately. The most widely used compilation of statistics has been that of Baron d'Unienville's *Statistique de l'île Maurice* published in 1838. Not only are the slave data contained in it estimates, but the published version of his work is believed to be full of mistakes. The manuscript version of his work lies in the Public Record Office and has yet to be compared with the published version. With the exception of Richard Allen and Barker who have been cautious in their use of d'Unienville's figures, most researchers seem to have adopted them as a reliable and accurate set of data. The slave registration returns compiled under British rule are the most complete sources of statistical data available to date. In the first official registration of 1815, the illegal slaves appear in the form of hundreds of young males born overseas and without parents. There were 51,452 male slaves and 28,594 female slaves in Mauritius at this time.

In 1826 the figures for the slave population were 66,656 slaves.

Table 2.4: Ethnic Origin of Slaves

Ethnic origin	Male	Female
Creoles	17,371	17,461
Mozambican	15,444	3,713
Malagasy	8,271	4,396
Total	41,086	25,570

Despite the numerous errors, particularly in ages and marks of imported slaves, the 1826 registration is considered the most complete yet and carried out with more care than ever before.

The Impact of Sugar Expansion on Slavery

By 1832, there were 2,605 slave-owners in Mauritius. Out of these, 1,192 owners owned four or fewer slaves and had a total of 2,372 slaves. These small slave-holding units were composed for the most part of the owner's family and a number of slave families. A 'medium'-sized unit had between 20 and 99 slaves, while a large slave holding unit, 100 or more slaves. 'Medium'-sized estates can be further categorised into sugar producing and others. The sugar producers on average owned over 49 slaves.

Sugar was increasingly grown from 1815 on large slave-holding units and principally in the three northern and western districts of the island: Pamplemousses, Rivière du Rempart and Flacq. The transformation of society and economy engendered by sugar expansion also had its effects on the slaves: reorganisation brought significant changes, for example in the spatial and occupational distribution of rural slaves in the districts and estates. The slave population became concentrated in the northernmost and western districts of Pamplemousses (15.6 %), Rivière du Rempart (12.7 %) and Flacq (14 %), i.e., the 'sugar' districts. Between 1825 and 1830, the slave population increased by over 3,700 slaves in Pamplemousses, Rivière du Rempart and Flacq while a substantial decrease took place in Savanne and in Plaines Wilhems. The abolition of the slave trade and the slowing down of illegal trade had led to an increasing number of slaves over the age of 45 years and an increasing proportion of locally-born slaves. According to the Commission of Eastern Enquiry (CEE), there were over 7,000 children in the districts alone, i.e., one-seventh of the total rural population and some 2,000 aged slaves over 60 years old.

Age was perhaps the most crucial factor in deciding occupational stratification: the ages preferred were from 15 to 39 years as slaves were at their most productive. Gender was especially important on sugar estates. Field work, especially the physically strenuous tasks of clearing, hoeing, planting and harvesting were tasks believed to be best carried out by men. But with the dearth of field hands, slave women in Mauritius were used in activities traditionally carried out by men such as clearing, hoeing and planting. According to the CEE, in 1826, deaths on large plantations exceeded births because of 'immoral intercourse, severe labour, insufficient food and comforts'.[25] By 1832, the census reveals continued persistent high mortality figures on most estates.

In the 1830s, there was thus little improvement in the provision of food and health care of slaves. The hurricanes destroyed straw huts regularly every year, and slaves were often left without any shelter for days on end.[26] However, an improvement had occurred because slaves were now vaccinated. During the period under French rule, diseases and infections such as smallpox, fevers, plague and leprosy depopulated the slave population.[27] The evidence from the Protector of Slaves showed the trauma that slaves underwent during the period of sugar expansion. By the 1830s, the use of steam engines and water mills had increased greatly. More field and mill slaves were thus needed. Far from saving slave labour, technological change actually created a demand for more and more labour as an increase in agricultural output was expected. It was estimated that the labour input required for preparing the land, digging holes and planting, was higher than cane cutting to a proportion of eight to one.[28]

Zanzibar: The Slave Trade and Slavery

The Slave Trade

The islands of Zanzibar lie less than 40 miles from the East African coast, and have enjoyed close social, economic, and at times even political relations with the Swahili coast across the narrow channel for at least two millennia of recorded history, and maybe even longer as archaeological evidence has begun to reveal. Moreover, Zanzibar and the rest of the Swahili coast have been part of the Muslim world for at least one millennium, and now Zanzibar is overwhelmingly Muslim. During this long millennium, evidence for slave trade can be traced in historical records from as early as the seventh century when Zanj slaves from the East African coast begin to appear in the annals of the Middle East, but from existing records it appears that there were probably only two major periods when slavery as a system of production was in operation.

The first was in the tenth century when a large number of Zanj from the East African coast and elsewhere in Africa, but also slaves from India and central Asia, were imported in large numbers to the Persian Gulf. An oppressive and highly exploitative system of slavery was set up within an overall tributary mode of production in southern Iraq. It led to the famous Zanj Rebellion during which the rebels set up their state and controlled the Basra region for 14 years.[29]

The second period that we are more immediately concerned developed from the eighteenth century and was connected with the transformation of Oman following the expulsion of the Portuguese from Muscat in 1650. It led to the growing importance of commerce in the political economy of Oman, and investment of commercial profit in date production based on slave labour. Slaves were exported from the Swahili coast northwards to Arabia and the Persian Gulf to supply labour for the date plantations and pearl diving in the Persian Gulf, as well as to meet the demand for domestic slaves that accompanied these developments.

This trade has been widely exaggerated by the British abolitionists in the nineteenth century and the colonial and post-colonial historians in the twentieth century without considering the potential for absorption of such large number of slaves by the economy and society in the deserts of Arabia. The only clue to the dimension of the slave trade in the eighteenth century comes from an Omani chronicle that states that Imam Saif b. Sultan (1692-1711), who had expelled the Portuguese from the East African coast in 1699, owned 1,700 slaves and one-third of all the date-palms in Oman. We can therefore hazard a guess that the slave populations on the date plantations in Oman may have been in the region of 5,000, although the numbers may have increased as the economy of Oman flourished in the mid-eighteenth century. Slaves were also ubiquitous among the dhow sailors and pearl divers of the Persian Gulf – an early nineteenth century detailed survey suggests that they constituted a third of the 27,000 to 30,000 pearl divers. Moreover, a smaller number of slaves was absorbed in the Sultan's army, and in 1802, it included 1,100 African slaves.[30] These developments also created a demand for domestic slaves for which it is difficult to estimate a global figure.

The most detailed estimates by British officials in the Persian Gulf in the early nineteenth century give a figure of between 1,400 and 1,700 slaves imported into the major Omani ports of Sur and Muscat, of whom three quarters were from the Swahili coast and the rest from Ethiopia. Some of these slaves were transhipped to the Persian Gulf which seems to have imported a much smaller number of slaves directly from the African coast – only one dhow carried 12 slaves directly from the Swahili coast. In 1841 the British kept a register of all dhows passing to the northern end of the Gulf, and they counted 1,217 slaves, almost equally divided between males and females. Based on these figures, Martin and Ryan estimated an annual average of only 2,500 for the period 1770 to 1829, and Austen has revised his figures down to 2,250 per annum for the period 1700 to 1815.[31]

The northern slave trade which had developed within the pre-capitalist mode of production had a fairly limited potential for expansion. On the other hand, from the eighteenth century eastern Africa was being drawn into the vortex of the Atlantic system of slavery that was encroaching into the south-western Indian Ocean. From the 1730s there was a growing demand for slaves in the previously uninhabited Mascarenes islands of Mauritius and Réunion that was initially met largely by Madagascar and intermittently by Mozambique and the Swahili coast. From the last third of that century, the market expanded to meet the growing demand for African slaves for the emerging sugar plantation economy and other infrastructural activities in those islands. In 1775, the French slave trader, Morice, inaugurated the southern branch of the slave trade of the Swahili coast on a large scale by making two voyages to Zanzibar, taking a total of 1,625 slaves. The following year he shifted his trade to the source at the major slave port of Kilwa, which was described as 'the entrepot for the slave trade for all the coast of Zanzibar'. He bought 700 slaves, and signed a treaty with the Sultan of Kilwa to supply 1,000 slaves a year. In 1784 Joseph Crassons de Medeuil listed 14 voyages that carried a total of 4,193 slaves over a period of 28 months, giving an average of nearly 2,000 slaves per annum.[32]

Therefore, the slave sector of the economy of the Swahili coast during the late eighteenth and early nineteenth century consisted largely of an export of about 2,250-2,500 slaves to the north, and perhaps an equal number going to the south. However, the intensifying Anglo-French warfare during the Napoleonic period began to disrupt this lucrative branch of trade of the Swahili coast, culminating in the capture of Mauritius by the British in 1810, and the prohibition of slave trade to the south by the Moresby Treaty of 1822. Only five vessels traded at Kilwa and Zanzibar in 1803-4 compared with at least eleven in 1788. James Prior commented in 1811 that 'the number of slaves formerly exported amounted to many thousands, but at present the demand is confined to the Arabs, who do not take many'.[33] The crisis resulting from the loss of the southern market forced Zanzibar and the Swahili coast to internalise the use of slave labour, thus giving a tremendous boost to the creation of a slave economy and society on the Swahili coast that consumed even more slaves by the 1860s than they were exported half a century earlier.[34]

Cloves were initially introduced to Mauritius during the eighteenth century, smuggled there from Dutch-controlled Indonesia.. However, Mauritius is located along the thoroughfare of hurricanes, and therefore the perennial could not thrive there, and was replaced by sugar. With the disruption of the slave trade on the Swahili coast, an enterprising Arab, who had previously been trading in slaves to the Mascarenes, probably in partnership with some French slave traders, introduced cloves from Mauritius in c. 1810. He planted them on his plantations at Mtoni and Kizimbani, and by the 1820s, small quantities of cloves had begun to reach the Bombay market from the East African coast. Because the Dutch were still exercising a monopoly over the spice, prices were very high. This led to what a French visitor in the 1840s described as a 'clove mania', clearing the coconut and other trees for cloves. By the end of the same decade production from Zanzibar had peaked, and overproduction led to a precipitous decline in the price of cloves and stagnation until the 1870s. The clove had been introduced to the smaller island of Pemba which was even more suitable, but the fall in prices and stagnation postponed the emergence of that island as the larger producer until after the hurricane of 1872.

This expansion of the clove economy was steered by Sultan Seyyid Said who visited Zanzibar in 1828, and immediately recognised the potential for his East African dominion. He is said to have compelled his subjects to plant a certain proportion of clove to coconut trees. The ruling dynasty and the Omani ruling class undoubtedly dominated the clove economy at that time, but they were soon joined by the indigenous Shirazi ruler, the Mwinyi Mkuu and other Swahili landowners. Even some of the Indian merchants had begun by the 1840s to pay 'their tribute to the mania', acquiring through foreclosures clove plantations worked by slaves. The source of capital for these plantations in many cases was trade that was flourishing at Zanzibar at that time, in which Arab, Swahili and Indian traders were involved, including the caravan trade into the interior which was the source of wealth of such people as Tipu Tip who reportedly owned seven plantations and 10,000 slaves by the end of the nineteenth century.

Unlike Mauritius, cloves were introduced to an island that was already long settled by the indigenous Shirazi population who were predominantly Muslim, and therefore could not be legally enslaved under Islamic law. Moreover, as peasants, they preferred to work on their own communal land to produce their subsistence rather than work on the clove plantations as workers, retreating to less fertile areas when their lands were encroached upon by the expanding clove plantations. Therefore, the clove economy was almost entirely dependent on slave labour imported from the mainland. Contemporary sources are replete with some wild guesses about the slave population of Zanzibar at various times on which some modern scholars have tried to construct hypothetical curves based on untenable assumptions (e.g. Martin & Ryan 1977). However, Albrand's and Burgess's first-hand accounts suggest a slave population of 15,000 and 17,000 in 1819 and 1839 respectively when the 'clove mania' was just getting underway. By the time the clove had peaked in the late 1840s, Putnam and Loarer give figures of 60,000 and 100,000 where it may have stagnated because of a drastic fall in the price of cloves. Customs house figures for the 1860s suggest that, by that time, about 12,000 of the nearly 20,000 slaves passing through Zanzibar were retained for local production and services, which seems to be realistic in view of the high mortality and low reproduction among slaves, estimated at about 10 per cent.[35]

The hurricane which hit Zanzibar in 1872 and totally destroyed the clove plantations of Unguja, followed by the 1873 treaty which prohibited all slave trade by sea, began to transform the clove economy of Zanzibar. Much of the replanting of cloves thereafter occurred in the more fertile Pemba, and many of the landowners shifted their slaves there. It is in this context that the list of slaves owned in Pemba compiled by an Arab official of the British Consulate, Sulaiman b. Saleh, should be seen. The detailed but partial estimate by this official in 1875 gives the number of slaves owned in Pemba just after the hurricane and the prohibition of all slave trade at 28,057, which he suspected to be half the total number; although his estimates may be exaggerated because he was doing the estimate secretly at the behest of the British Consul charged with the stoppage of the slave trade.[36]

The growth of the slave trade during the nineteenth century was due, therefore, not to any expansion in the demand for slaves in the desiccated coasts of Arabia, but to a fundamental transformation of the slave economy from one that had depended on the export of slaves, to one that retained slave labour within East Africa to produce agricultural commodities for export, especially cloves on Zanzibar, and oil-producing grains on the coast of Kenya, for export to the East and the West. In fact, British efforts to prohibit the export of slaves to the south by the Moresby Treaty of 1822, and to the north by the Hammerton Treaty of 1845, ironically, contributed to the localisation of the slave economy along the East African coast. This had a much greater potential for expansion since slaves were a vital means of production. It developed its own momentum once it was connected to the more vibrant industrial economies of Europe, more than making up for the losses in the export markets for slaves in the Mascarenes.

Slavery

Unfortunately, the registers of the emancipated slaves of 1897 have not yet been found in the Zanzibar Archives to give a more reliable overall picture of the characteristics of the slave population in Zanzibar. The annual reports of the Slave Commissioners give an overall number of slaves who were freed between 1897 and 1907. Surprisingly, only 11,837 were emancipated out of a figure of between 60,000 and 100,000 who may have been there at the height of the clove economy before the hurricane of 1872.[37] Part of the reason may have been the cut-off of the supply of slaves from the mainland after the prohibition of the slave trade by the 1873 treaty. This was a full quarter century before official emancipation during which the number may have been depleted by high mortality and low reproduction among slaves without being replaced. Part of the reason also is the manumission of 3,776 slaves by Muslim owners between 1897 and 1901, apart from others who may not have been reported, who preferred rewards in the afterworld rather than worldly compensation from the hand of the British, as Saada Wahab shows in her study, to which we shall return.

As regards the profile of the slave population, the emancipation figures fortunately give a gender breakdown, showing 47 per cent were male and 53 per cent were female. A larger proportion of women may come as a surprise to those familiar with the Atlantic slave trade where there was a heavy preponderance of able-bodied men. However, since emancipation came nearly a quarter of a century after the prohibition of the slave trade, the larger female proportion may also to some extent be due to the longevity of women common in many populations. It may also be explained by the larger proportion of domestic slaves in the Unguja island of Zanzibar, although they also included male domestic slaves, and women may have been used to a larger extent even on the plantations where they could help in picking cloves from the lower branches and separating the cloves from the stems. Other evidence from captured slave dhows show a surprisingly larger number of children, as much as 30 per cent, because the owners preferred to socialise younger children at an early age especially for domestic work.[38]

For further elaboration of the characteristics of the slave population, we are fortunate to have a register of about 1,620 slaves who were held illegally by Indians that were considered British subjects by British Consul Charles Rigby, and were thus freed by him in the 1860s. However, since Indians in Zanzibar were primarily urban-based merchants and traders who used their slaves mostly to transport goods, and only a few seem to have had any plantations, it may not be representative of the total slave population. Among the Indian-owned slaves, a vast majority of the owners (82 per cent) held less than 9 slaves, probably mostly as domestics, while 18 per cent held between 10 and 69 slaves who may have been used for transportation of goods, and only one owner, the foremost merchant and customs master, who had 446 slaves. He was one of the few who employed them on his plantations as well as for his commercial activities in the town. Among the emancipated slaves, only 16 per cent were over the age of 40. The largest category of slaves, who constituted 61 per cent of all the emancipated slaves, were between the ages of 20 and 39, and were almost equally balanced in terms sex. On the other hand, 22 per cent were children under the age of 19, but in this category males predominated (56 per cent) over females. Among the last class, particularly notable is the class of *wazalia* (locally born) who constituted 13 per cent of the emancipated slave population. Commenting on the fertility of slave women, Rigby had claimed that fewer than five per cent of the adult females bore children because they were liable to be deprived of their offspring. However, statistics show that of the 124 children of both sexes under the age of 10, 104 were born in Zanzibar, showing that slaves were able to reproduce themselves, and some were in their forties.[39]

Conclusion

This chapter has highlighted the similarities and differences between the two islands in terms of composition of the slave population and their owners as well as the emerging structure of the economy based essentially on slave labour. Culturally, it is clear both islands had very different orientations as Mauritius was ruled by a French administration intent on 'civilising' its slave and non-white free population by integrating them into the Catholic faith, the only religion allowed in Mauritius at the time. In Zanzibar, the British could not displace the religions and cultures they found there, and so were forced to accommodate them. The varying ethnic and cultural organisation of society found in each island operated in equally varying ways during the transition to freedom, and influenced emancipation outcomes for ex-slaves and their former owners.

Photo 2.1: Clove picking
Source: Zanzibar National Archives

Photo 2.2: Female slaves and their overseer
Source: Zanzibar National Archives

Notes

1. Richard Allen, 'Satisfying the "Want for Labouring People": European Slave Trading in the Indian Ocean', *Journal of World History*, Vol. 21, No.1, 2010, p.45-73.

2. These figures have not been disaggregated by historians as yet, although the Truth and Justice Commission has started this process. However, there are local censuses which can give an indication of how many slaves there were on the island.

3. Filliot, Volume 2, p. 40.

4. See Filliot, volume 2, p.84 and Eric Saugera, '*La traite des noirs en trente questions.*' Document downloaded from, http://hgc.ac-creteil.fr. Editions Geste. 2003, p. 34

5. Hubert Gerbeau, L'Océan Indien n'est pas L'Atlantique. La Traite illégale à Bourbon au XIXe siècle.' Un article publié dans *Outre-mer*, No 336-337, Décembre 2002, Paris, p. 79-108 par Olivier Pétré-Grenouilleau, pp.1-282).

6. COL-C4-7-2 1751-1753 Corr. Gén. David, de Lozier Bouvet, 1753 Mémoire concernant les îles de France et de Bourbon, Distinction par classes de noirs, tarifs pour chaque espèce.

7. COL-C4-7-2 1751-1753 Corr. Gén. David, de Lozier Bouvet,1753 M. Projet de L'abbé de la Tour.

8. COL-C4 -7 Mémoire concernant les îles de France et Bourbon 1753.

9. Benigna Zimba, *The slave trade to Mauritius and the Mascarenes 1780s to the 1870s*, Truth and Justice Commission Report, Vol 4: Part VI Slave trade and Slavery.

10. M. Jackson-Haight, *European Powers and South-East Africa.., 1796-1856*, London,1942, p.108.

11. T. Vernet, *La première traite francaise à Zanzibar...l'Espérance 1774-1775*, 2011, p.518.

12. Vernet, *La première traite*, p. 478.

13. G.S.P Freeman-Grenville, *The French at Kilwa Island*, Clarendon Press,1965, p.71.

14. COL–C4-15 1763-1765 Corr gén. Desforges Boucher Mémoire sur la position actuelle des établissements français.

15. Abdul Sheriff, *Slaves, Spices & Ivory in Zanzibar*, London, Currey, 1987, p.46.

16. Le Lan, p.3. For more information on the French slave trade with West Africa, see Philippe Haudrère and G. Le Bouëdec, Les Compagnies des Indes, Collection Ouest-France, 2001 and Patrick Villiers, 'Les établissements français et les débuts de la station navale française sur les côtes occidentales d'Afrique de 1755 à 1792' in A la découverte de l'Afrique noire par les marins français (XV° - XIX° siècle), Rochefort et la mer, Vol. 12, Publications à l'Université Francophone d'Eté-Jonzac,1998.

17. COL-C4-3 1738-1739 Correspondances générales M. de la Bourdonnais, gouverneur1739 M. de Cossigny, ingénieur.

18. COL-C4-6 1749-1750 Corr. Gén.David, 1750,Réflexions anonymes pour l'intérêt de la Compagnie des Indes.

19. COL-C4-6 1749-1750 Corr. Gén.David, 1750,Réflexions.

20. R. Allen, 'The Constant Demand of the French', *Journal of African History*, 2008.

21. Filliot, Tome II, p.29.

22. Filliot, Tome II, p. 33.

23. One hectare is equivalent to 2.47 *arpents*, an old French measure still in use in Mauritius.

24. MNA : OA 109 (1769), dossier 4, ff 32.
25. PRO: CO 167/118, Colebrooke and Blair to Lord Howick, 17 December 1828.
26. PRO: CO 167/16, Report of Dr. Burke to Kelso, 13 July 1813.
27. PRO: CO 167/16, Dr. Burke to Farquhar, 15 October 1813.
28. F. Scarano, *Sugar and Slavery in Puerto Rico*, 1984.
29. Alexandre Popovic, *The Revolt of African Slaves in Iraq in the 3rd/9th Century*, Princeton, Marcus Wiener, 1999.
30. Sheriff, 1987, pp. 18-20, 37-8.
31. Sheriff, 1987, p. 35-40, also quoting Martin & Ryan and Austen.
32. Sheriff, 1987, p. 43-4.
33. Freeman-Grenville, *East African Coast*, p. 210.
34. Sheriff, 1987, pp. 48-60.
35. Sheriff, 1987, p. 60.
36. ZNA: AA 12/4, Reports on Slaves & Slave Owners in Pemba & Mombasa.
37. A. Sheriff, 'Localisation and social composition of the East African slave trade, 1858-873', in W. G. Clarence-Smith, ed., *The Economics of the Indian Ocean Slave Trade*, London, Cass, 1989, p.144.
38. Sheriff, 1987, pp.139, 144.
39. Sheriff, 1987, p.140.

3

Emancipation and Post-emancipation in Zanzibar

Saada Omar Wahab

There has been a heated debate on slavery and transition from it in the Atlantic region and the rest of the world, and a comparative study of two islands in the Indian Ocean where the two types of slavery come together offers a very good opportunity to contribute to the debate. Both these two islands underwent intertwined histories of the establishment of slave economies in the eighteenth and nineteenth centuries respectively, and the consequent abolition of slavery.

The slave trade between Mauritius and Zanzibar which had started in the eighteenth century began to be disrupted at the end of the eighteenth and beginning of the nineteenth century with the British blockade and subsequent anti-slave trade treaty signed between Captain Moresby and Sultan Said bin Sultan in 1822. This treaty prohibited the Sultan from shipment of slaves to Christian colonies, including Mauritius.

In 1840 when the Imam of Oman shifted his capital to Zanzibar, the islands were integrated into the world economic system. This ruler intensified the agricultural system of large plantations. By the mid-nineteenth century the demand for slaves had increased not only for export but for internal use as well, following the establishment of clove and coconut plantations in Zanzibar which required massive labour power. At this time, many slaves worked in clove and coconut plantations owned by Arabs and some Africans scattered in the islands.

By the end of the nineteenth century, the slaves in Zanzibar were divided into three categories: plantation (*shamba*) slaves, who devoted most of their time to coconut and clove plantations; domestic (household) slaves, who worked full-time in the houses of their owners, as personal attendants of the master; *suria* who were legally the secondary slave wives of the master; and skilled workmen, for example masons, carpenters, coolies (*wachukuzi*), daily labourers (*vibarua*), and in general those slaves employed in the town by European, Indian and other merchants of various nationalities.

This chapter will document the life after emancipation of the two mentioned classes of slaves in Zanzibar, i.e., plantation and town slaves. Domestic slaves will be covered in chapter four.

Suppression of the Slave Trade

In the nineteenth century the European factor became important in the transformation of the lives of slaves in Zanzibar. The Abolition movement which had begun in Britain and her overseas territories first took effect in West Africa.[1] The decline in West African slave trade encouraged the expansion of the trade in East Africa especially to the Americas and the West Indies.

In the early nineteenth century, the British had begun to put pressure on Seyyid Said, Sultan of Zanzibar, to confine the slave trade to the islands. The question could be asked as to why the Sultan accepted the British demand for the abolition of the slave trade, considering the fact that this trade was very lucrative to the Arab State not only of Zanzibar but also in Oman. Two explanations will serve. First, it has to be remembered that Seyyid Said originated from the Busaidi dynasty of Oman and owed his position to the British who helped him and his dynasty against the Mazrui family (the former rulers of Mombasa). Secondly, Seyyid Said had a farsighted approach and had observed the expansion of Europeans in different parts of the world. To secure his position, Seyyid Said entered into good relations with the British in the early 1800s. His relations with the British were friendly and they ensured security for him and his territories. He was therefore obliged to support the British anti-slave trade campaigns.

In 1822 the British concluded the first treaty, the Moresby treaty, for the suppression of the slave trade with Sultan Said of Zanzibar. In the treaty, the Sultan agreed to proscribe and stop the sale of slaves to any Christian nation, and allowed British warships to seize all Arab vessels carrying slaves to the south of the East African coast.[2]

In 1845, another treaty was signed between Colonel Hamerton and Sultan Said. This time the treaty forbade the shipping of slaves outside the Sultan's East African possessions, i.e., beyond Brava to the north, but local trading of slaves was legal within East Africa. The 1840s was an opportune time for the British to impose a new treaty on the Sultan of Zanzibar. They had successfully imposed the first treaty on the Sultan. Familiarity had developed between the two as a result of working together for twenty-three years. Secondly, in 1840 Britain established diplomatic relations with Zanzibar, and posted its consul there.[3] Primarily, the British wanted to keep an eye on Sultan Said's movement and control Indian Ocean trade, including acting against the island's position in controlling and supplying slaves.

Compared to the earlier treaty, the Hamerton treaty had a significant impact on the Sultan and his subjects in East Africa as well as Oman. It provided additional authority to the British to stick their noses along the East African coast and its trading system. Together with this, the treaty acted as an initial step in the disintegration of the Sultan's empire, and it triggered bitter resentment and anger among his subjects.

David Livingstone's figures, though exaggerated, pointed to the failure of the 1845 treaty, as large numbers of slaves were still being trafficked beyond the Sultan's empire. He stated that between 1867 and 1869, about 37,000 slaves had been successfully smuggled overseas.[4] A study by Sheriff for the 1860s shows that the majority of the slaves were not smuggled overseas but were used in Zanzibar. He shows that of the 100 dhows captured by the British ships during the 15 years of slave trafficking '40 had no slaves at all, 35 dhows were involved in a local trade carrying an average of 27 slaves, whereas the 12 involved in the foreign trade to Arabia carried an average of 70 slaves, including one that had a cargo of 283 slaves'.[5] The Sultan's subjects were also very dissatisfied with this treaty. While the Sultan had signed this treaty, his subjects were in no position to object to the terms of the treaty as it limited their profits in this lucrative trade.

Photo 3.1: Freed slaves on a British warship
(Note the different age groups and gender of the freed slaves)
Source: Zanzibar National Archives.

In 1873, Sir Bartle Frere, British Governor of Bombay, went to Zanzibar armed with another treaty to end the slave trade. Frere was sent to persuade the new Sultan of Zanzibar to end the slave trade in his dominions. However, Seyyid Barghash was not in a position to accept British demands so easily. He found himself in a most awkward position and stated to the British Consul: 'A spear is held at each of my eyes; with which shall I choose to be pierced?'[6] He faced the same dilemma as his father as, on one hand, he faced Great Britain insisting on suppression of the slave trade while, at the same time, helping him to sustain his dominion. He knew, however, that the British could employ any tactic to enforce their demands. On the other hand, his Afro-Arab brothers and subjects who were slave owners, strongly opposed the British demands.

The problem had been compounded because in 1872 a terrible cyclone had struck Zanzibar and uprooted almost all the clove trees, thus destroying the clove plantations, especially those of Unguja. Since many planters lost their plantations, Barghash was intent on resolving their problems but had to tread carefully. He knew that he could not get any support from his subjects regarding the issue of ending the slave trade, especially now after they had lost their plantations. Barghash assumed that if he accepted the British demand, he would invite the anger of his Arab subjects, and his life and position as the Sultan would be jeopardised. This situation led Barghash to refuse to sign the treaty. As a result of his refusal, the British used the threat of a naval blockade. Frere had angrily left Zanzibar, leaving a copy of the treaty with the British Consul, John Kirk, who persuaded Seyyid Barghash to sign the treaty in June 1873. The Frere treaty prohibited the export of slaves from the mainland, and closed the slave market of Zanzibar.[7]

Officially, the Frere treaty of 1873 marked the end of the export of slaves to Zanzibar, other ports and overseas, but the legal status of slavery in Zanzibar was not abolished until 1897. However, the trade still continued illegally. After 1873 many slaves being smuggled for export were rescued from different dhows. Following the three mentioned treaties for the suppression of the slave trade, the sultans of Zanzibar began to lose their independence and influence over the East African coast, and started to act as British puppets in East Africa. They lost their legitimacy with many Afro-Arab planters and merchants who had been slave dealers.

The legal ending of slave trade in Zanzibar marked the beginning of the inflow of European agents in coastal towns as well as the interior of East Africa. For instance, Bishop Tozer arrived in Zanzibar in 1864 to preach Christianity,[8] and an Anglican cathedral was built on the site of the last slave market in Zanzibar soon after the Frere treaty of 1873.

Zanzibar Slavery Emancipation, 1860s – 1900s

Emancipation in the 1860s

The treaties for the suppression of the slave trade concluded between the Zanzibari sultans and the British consuls marked the beginning of freedom for the slaves in East Africa. But before this, the 1860s were marked by another momentous event for slaves. Those slaves that had belonged to Indians who were British subjects, were freed as the 1833 Abolition of Slavery Act began to take effect in Zanzibar. The Indians were thus obliged to obey British laws, and in the 1860s they were required to free their slaves. This was a surprise to many of them who expected to be protected from British laws as they originated from Indian princely states. The Indians in Zanzibar were traditionally merchants, but a few also became planters. As Princess Salme pointed out, 'some of them have hundreds and more slaves for cultivation of their estates'. Unlike Arab slave owners whose slaves were emancipated gradually, Indians were required to end ownership of slaves with immediate effect.[9]

There is no reliable estimate for the total number of slaves freed during the period 1822 to 1870. However, available evidence from slave registers in the Zanzibar Archives show that there were about 8,213 slaves freed in the 1860s. These included slaves who were unlawfully held by British Indian subjects who were emancipated at the consulate. However, no compensation was paid to any slave owner, as they had held them illegally. Between 1874 and 1876 there were 1,380 more slaves registered for emancipation. This brings the total number of slaves freed in the 1860s and 1870s to 9,593, of whom 75 per cent were emancipated from the Indians, and the rest were captured by British anti-slavery naval patrols.[10]

However, slave ownership in Zanzibar was not a matter of ethnicity. Anyone could own as many slaves as s/he could afford. In a slave society where there was no free labour, Indians (British subjects) used slave labour in their economic activities. As noted earlier, the Indians were predominantly merchants, and slaves worked in shops in towns, as coolies, and performed other skilled works. But since the 1840s a few had also begun to acquire clove plantations which was naturally accompanied by slave ownership.[11] Moreover, the nature of the nineteenth century Zanzibar economy encouraged many rich and middle class men to own and utilise slaves not only as labourers but also as prestigious status items.

While the available evidence shows that 9,593 slaves were emancipated in the period under discussion, this figure is not reliable in assessing the total number of slaves in Zanzibar in this period. There were also illegally traded fresh slaves who were caught by British warships. Nevertheless, sex, age and tribe proportion represented by this data can give some indication about the characteristics of the slave population at the time.

The sex and age proportion discussed in this chapter is based on a sample of 6,200 slaves emancipated from British Indian subjects residing in Zanzibar in 1860. The registers show that 51 per cent of the total emancipated slaves in this period were female, while men formed 49 per cent. These figures suggest that in the nineteenth century there was a fair ratio between male and female slaves.

The age profile of the same sample of emancipated slaves shows that 852 slaves (14 % of the total) were children ranging between 2 and 16 years of age; 4,456 slaves (72 %) were at the productive age of between 18 to 47 years; and the remaining 896 (14%) slaves were aged above 50 years.[12] It is evident that many of the freed slaves emancipated during this time constituted effective labour.

It is regrettable that the registers did not indicate the trajectory of the emancipated slaves after freedom. This would have allowed us to trace their post-emancipation movements and life. Stereotypes do abound, for example, in the work of Princess Salme, one of the Sultan's daughters, who takes an apologetic stand on behalf of slave owners, describing ex-slaves as idlers, vagabonds and thieves:

> The freed grown-up children considered the fact that they did not have to work anymore as an essential element of freedom, and they wanted to really celebrate this freedom, totally unconcerned that they could not expect neither lodging nor maintenance from their masters anymore.[13]

What can be observed from the above statement is that according to slave owners, the anti-slavery campaigns in Zanzibar had liberated slaves from the hand of their masters only to create an unproductive social class. Anti-slavery campaigners were less concerned about what became of the freed slaves.

Emancipation in 1897–1900s Period

The legal ending of slave trade in Zanzibar did not mark the end of slave labour in both islands. The island of Pemba became even more dependent on slave labour after the hurricane of 1872. The list of slaves held in Pemba mentioned in chapter 1 allows us to gain an overview of the size of slave-holding by landowners in 1875. It shows that the 255 landowners held a total of 521 plantations, or an average of 2 plantations each. Of these landowners, 27 per cent held less than 50 slaves; another 31 per cent held between 50 and 99 slaves; a further 35 per cent held between 100 and 299 slaves; and only 7 per cent held more than 300 slaves, with an overall average of 54 slaves per owner. One interesting aspect that emerges from this list is that there were at least eight land- and slave-owners who are described as slaves or freedmen, and two of them are described as *nokoa* or supervisors who were probably freed slaves. Between them they owned 13 plantations with a total of 300 slaves, or an average of 38 slaves each. This shows that slaves who were freed under Islamic law (discussed below) before the general emancipation may have been trusted servants who were given plots of land by their masters, and even sizeable numbers of slaves.

Table 3.1: Freed slaves owning land and slaves in Pemba, 1875

No. of plantations	Land/slave owners	No. of slaves
2	Towfeek slave of Hamood b Muhammad Il Mawli	40
1	Baba Kondo freed man	30
1	Lewela the Nokowa	60
2	Hamees b Khamas slave of Ismail	20
3	Juma b Said slave of Ismail	40
2	Nasor b Fahum slave of Ismail	20
1	Nocowa of Surbok	60
1	Imreeko freed by some Arab	30

Source: ZNA/ AA 12/4 Records of slave and slave owners in Pemba and Mombasa

The suppression of the slave trade was in many ways only the commencement rather than the end of the tale. The abolitionists never made any secret of the fact that their definitive intent was total emancipation throughout the islands, but it was to take another quarter of a century of campaigning before this was achieved. The explanation for the Sultan accepting this decree was the British bombardment of the palace in 1896.[14] It forced the rebellious Prince Khalid to escape, and Arab resistance to British rule and to the abolition of slavery was thus broken. The British moved quickly and imposed the compliant Seyyid Hamoud Bin Muhammed who abolished slavery, and changed the legal system to facilitate emancipation: 'It was easy to introduce many reforms without tension between the palace and the British Consulate General as it happened during the previous three sultans.'[15] The bombardment was a lesson to the Sultans of Zanzibar not to oppose British wishes and reforms, as they were capable of employing force to enforce their decisions.

Slave emancipation in Zanzibar was a long process, which went through several stages of approvals at different levels. By 1897 the British Cabinet had decided that after the fasting month of Ramadhan, British officials should invite the Sultan to issue a decree abolishing the legal status of slavery in Zanzibar, and give compensation to owners who could prove legal ownership of the slaves and the damage resulting from the abolition. The British Consul put it very clearly that no interference with the Arabs' family structure was contemplated.[16]

The Emancipation Decree was signed by Seyyid Hamoud on 5 April 1897 centred on the abolition of the legal status of slavery. While the earlier treaties suppressed the slave trade and made it illegal, slavery per-se was not abolished. The 1897 Decree gave the slaves the right to claim their freedom whenever they needed it. The replacement of the Consular Court by Her Majesty's Court in Zanzibar, consisting of a judge and an assistant Judge appointed by the Crown, further helped in implementing the Decree.

On 8 April 1897 the Sultan held a meeting at which he announced the contents of the decree, and ordered the Arabs' representative to explain the decree to others throughout the country. This notification was applicable not only in Zanzibar but also in the dominions of His Highness the Sultan of Zanzibar. However, this did not include the coast of Kenya, especially Lamu. As Romero's study shows, 'News of the legal emancipation came to Lamu at the same time as it reached the mainland, but the Slavery Commission which was empowered to enforce the Ordinance did not actively interfere in Lamu until 1910".[17]

The Emancipation Decree included six important articles on abolition of slavery in Zanzibar.

Art. 1: From and after this 1st day of Zilkaada [April 1897], all claims of whatever description made before any court or public authority in respect of the alleged relations of masters and slaves shall be referred to the District Court (Mehkemet-ele-wilaya), within those jurisdiction they may arise, and shall be cognizable by the court alone.

Art. 2: From and after this 1st day of first of Zilkaada, the District court shall decline to enforce any alleged rights over the bodies, services or property of any person on the ground that such person is a slave, but wherever any person shall claim that he was lawfully possessed of such rights in accordance with the Decrees of our predecessors.

Art. 3: The compensation money thus awarded shall not be liable to be claimed in respect of any debt for which the person of the slave for whom it was granted could not previously by law be seized.

Art. 4: Any person whose right to freedom shall have been formally recognized under the 2nd article shall be liable to any tax, abatement, corvée or payment in lieu of corvée' which our government may at any time hereafter see fit to impose on the general body of its subjects and shall be bound, on pain of being declared a vagrant, to show that he possesses a regular domicile and means of subsistence, and where such domicile is situated on land owned by any other person, to pay the owner of such land such rent as may be agreed upon between them before the District Court.

Art. 5: Concubine shall be regarded as inmates of the Harem in the same sense as wives, and shall remain in their present relations unless they should demand their dissolution on the ground of cruelty, in which case the District Court shall grant it if the alleged cruelty has been proved to its satisfaction.

Art. 6: Any person making any claim under any of the provisions of this Decree shall have the right to appeal from the decision of the District court to ourselves or to such Judge or other public authority.[18]

A number of issues deserve special consideration as the various articles of the decree were implemented in Zanzibar. The first is the question of compensation paid to slave owners. Unlike Mauritius where compensation was paid out of British revenue, in Zanzibar it came from Zanzibar's revenue, and £ 81,000 was borrowed from the National Bank of India to meet the expenditure. The decree stated that the slave owners were to be paid compensation for any legally-held slaves, and such compensation money could not be seized for past debt. The decree did not provide a fixed amount as compensation, but promised fair compensation for an able-bodied slave. It was meant to silence opposition to the decree, and the reference to the debt was to protect the owners from moneylenders and protect the clove economy.[19]

The compensation varied depending on the type of slave owned such as physical condition and ability, including skills, health and age of the slave. For an able-bodied slave the higher fixed amount was Rs. 60, equal to five months wages a master could earn from his slave.[20] This amount was paid only for those slaves who were above average in intelligence and skills, such as carpenters, masons, trainers, and workmen of any kind, including women slaves who worked in the house, cooks for their households and those who occupied the position of housekeepers. Other slaves were worth less than the average, such as sickly and weak, old and worn-out slaves, whose compensation ranged between Rs. 40 to 50.[21] A total of £38,889.75 (Rs. 15 = £ 1) was paid as compensation to slave owners between 1897 and 1899 – 53 per cent to Pemba slave owners and 47 per cent to those in Unguja.[22] This provides an insight into the relative positions of Pemba and Unguja regarding the question of the number of slaves in the two islands.

It is clear that there were a larger number of slaves in Pemba than in Unguja, and this was highlighted by many factors including the cyclone of 1872 which affected Unguja more than Pemba, and a larger number of clove plantations were established in Pemba thereafter. Secondly, it is possible that after the hurricane, a larger number of slaves in Unguja were domestic while in Pemba there were more plantation slaves, although lack of enough information regarding domestic slaves of Zanzibar makes it hard to draw a definite conclusion for this variation. If the above supposition is correct, then it is possible that more slave owners in Unguja may have voluntarily emancipated their slaves without asking for compensation, but expecting a huge reward in afterlife.

Another important issue is how the slave owners spent their compensation money. It is believed that part of the money, some £ 11,000 received by the Arabs was used to pay off or reduce mortgages on their *shambas*[23] as they were heavily indebted after taking mortgages from Indian merchants. In 1900, the total indebtedness incurred by the Pemba Arabs to moneylenders, and in connection to which they had pawned their *shambas*, amounted to a little over £6,000. Outstanding mortgages executed prior to 1900 amounted about £3,000.[24]

Court Emancipation

Since the declaration of the decree for emancipation in 1897, the courts were legally authorised to grant freedom to slaves with a freedom certificate. Any slave who wished to be freed had to send his/her application to the courts for certification. This was quite a contrast with Mauritius as in Zanzibar slaves were free to apply for their freedom and the Zanzibar Protectorate government paid compensation fee to their masters. This did not occur in Mauritius where a slave was required to serve as an apprentice or buy his own freedom (by paying a non-fixed amount of money to his former owner) before the court.

However, many conditions were considered when a slave applied for freedom in Zanzibar. For instance, to be granted freedom, a slave had to provide enough information on what s/he was going to do and where s/he intended to stay, to minimise the problem of vagabondage. At the beginning, the speed of this kind of emancipation was very slow partly because many slaves were afraid of change. They had lived in the owner's compound all their lives and worked under his instructions and eyes, eating what the owner assigned to them, sleeping where the owner wished.[25]

I.P. Farler (Commissioner in Pemba) reported that in the interval between the end of the clove harvest and the coming of the new season (rainy season), many slaves applied for their freedom and were subsequently freed at the rate of 160 slaves a week.[26]

In the initial stage, slaves had only to state what they were going to do, and on whose *shamba* they had obtained permission to settle.[27] Slaves had all the freedom to choose where to stay. The decree stated that neither the late owner of the *shamba* himself nor any local authority could effect the removal of the slaves against their will. Many applicants went to the courts when agricultural conditions were bad, and fewer when conditions were good. Many of them were affected by the success or failure of the system of labour contract.

Complaints were brought to the Commission, and many *shamba* owners made a formal appeal to the government for help and protection.[28] The state found it necessary not only for the benefit of the *shamba* owners but also for the freed slaves to put into the emancipation decree an article of the supplementary decree of the Sultan 'that any person whose right to freedom shall have been formally recognized, shall be free on pain of being declared a vagrant to show that he possessed a regular domicile and means of subsistence.'[29] To make this effective, a notice was given that all slaves who were asking for court freedom had to bring with them a person on whose land they had obtained permission to settle, or if he was unable to come, someone in his place, and a letter would also suffice. The name of this person was then registered as responsible for the wellbeing of the particular freed slaves. This rule worked, and the slaves found no difficulty in getting their patron and a new home.

To be assured with a livelihood, the department did not place any obstacle in the way of those applicants who were willing to work on fair terms. The demand for free labour on the part of the Arabs greatly exceeded the supply, and if any slaves applying for their freedom failed to make a satisfactory agreement with the Arabs, there was always a demand for their labour on the various *shambas* owned by the Sultan and in connection with the Department of Public Works (PWD). While slaves were being freed, a large number of *shamba* owners or their deputies were waiting near the office, ready to make arrangements with the slaves being freed, to propose to them to live on their lands on government terms. However, many slaves stated openly that since they were free, they did not intend to work, especially on plantations.[30]

The report of the Slavery Commissioners of Unguja and Pemba on the working of the decree for the year 1901 stated that the number of slaves freed by the court in the course of 1901 was 844, of whom 589 received their papers in Unguja and 255 in Pemba.[31] However, the total number of slaves freed by the courts since the abolition of the legal status of slavery is hard to assess as data are not available. Table 3.2 shows the number of slaves voluntarily freed by their owners which will form the subject of the next section.

Table 3.2: Total Number of Slaves Freed by Court and by their Owners in Zanzibar

Year	Slaves freed by court			Slaves freed by owners and % of total	Total
	Unguja	Pemba	Total	Unguja & Pemba	
April 1897 to April 1898	469	778	1,247	799 (39%)	2,046
April to December 1898	704	1,316	2,024	709 (26%)	2,733
January to December 1899	1,427	2,230	3,657	798 (18%)	4,455
January to December 1900	1,126	594	1,720	770 (31%)	2,490
January to December 1901	589	255	844	624 (43%)	1,468
Total	**4,315**	**5,173**	**9,488**	**3,700 (28%)**	**13,264**

Source: Compiled from Mr Last to General Raikes, February 6th, 1902. ZNA DL10/12; Mr Cave to the Marquess of Lansdowne Zanzibar, February 21, 1902.

The above table shows that the number of freedom papers granted by the courts in 1901 was less than half of the number recorded in the previous year. Several reasons contributed to this situation. In the first place, unusually heavy rainfall enabled the slaves in agricultural districts to grow such abundant crops of various kinds of grain, fruits and vegetables on which they depended for their food supply that they had not only enough for themselves, but a sufficient margin with which to make a respectable profit in the neighbouring towns and villages, and consequently there was little inducement for them to leave the plantations on which they were employed. Secondly, the condition of slave labour was considerably improved by the knowledge, which was shared by master and slave alike, that freedom could be had for the asking, and there was therefore less need to abandon their slave status. In any case, the rush for freedom which took place when the decree first become known had apparently expended itself, and the slaves who had real cause for complaint or real longing for emancipation, as well as those, according to a colonial official, who were 'attracted by a sense of novelty or by visions of idleness and indulgence, had their desire satisfied, and the remainder had made up their minds that it was better to remain as they were in comparative peace and contentment than tempt providence in some new and untried form'.[32]

Court emancipation was perceived differently by different slaves, at different times and by different age groups (between youth and old-age slaves). The study found that at the beginning of the process many slaves had a negative perception towards this kind of freedom, and this factor was among many that delayed the process of emancipation. However, as time went by they learnt to accept the process.

Soon after they submitted their application for freedom at the courts, the slaves were taught by the colonial officials that they had to live an honest life and be respectable members of the society; that this kind of life could only be attained by work. Africans were taught to believe that a hardworking man was always a respectable one, who could achieve much economically, while lazy persons would gain nothing but disrespect from the community members.[33]

Voluntary Emancipation

What was very striking about emancipation in Zanzibar was the large percentage of slaves who were emancipated by their owners voluntarily and without compensation. In comparison with the court emancipation, this type of emancipation did not include the various conditions for a slave to be granted freedom. What was needed was only an agreement between a master and a slave. Many slave owners who decided to grant freedom to their slaves using this method were influenced by two factors. The first was the religious motivation, as they expected a better reward in the afterlife.[34] The whole idea was initiated by the fact that money was nothing but material that always diminished. The second reason was the nature of the bond that had developed between the slaves and their masters. Many slave owners who applied this approach had a well-established attachment with their slaves. Between 1897 and 1901, voluntary emancipation granted and registered covered 3,776 cases from both islands, i.e., 28 per cent of the total number of 13,264 slaves who had received their freedom during this period.[35] (see Table 3.3).

Table 3.3: Statement showing the total number of slaves freed by their owners, 1897–1901

Month	1897	1898	1899	1900	1901	Total
January	43	61	33	65	20	222
February	39	32	50	26	68	215
March	35	115	33	58	28	271
April	84	69	46	30	28	257
May	52	48	182	75	125	492
June	55	66	61	106	71	359
July	68	84	76	25	59	312
August	72	68	74	66	44	324
September	54	47	61	69	63	294
October	64	43	76	65	52	300
November	171	57	70	107	49	454
December	60	19	36	78	17	210
Total	799	709	798	770	624	3,700

Source: Mr Last to General Raikes, Zanzibar. February 6, 1902. ZNA/DL. 10/12, p. 8.

Table 3.3 shows that slave owners in Zanzibar were ready to free their slaves before the issue of the emancipation decree, and they continued to do so after the decree was issued. While the decree was issued in April 1897, there were already 117 cases of slaves freed by their owners from January to March 1897. Although further research is required, it appears that a larger number of emancipations occurred from May to November, in other words, soon after the clove harvest and beginning of the rains. An average of 30 slaves were freed each month, while between December and April an average of only 19 slaves were freed.

There may also have been a motivation for owners to be more generous after harvest time when more money circulated. Unfortunately, the records do not show what kind of slaves were freed at this particular time, what were their age groups, sex, tribes and so on.

Although voluntary emancipation covered 28 per cent of the total number of freed slaves in Zanzibar, this proportion was not the same throughout the emancipation period, as shown in Table 6. It was reported that the number of slaves freed by the courts in the course of 1901 was 844, while slaves freed by their owners voluntarily during the same period numbered 624, i.e., 43 per cent of 1,468 freed that year, which was the highest, while they constituted only 18 per cent in 1899 when the largest number were freed in a single year. In addition, there were many slaves who never applied for their freedom for whatever reasons. These included very old slaves living on the plantations, and did not wish to move as this was the only place they had ever known and had nowhere else to go.[36] This same phenomenon was observed in Mauritius after abolition of apprenticeship in 1839.

A report from Mr. Last to General Raikes in February 1902 stated that there was also a considerable number of younger slaves who were attached to their owners by ties of respect and regard, and who were also sympathetic towards them because of their depressed status. 'They were determined to stick to their slave status, and no personal advantages would provoke them to abscond from their owners.'[37] They were generally personal attendants and house slaves, who had probably been brought up from childhood by their owners (*wazalia* – born slaves), and had received from them the consideration and care which was due to them from the owners, and by this treatment the owners had won the regard and fidelity of their slaves.[38] Even if their owner had decided to move his capital elsewhere and farther away, these former slaves found no reason to leave him.

One good example was that of an Arab, Hamaid bin Amor El-Hinawi, who was about to leave Zanzibar for Muscat in April 1898. He wished to take with him 36 of his former slaves, male and female. When those slaves were examined, all of them had freedom papers. When they were interviewed, all of them without exception stated that they were willing to follow their master to Muscat.[39] However, Basil S. Cave expressed his opinion that it was undesirable to permit him due to the fact that this case might set a very undesirable precedent. Nevertheless, this case confirms the close relationship that existed in Zanzibar between some ex-slaves and their masters.

The Contract System

Although the British had pushed through emancipation in Zanzibar, they were concerned about disrupting their protectorate's economy, which was now their responsibility. Therefore, the same courts were summoned to regulate new relations between master and slave, and up to 1901, some 4,000 labour contracts were drawn up and signed between them, although some of the slaves were frightened to have their privileges and responsibilities more plainly and precisely defined.[40] In 1902 there were 448 contracts approved by the courts, 664 in 1903, 91 in 1904 and 14 in 1905, totalling some 5,217 contracts.

The contract system was a mechanism that was introduced to ensure the former slave maintains his/her bond with the former owner, or with any other interested employer in order that cloves would continue to be produced. The courts stated very clearly that in a labour contract, a freed slave must be assured of sufficient land for his personal usage, care during sickness, supplied material for building his house, and food at least for a short period until his first crop was gathered. These terms were applicable mostly to plantation slaves. In return, a freed slave was required to work for three days in every week on a specified plantation. The courts made it clear that the labourer did not have any right to run away from the assigned plantation, and if he refused to work, the courts could punish him. The courts had the authority to enforce the condition under which the labourer had agreed to serve, and at the same time insist on the due fulfilment of the terms on the side of employers as agreed to in the contract.

However, objections have been raised to this system of labour contracts on the ground that the free man had lost much of the liberty in that he could not leave the plantation to which he was sent without the court's consent. In entertaining that objection the court assured the applicant labourer that it would welcome and consider a request for a transfer to another plantation if the grounds were in any way reasonable.[41]

There was also objection to the contract system because under this system, the freed slave could not, except at harvest time, earn sufficient money to provide him with more than basic necessities such as clothes, food and goods to satisfy the requirements of his household. For three days of the week he had to work for his employer, and as the daily task which was apportioned to him could be got through, if he was fairly industrious, in three or four hours, it amounted to not more than twelve hours' labour that he had to perform in every seven days. For the remainder of the week, he was his own master, either to spend his time in cultivating his own plot of land or earn monetary wages elsewhere. In this context it was possible for a plantation worker to work in the plantations and work elsewhere for wages.

A freed labourer was free to select where to work on his four remaining days. If he selected to work for cash wages he could do so either on his employer's *shamba*, where his services were occasionally required for more than the stipulated number of days, or on that of some neighbouring landowner where paid labour was in greater demand. Vagrancy laws similar to the Mauritian ones thus ensured a restricted labour mobility. However, as with the Mauritian case, when labourers were not happy they simply deserted the plantations.

The consolidation of the new labour/ working discipline with the rise of imperialism and based on western work ethics and free labour ideology in the post-slave era in Zanzibar was in some cases seen by many slaves as a condition comparable to slavery. In Zanzibar it is very clear that beyond slavery there was simply no freedom as it was proposed within the emancipation decree, but instead a hazy shading into various forms of coerced and forced labour, with free labour itself being a severely defective ideal.

Slave Categories

Town Slaves

Between 1897 and 1904 reports show that the freed slaves had shown preference for living in the town rather than in the country. Town slaves included a large group of slaves who employed themselves in skilled work. This group included domestic and skilled slaves. For instance, of the 589 slaves freed in 1901, 357 (218 male and 139 female), or 60.7 per cent, elected to live in town. The remaining 232 preferred to take up their abode in the country. Two questions need answers here. First, why were the numbers for town slaves higher than for the plantation slaves, and secondly, why did male slaves opt to live in town compared to female slaves?

Many of the slaves who had run off to town after they had been issued their freedom certificates were young and skilled, such as artisans, masons, carpenters, tailors and fishermen.[42] By far, the greater number of those who elected to live in town, both male and female, engaged themselves as daily labourers or *vibarua* as they were called. They were employed in loading and unloading ships, carrying loads to various parts of the town and country, drawing trolleys, assistants to masons and other artisans, and in any other kind of unskilled labour which happened their way. This nature of work attracted more male than female freed slaves. Apart from them, there was a considerable number of freed slaves, male and female, who were employed as house servants by the Europeans and other foreign residents in the town. Others were engaged as water-carriers, grass-cutters and petty trade dealers. Fortunately, there was work for all who were willing to work in town.

The economic future of the freed slaves who opted to live in town depended very much on their own efforts and actions, whether they would be fairly prosperous and comfortable or in poverty and wretchedness. The 1925 Ethnicity and Occupation census revealed that town ex-slaves numbered 1,654 out of a total of 5,695 town dwellers, equal to 29 per cent of the general town population.[43]

However, there were many cases of immorality reported. Among the expected negative impacts from the implementation of emancipation was an increase of immorality. In 1901 the number of convictions for offences such as assault, drunkenness, theft, and vagrancy for Unguja only numbered 2,543. This figure was similar to that of 1898, a year after the enforcement of the decree; and in 1900 there were 2,057 convictions.[44] The state tried hard to prevent this situation but they found it impossible to prevent the freed slaves from embarking on a career of idleness and vice. In Pemba, things were different - each year there was a reduction in the number of vagrancy cases as pointed out by Farler: 'every effort is being made to provide respected employment for the freed slaves'.[45] To control the vagrants the colonial state consolidated a system of labour contract.

Another important feature as shown by the town slaves is widespread drunkenness. It was reported that the principal towns and streets after dark were habitually scenes of uproar and of brawling in which sticks and knives were freely used.[46] O'Sullivan, Vice consul in Pemba, reported that soon after the issue of the decree, Indian shopkeepers repeatedly complained to him that their stores were constantly being broken into and their goods looted by drunken bands.[47] These bands, however, consisted of not only ex-slaves, as there were also squatters imported from the mainland.

Moreover, in a report from the Slavery Commissioners in Unguja and Pemba during the year 1901, there was a shocking statement that nearly every unmarried freed female slave in Pemba had become a prostitute since the abolition of the legal status of slavery. This statement was made by Mr. Cave, and was strongly corroborated by Mr. Farler. In the town of Zanzibar the number of brothels was considerably greater than it had been five years before emancipation, and whenever there was a cause to enter and search one of these houses, it was generally found that a considerable proportion of its inmates were women who had been freed by the courts. By early 1900, it was found necessary to clear away some huts which had been built for immoral purposes on the outskirts of the town, and 75 per cent of the women who occupied them were found to be freed slaves.[48]

British officials believed that amongst the lower-class Africans, voluntary morality was a virtue almost unknown. In previous years, before the abolition of the legal status of slavery, any laxity in this respect on the part of the female slaves of a house or a harem was severely punished and chastity was to a certain extent, compulsory. After emancipation, however, every Arab master or mistress was well aware that any severity or restraint would be met by an immediate application to the courts, and domestic slaves as well as their emancipated sisters followed their own inclinations.[49] For these reasons, it was felt that the issue of the decree had to be followed by a wholesome check upon the number of women who deliberately adopted prostitution as a profession and depended upon it for their livelihood.

Another important issue regarding freed slaves was socialisation in the town among themselves as a social group and their relation with their former masters. Many of them, while they stayed in town, shared the common idea that at one time in their lives they were slaves. The ex-slaves with the same skills formed a guild to make their services more profitable and protect their technology and skills.[50]

On the other hand, some of the ex-slaves who lived in the town maintained their bonds with their former masters, by being employed in their economic projects as houseboys, water girls, shopkeepers, and daily labourers (*vibarua*). Others greeted them and paid their respect to them even after they became free. These slaves were skilled workmen before emancipation, and they had lived in town with their masters.

Plantation Slaves

It is more than likely that the action of the owners towards their slaves had a considerable influence in regulating the number of slaves applying for freedom. The owners recognised more and more that it was to their advantage to keep their slaves on their estates, and that in order to do this they had to respect their natural rights and wants as workers, before the workers would be willing to do and act for their owners as in the past.

But in many cases, the slaves were as anxious to remain on their owner's estates as their owners were to keep them. They knew that they had no other home to go to, and that the probabilities of improving on their prevailing state by living with their owners and in their homes would be very small. They realised that their status was not what it was a few years before, and so, without wishing to leave their prevailing homes and occupations, they were naturally desirous of improving their condition by making more advantageous arrangements with their masters. They knew that they could have freedom by simply applying for it, but they preferred to remain with their owners and in their environment, but only asking that the conditions of their relationship with their masters may be somewhat modified. Cases of this kind were frequently brought before the Walis (governors) of the various provinces of Zanzibar by owners and slaves, in which they requested the Walis services to arrange and place on an equitable basis their mutual obligations in a manner satisfactory to all concerned.

Generally, it is the aged and somewhat infirm slaves who, having lived all their lives in the country, preferred to remain rather than to make a fresh start in life in town, under circumstances that were very different to those they were accustomed to. However there were also a large number of young freed slaves between 18 and 30 years who also preferred to live in the country rather than in town.[51]

After total emancipation of slaves in Zanzibar, many slaves who were used to work in clove and coconut plantations owned by their owners signed new labour contracts with their former masters. As a matter of fact, the great majority of those slaves who presented themselves at the courts had already made their own arrangements as to their future, and what remained was for the court to give their blessing to the contracts. However, those slaves who had not done so, and did not have any preference for any particular district, were given a choice of several plantations where more labour was required, and they were sent there.

The contract labour system was constituted after the end of slavery. The institution of a system of labour bureau was an experiment which was watched with a good deal of interest. Farler explained in his report that, 'Some such system is urgently needed to equalize the supply of labour in the agricultural districts, and if it is successful, it will at once assist the Arab planters to gather a larger portion of their crops than they could under the existing condition, and enable the labourers to accumulate during the clove picking season a reserve fund which, if they were frugally inclined, will be of a great service to them during the remaining months of the year."[52]

In allotting freed slaves to the *shamba*, the court which as stated earlier had the responsibility of arranging for new contracts between ex-slaves and planters, had adopted the sound principle of distributing slaves to various *shambas*. Any *shamba* owner who was looking for labourers had to satisfy the court upon two points: 'First as to the number of bearing trees upon his property and second as to the total number of slaves which he possesses.' [53] The court distributed freed slave labour proportionately to the various *shambas*. The desirable proportion of hands for cultivating and picking cloves was about 10 men to 100 clove trees. However, due to the scantiness of the supply of freed slaves, it became impossible to do so. Indeed, the proportion of the number of labour of freed slaves in clove plantations 'throughout the island [Pemba, was] more than 5 persons to every 100 bearing trees'.[54]

As with the experience of town slaves, there was a similar problem of vagrancy even among plantation slaves. The colonial state tried to consolidate a system of labour contract to deal with this problem. These contracts were supplied and registered by the court, provided that the freed slave who was engaged under them 'shall' work for his employer on a personal plantation for three days in every week. This arrangement appeared to be a very fair one and was in writing and signed by both parties to it.

The liability of each side was observed with a certain amount of respect, and could if necessary be enforced in a court of law. These arrangements gave the impression that the court tried to recall the pre-existing relation between masters and slaves. Many of the terms applied here were rehearsing the bond that had existed between those two sides.

A plantation slave had three working days, but during harvest time even his regular employer had to pay him for picking his cloves, so that for seven days in the week during three months of each year he was engaged in piece work, which was paid for on a moderate scale. As for the proceeds, he could either squander them in a month's riotous living, or employed in the purchase of clothes and other requisites or to invest as was frequently done by the more thrifty, with a view to eventually becoming a landowner on a small scale himself – each according to his temperament – but, at any rate, each individual had the opportunity offered him of living a respectable life.

However, there was a considerable number of ex-slaves who were employed in the plantation but they did not have written contracts. At Mkanjuni (Pemba), a plantation owned by Suleiman bin Mbaruk, the Wali of Chake Chake, consisting of some 10,000 clove trees, there were 200 labourers, 150 of whom were freed slaves who did not have written contracts, but had all made verbal arrangements with their employer under which they picked his cloves. At another *shamba* belonging jointly to the four sons of Suleiman bin Mbaruk containing some 3,000 trees, there were 150 men employed, 80 of whom were freed slaves with no written contracts.[55] The implication of these cases is that many slaves in plantations were working under the close bond that existed with their former masters. It is obvious that even after emancipation the ex-slave still persisted in the ideology of trusting their former masters.

After emancipation, many landowners and traders possessed the same ideas that ex-slaves were the only ideal manpower for the progress of their economic projects including plantations. It was found that during the time of clove picking, the Arabs claimed that Indian merchants took their labourers and used them as '*wachukuzi*' (porters). This made Arabs suffer great losses.[56]

Both landowners and merchants were not ready to impart new working discipline to other communities. Farler once advised Indians to speak with Watumbatu and Wapemba (native of Zanzibar) to act as *wachukuzi* and leave those energetic men (mostly ex-slaves) for the plantations. Many Indian merchants objected to the use of Swahili or Wapemba and Watumbatu as these people wanted much more pay than the *shamba* workers, and it would be a great loss to them if they could not have the *shamba* hands.[57]

As the labour problem had become acute, the colonial official thought of the possibility of opening labour bureaux in Zanzibar and Pemba, and they were started under two commissioners and a branch office was opened at the Dunga plantation under Mr. Lyne. The objective was to organise and utilise all available labour, and employ it where it was most needed.

Conclusion

Emancipation history should be regarded as a transition period for slaves, their owners as well as the system itself. Slave owners, mainly Afro–Arabs and the Sultan's estates were dependent on the slave trade and slavery for profits and prosperity. This dependence was disturbed by the suppression of the slave trade by the British, and later by the legal emancipation of the slaves. The economic situation of Zanzibar was placed in a shaky position. The situation caused unease among many slave owners who did not accept changes easily, and reacted by organising smuggling to distribute slaves in and outside Zanzibar and East Africa dominions. In the earlier period the state had transformed the sector from being primarily an export trade that took slaves to work outside Zanzibar, to consolidation of clove and coconut plantations where slave labour became an important human force for production.

The slaves, on the other hand, had different understanding regarding their freedom. There was a group of slaves who decided to leave their masters and established their free life in distant areas. There was also a group of slaves who chose not to leave their masters, but maintained and renewed their former bond with their masters. In their new status as free men, they lived with their former masters as labourers.

Historians have been debating why slave revolts were not frequent in the Indian Ocean, for example in Zanzibar and Mauritius. It is important to highlight that if they occurred, there is not enough information in the Zanzibar national archives regarding this issue despite its importance in a slave society in transition. In Zanzibar, the British government established clear distinction between slaves of Unguja and Pemba in terms of understanding and controlling them. There was a famous saying that '*watumwa wa Unguja wajanja sana, watumwa wa Pemba wajinga kabisa*' (Zanzibar slaves are a very cunning lot; the Pemba slaves are absolute fools).'[58] This was a colonial perception; in reality slaves from both islands rioted when there was a need to do so. At different times it was reported that slaves in various parts of the island went on strike from time to time. But this was mainly after the issue of the emancipation decree. In one instance, an Arab planter applied for advice to the vice consul in Pemba in the following circumstances: 'it appears that the slaves on one of his plantations, which was at that time under rice, had gone on strike and absolutely refused to do any work; even the boys declined to mount guard as usual and scare away animals from the growing crops. The slaves had no special grievance to urge, but they boldly told their master that he no longer had any power to punish them.'[59] A similar strike was reported in other parts of Pemba island where slaves organised a strike as they claimed that they did not receive the usual two days per week of free time or that they were kept too long at work.[60] Although there appears to have been no major slave revolts in both islands, slaves showed their distaste for their enslavement.

One of the most significant transformations on the part of the slaves as a result of the abolition of the legal status of slavery in Zanzibar was the increasing tendency of the best of the freed slaves to save their harvest money or collect their salaries from town work and add to it to by selling the product of their allotment, until they had saved up enough money to buy a small *shamba* of their own.[61] Farler, the Slavery Commissioner in Pemba, reported that there was a large number of freed slaves in Pemba who had borrowed money from Indians at an exorbitant rate of compound interest to buy *shambas* which they had agreed to pledge to the Indians as security until the purchase was completed. Thus the emancipation decree can be said to have opened the possibility for the African ex-slaves to become small landowners themselves.

Photo 3.2: A manumitted slave woman in early nineteenth century Mauritius
Source: Mauritius National Archives

Photo 3.3: A female slave with her children in late eighteenth century Mauritius
Source: Mauritius National Archives

Notes

1. S. G. Ayany, *A History of Zanzibar: A Study in Constitutional Development 1934–1964,* Nairobi, Kenya Literature Bureau, 1983), p. 11.
2. A. H. Al- Maamiry, *Omani Sultans in Zanzibar 1832-1964,* New Delhi, S. Kumar, 1988, p. 6.
3. Ayang, p. 13.
4. A. Sheriff, 'Localization and Social Composition of the East Africa Slave Trade, 1858–1873'. In Clarence-Smith, 1989, p.134.
5. Ibid.
6. Ibid.
7. Ibid., p.19.
8. Ibid., p 17.
9. Salme.
10. ZNA 12/3, Register of Freed slaves. Slave Relief Book.
11. Sheriff, A., 1989, p. 140.
12. ZNA: AA/12/3, Register of freed slaves, Slave Relief book.
13. ZNA: AA/12/3, Register of freed slaves, Slave Relief book.
14. Patricia W. Romero, 'Slave Emancipation in Lamu', p. 500 .
15. Al- Maamiry, p. 53.
16. Salme, Ibid., p 327.
17. ZNA AB71/1, The Slavery Decree No. 11 of 1909.
18. Ibid.
19. ZNA AC/8, Vice Consulate Pemba to Consul General of Zanzibar, 3rd August 1903.
20. ZNA, Colonial Office to Foreign Office, January 9, 1910.AB71/1. The Slavery Decree No. 11 of 1909
21. ZNA AB 71/1, Mr Sinclair to Edwards Grey, Zanzibar. January 19, 1909. The Slavery Decree No. 11 of 1909.
22. Ibid.
23. Vice Consul, Mr. O' Sullivan to Foreign Office, May 13, 1901. *British Parliamentary Paper (BPP)* 1901, Vol. 81.
24. Ibid.
25. ZNA DL 10/12, Mr Cave to the Marquess of Lansdowne, Zanziabar, Ferbruary 21, 1902.
26. ZNA AC 1/11,Cave to Landsdowne, 24, 9, 1902.
27. ZNA AC/1/11, Mr. Armitage to Consul Cave, Pemba, August 20, 1902.
28. Ibid.
29. Ibid.
30. ZNA AC1/11, Cave to Marquess of Salisbury (Received November) Zanzibar, October 26, 1897.
31. ZNA DL/ 10/12, Mr Cave to the Marquess of Lansdowne, Zanzibar, February 2, 1902.
32. ZNA DL 10/12, Colonial to Foreign Office, Zanzibar, Received April 20. 1902.
33. ZNA DL/10/12, Mr Last to General Raikes, Zanzibar, February 6, 1902.
34. Ibid.

35. Ibid.
36. Ibid.
37. ZNA DL10/12, Mr Last to General Raikes, Zanzibar, February 6, 1902.
38. Ibid.
39. ZNA AC 5/4, Vice Consul, Mr. O' Sullivan to Foreign Office, May 15, 1900
40. ZNA/DL/10/12, Colonial office to Foreign Office, Received April 1902.
41. Ibid.
42. Ibid.
43. F. Cooper, *From Slaves to Squatters, 1980,* p. 161.
44. ZNA/DL/10/12, Colonial Office to Foreign Office, Received April 1902.
45. Ibid.
46. Vice Consul, O' Sullivan to Consul General Zanzibar, Zanzibar October 26 1897, BPP, 1898, Vol. LX, No.144. C.8701
47. Ibid.
48. ZNA/ DL/ 10.12, Mr. Last to General Raikes, Zanzibar. February 6, 1902.
49. Ibid.
50. O' Sullivan, Vice Consul Pemba to General Consul, December, 30, 1901. BPP,p.6.
51. Ibid.
52 Ibid.
53. O' Sullivan, Vice Consul Pemba Received at Foreign Office, May, 1901, BPP, 1901, Vol. 81
54 Ibid
55. O' Sullivan, Vice Consul Pemba to General Consul. 30 December 1901, BPP, p.6.
56. ZNA AC 5/ Vice Consulate Mr. O' Sullivan to Foreign Office, May 15, 1900.
57. Ibid.
58. O' Sullivan, Vice Consul Pemba to General Consul. September 30, 1897, BPP 7.
59 Ibid. 6
60. Ibid.
61. ZNA, DL/10/12, Mr. Farler to Cave, A slavery Report for 1901, January 1902.

4

'Fit for Freedom'[1]: Manumission and Freedom in Early British Mauritius, 1811–1839

Satyendra Peerthum

…it was often possible for the slave [and apprentice], by great perseverance and labour to purchase his own freedom and, this being accomplished the freedom of those dear to him.[2]

The slaves, however, were not prepared to wait for freedom to come to them as a dispensation from above….They were fully impressed with the belief that they were entitled to their freedom and that the cause they had embraced was just and in vindication of their own rights.[3]

Introduction

The objective of this chapter is to explore the experience of slaves during the Slave Amelioration Period and of apprentices during the Apprenticeship era in Mauritius. It focuses on slaves' and apprentices' attempts to free themselves through manumission, their motives and the methods used to achieve this between 1829 and 1839. The aim is to show that slaves did not wait for the official abolition of slavery by the British government to attempt to change their servile status and instead used innovative attempts to improve their lives. As stated by Saunders for South Africa:

Historians of slavery…may lay too great a stress on the great day of freedom…or the more important day four years later. Freedom had come to many individuals long before either of those dates … Individually and collectively they moved from effective slavery to 'freedom' before emancipation day dawned for the slaves.[4]

The slaves' and apprentices' attempts at manumission were interpreted in a number of ways by colonial officials and local colonists, and thus this chapter will also seek to extract all available information from sources to try to understand the world view of the slaves as this is rarely seen or stated explicitly in the sources.

Finally, this section of the study pays particular attention to female slaves and apprentices and their efforts to secure their freedom and that of their children. In all these aims, therefore, the underlying objective is to better understand slave/ apprentice 'agency' in Mauritius and Zanzibar and seek to define a gendered view of slavery. It is not often that female slaves come to the forefront in the historiography of slavery, but the Zanzibari suria and Mauritian female *manumitted* slaves are examples of women overcoming the worse conditions of servitude.

Manumitted Slaves in the Early British Period, 1811–1831

The manumission of Mauritian slaves and apprentices is one of the largely neglected themes of Mauritian slave historiography and deserves further study. This approach is necessary in order for social historians, other scholars and ordinary Mauritians to understand how the Mauritian slaves and apprentices were able to secure their own freedom before the abolition of slavery in 1835 and the advent of final freedom in 1839, and how they epitomise the idea of human agency in this island's history.

Although Richard B. Allen has shown how in Mauritius, during the late 1700s and early 1800s, 'the manumission rate remained low and relatively constant over time',[5] this observation does not apply to the later manumission that occurred between 1811 and the 1830s. However there is some discrepancy in the sources on numbers being manumitted. In one source, out of a slave population of some 80,000, from 1811 to 1826, there was an average of 100 to 119 manumissions per year,[6] this despite manumission laws which were not very liberal.[7] Another estimate shows that an average of 135 manumissions per year occurred.[8] Yet another mentions that between 1818 and 1821, there was an annual average of 121 manumissions.[9]

Whatever the source, there is clear evidence that during the mid-1820s, there began to be a sharp decline in the number of slaves being manumitted, especially between 1823 and 1826, when the annual average dropped to 60 manumissions. There is also clear evidence that, by 1827, the colony's manumission rate increased once again because, during the first nine months of that year, more than 127 slaves were manumitted and it would continue to increase sharply between 1828 and 1834.[10]

In 1828, while commenting on the colony's manumission trend during the late 1820s, the Commissioners of Eastern Inquiry observed that 'emancipations are not infrequent even under the present restrictions'.[11] Furthermore, the figures also show that the even before the introduction of British amelioration legislation to liberalise the colony's manumission law, hundreds of slaves had already obtained their freedom. When they were freed, they joined the ranks of the group known in census records as Free Coloured who were composed of both free-born people of non-European descent and of manumitted slaves. The Free Coloured population was also characterised by a very high birth rate and low mortality, and they made a significant impact in the demographics of the island in the first half of the nineteenth century.[12]

The sharp drop of manumission during the 1820s can be attributed to Mauritian slaveholders becoming reluctant to free their slaves.[13] At this stage, it is important to point out that the 1820s were a period of dramatic economic transition for Mauritius with the emergence of the sugar plantation economy, and this brought about major changes in the lives of the Mauritian slaves. While there was a sharp decline in the colony's manumission rate, maroonage levels increased dramatically throughout the island, thus signifying that many slaves were bent on securing freedom even at the risk of losing lives as punishments for maroonage were severe. The increase in maroonage could also be explained by the economic changes in Mauritius: sugar production increased the workload for existing slaves as the labour force was gradually shrinking. Each year, thousands of slaves were being sold, transferred or hired out by their owners and thus high mobility between sugar estates characterised the state of the 'sugar' slaves. This was not to the liking of slaves, and each year thousands of slaves escaped from their owners for periods of anywhere from a one week to more than one month, and many hundreds of them remained uncaught. This period represents a decade of great social upheaval for Mauritian slaves.[14]

Another possible reason for the drop in manumission rates were the manumission laws themselves. It must be remembered that the slave amelioration laws were not introduced into Mauritius until the late 1820s, but, without a doubt, the mere contemplation of its eventual introduction made the slave-owners even more reluctant to manumit their slaves. As mentioned earlier, the amelioration measures included the passing of laws which liberalised the manumission process for the slaves and encouraged their manumission.[15] During the second half of the 1820s, there was a growing labour shortage in the colony and the manumission of some of the skilled slaves and slaves who were domestics greatly affected certain slaveholders. The slave-owners were extremely unwilling to manumit their slaves because they needed to secure their labour.

During the mid-1820s, another major reason for the decline in the colony's manumission rate and in gratuitous manumissions would be the sharp rise in the price of slaves which almost tripled from £36 in 1824 to £102 in 1829.[16] It must be remembered that during this period, just like in the previous decades and in other slave colonies, Mauritian slaves seeking to buy their freedom were appraised, most of the time, in comparison with colonial slave prices.[17] In 1831, in his despatch to Governor Colville, Goderich, the Secretary of State for Colonies, was greatly perturbed by this dramatic increase in the colony's slave prices. He firmly believed that such an increase made it more difficult for slaves to purchase their freedom and it would make slave-owners even more reluctant to manumit their slaves.[18]

Goderich's concern was only partly justified because between 1828 and 1829, out of 643 slaves who were manumitted, eight per cent had been freed by will or bequest by their owners. But even more significant, was the fact that almost 92 per cent had been manumitted through self-purchase, with the financial help of their relatives and loved ones, and through marriage.[19] Therefore, during the late 1820s, despite a sharp rise in the price of slaves, hundreds of slaves were still able to secure their freedom, while, at the same time, very few were manumitted gratuitously by their owners.

The Impact of British Manumission Laws

Several laws were introduced in the island when the British took over: in 1814 by Governor Farquhar; in 1827 by Lowry Cole; and, finally, in 1829 by Governor Colville. In January 1827, Governor Sir Lowry Cole passed Ordinance No.21. Its purpose was to amend the restrictive manumission law enacted by Farquhar in 1814.[20] Apart from reducing the donation to the colony's poor fund from 100 to 25 rix dollars, which was one of the requirements in the manumission process, it quickly became evident that Governor Cole's new law differed very little from the one passed by his predecessor. In fact, it was truly out of touch with the objectives of British amelioration legislation because it consisted of a number of complex and costly manumission procedures.[21] Therefore, it is not surprising that it did not receive the official sanction of the British imperial government, and Huskisson, Secretary of State for Colonies, ordered the British governor to draft a new and more liberal manumission law.[22]

But in his defence, Governor Cole pointed out to his superior in London that 'as a proof that the ordinance of January 1827 did not operate as a bar to emancipations' because from '27th January 1827 until the end of February of the present year, a period of 13 months, the number of enfranchisements (or manumissions) amounted to 212'.[23] He also sent a statement to Huskisson which contained an estimate of the number of slaves who were manumitted from 1814 to 1826. It showed that between 1823 and 1826, only 240 slaves were freed, or an annual average of 60 manumissions.[24] Governor Cole's figures and arguments, however, failed to convince and impress the Commissioners of Eastern Inquiry who were in the colony during this period.

In May 1828, Commissioners Colebrooke and Blair observed,

> it appears from a return made to us, that one hundred and fifty-nine petitions to emancipate slaves have been received by the Governor since April 1825, and which have not been completed, owing (we may presume) to the forms and securities required by the Colonial Ordinance.

which regulated manumission in the colony during that period.[25] In addition, it must be remembered that even Secretary Huskisson considered Cole's manumission law as being too restrictive because it limited the access of the slaves to freedom through manumission.[26] As a result of this situation, Colebrooke and Blair strongly recommended that, without any delay, 'all obstructions' for the manumission of the Mauritian slaves 'should be removed, and that any emancipation should be stated to the Protector instead of the Procureur General (Attorney General), and none should be considered excepting those involving the just right of creditors'.[27]

It was only the following year that most of the restrictions for the manumission of slaves were removed and between 1829 and January 1835, a sharp rise in the number of slaves being manumitted was observed. This dramatic increase in the colony's manumission during this period has received very little attention in recent years in some of the major academic studies on Mauritian slavery during the British period.[28]

In February 1829, after endless delays and in the face of fierce slave-owner resistance, the local colonial government, under Governor Colville, implemented Ordinance No.43 'for the amelioration of the condition of the slave population'.[29] This new law created the office of the Protector of Slaves, and it also liberalised the process of manumission for the slaves.[30] Within the first three months that Protector Thomas assumed his new position, some 28 slaves were manumitted and 101 requests for manumission were being processed. After this slow start, the number of slaves being manumitted rapidly increased.[31]

Robert Shell explains that 'the legal background, on its own, does not illuminate the practical process of manumission. The legislation dealing with manumission, just as in other slave regimes, was not an important guide to the process itself; indeed most manumission laws were irrelevant to the process'.[32] However, Shell's argument about manumission laws and procedure is not valid for Mauritius when we examine the impact of Ordinance No.43, which can be assessed from a reading of the *Reports of the Protector of Slaves*.

By December 1829, nine months after its enactment, Protector Thomas reported that between June and December of that year, more than 280 slaves had been manumitted and with another 159 slaves waiting for their acts of manumission to be approved. With this dramatic increase in the colony's manumission, he reported, with a great deal of satisfaction: 'The movement in this branch of the Protector's duties has been very active for the last six months'.[33] Overall, between 1829 and 1831, the records of the Protector of Slaves show that hundreds of slaves were manumitted each year.[34]

In his report, R.M. Thomas observed that, the passage of Ordinance No.43, 'has not only had the effect of lessening, by reducing to a mere trifle, the expenses attendant on manumission, but has essentially facilitated their progress, by removing the impediment consequent upon an attempt on the part of the Procureur-general to impose of his own accord upon enfranchisements (or manumissions) the conditions of an old colonial law, which in common with all other anterior laws and regulations relating to manumissions, was by the Ordinance No.43 declared to be abrogated and repealed'.[35] Therefore, the significance of this new law cannot be underestimated, because it swept away the costly and complex process of the old manumission laws and, as a result, it greatly facilitated the access of the Mauritian slaves to freedom.

During the concluding months of 1828 and the first half of 1829, eight per cent of the slaves had been freed by will or bequest by their owners, while almost 92 per cent had been manumitted through self-purchase, with the help of their relatives and friends, and through marriage.[36] Furthermore, before the passage of Ordinance 43, the final stage in the complex process of manumission was when the slave's act of manumission was approved by the procureur-general, or attorney general, and even by the governor. It was evident that many high-ranking officials in the local colonial government were either themselves slave-owners or favoured the interests of the Franco-Mauritian colonists; thus, they were biased against the slaves who tried to obtain their manumission. Therefore, Ordinance No.43 removed the responsibility for the approval of the slave's act of manumission from the hands of the procureur-general and the governor and placed it under the authority of the protector of slaves.

From October 1826 to December 1829, an annual average of 345 manumissions occurred.[37] Here too, as for the earlier period, estimates vary, ranging from 2,235 slaves who were given their freedom to around 3,753 slaves (annual average of 750).[38] Nevertheless, the figures indicate that there were three times more being freed in the 1830s than in the late 1820s. Thus, the introduction of Ordinance No.43, as well as the creation of the office of the protector of slaves, which were both the products of British amelioration legislation, did have a major impact on the colony's manumission after 1830.

Table 4.1: Categories of Slaves Manumitted in Mauritius, 1829–1835

Categories of Slaves	Number of Slaves	Percentage
Female	2,648	62
Male	1,622	38
Total	**4,270**	**100**

Source: Calculated from MNA/IE 8-10, 12-16, 37-40, 42, 63-84, Affranchissements or Manumissions, January 1829-January 1835.

During the Amelioration Period, an estimated 4,270 slaves were manumitted and the conclusions which are drawn from the IE series are quite revealing. There were 2,648 female slaves or 62 per cent of all those who were liberated, and 38 per cent consisted of male slaves or 1,622 individuals. Around 70 per cent of all manumissions or 2,989 individuals were freed through self-purchase and the overwhelming majority were skilled and semi-skilled slaves. Even more interesting is the fact that female slaves consisted around 57 per cent of all manumitted slaves or 1,704 individuals, and the male slaves around 43 per cent or 1,285 individuals who bought their freedom through self-purchase.[39]

Table 4.2: Categories of Slaves Manumitted through self-purchase in Mauritius, 1829–1835

Categories of Slaves	Number of Slaves	Per cent
Female	1,704	57
Male	1,285	43
Total	2,989	100

Source: Calculated from MNA/IE 8-10, 12-16, 37-40, 42, 63-84.

In 1832 and 1833, around 2,900 slaves received their freedom which was almost five times more when compared with the number of slaves manumitted in 1830 and 1831.[40] Overall, between 1826 and 1834, around 4,894 slaves were manumitted. The impact of the law was therefore to reduce the slave population's numbers further, and it shrunk between 1826 and 1835 from 69,076 to 61,045.[41] It must be said that there was also a high death rate and low birth rate, during this period.

The trend in the increasing number of manumissions continued throughout the 1830s, the last years of slavery and into the Apprenticeship era in Mauritius. The slaves' quest for freedom thus did not end with the abolition of slavery. The determination of the remaining slaves to obtain their freedom would only increase during the Apprenticeship Period.[42]

The concept that slaves desired freedom is not based on analysis of manumission alone. During this same period, maroonage rates also increased during both slavery and apprenticeship. This is further evidence of the existence of a strong desire of slaves to be free.

Profile of Slaves who Purchased their Freedom

Herbert Aptheker once observed that 'it was often possible for the slave, by great perseverance and labour to purchase his own freedom and, this being accomplished, the freedom of those dear to him'. This great American slave historian also described the act of the slave purchasing his freedom as an individual act of resistance against slavery.[43] Furthermore, manumission can be seen as 'being a passive form of resistance' because 'the slaves sought not to abolish slavery but to ameliorate conditions for themselves by freeing themselves'.[44] Thus, the slaves who bought their freedom showed that they rejected their inferior status vis-à-vis their owners and they wanted to improve their lives as free individuals in colonial society.[45]

The symbolism of an act of manumission cannot be underestimated because it was 'the most profound event in a slave's life'. However, it was experienced only by a few fortunate slaves.[46] Manumission was an 'extremely profound and dramatic act' because it was 'a judicial act in which the property rights in the slave' were surrendered by the slave-owners, and a new status and identity was being created for the manumitted as a free individual.[47] While referring to Hegel on slavery, Orlando Patterson explains that in the slave's struggle for freedom and 'in his disenslavement'; he evidently 'becomes a new man for himself'. Then, how does the slave become free and becomes a new man? According to Hegel, this is achieved 'through work and labour' which the slave gradually realises and this is truly when the slave's psychological and physical journey to freedom begins.[48] Eric Foner points out that one of the freedoms which the slaves immediately sought was self-ownership.[49]

Therefore, by purchasing their freedom with their hard-earned money as well as with the financial help of their relatives, the manumitted slaves showed that they asserted 'their ownership over their bodies'. In the process, through their actions, they completely rejected their owners' claims over them as a piece of property.[50] Manumission was also a major opportunity for some of these former slaves to buy the freedom of their enslaved relatives. As has been mentioned in this chapter, it was extremely common for slaves to be manumitted by their Free Coloured relatives and friends.[51]

As the above studies have been carried out from the Caribbean and the USA experience, it is important to have similar studies in Mauritius and Indian Ocean region. What type of slaves secured their manumission in Mauritius in the late 1820s and early 1830s? There is much evidence on this, and a short typology will be drawn up in this section.

Many of the slaves who were manumitted were skilled artisans and craftsmen as well as those who held a privileged position among the slaves and had access to financial resources.[52]

Another group were those who marketed their produce or goods. In May 1828, the Commissioners of Eastern Inquiry reported:

> We may observe, that the slave artificers and mechanics frequent the Sunday markets with articles for sale and the production of their leisure hours,....; indeed we have been assured that many of those enfranchisements, apparently gratuitous, have in fact been obtained by purchase from their masters by slaves from the fruit of their own exertions.

Therefore, many Mauritian slaves who were supposedly freed by their owners gratuitously had in fact paid for their manumissions themselves.

Another group seeking manumission were the trusted personnel of the sugar estate: in a letter to Governor Colville, the Franco-Mauritian slave-owning elite admitted that they were concerned by the fact that 'the commanders [headmen], workmen, and servants were generally those who have the means of purchasing their freedom'.[53] Thus, as in Jamaica, in Mauritius, those who had the best chance of buying their freedom were the headmen who were put in charge of the field slaves, those in charge of the estate workshops, the skilled slaves, and the servants or the domestics.

The concern of the Mauritian slave-owners was not unfounded. They were heavily dependent on the labour of skilled slaves such as masons, blacksmiths, coopers, joiners, and locksmiths for their sugar estates,[54] and fiercely resisted attempts at manumission. In particular, owners were against compulsory manumission by purchase, i.e., slaves paying a certain sum for their freedom, because freedom often would be bought by the most intelligent and hard-working slaves.

A fourth but no less important group were female slaves who were manumitted through marriage.[55] These will be the subject of attention in succeeding sections of this chapter.

The skilled males, market men and estate personnel formed a formidable group. In 1835, according to the *Abstract of District Returns of Slaves in Mauritius at the time Emancipation,* there were 5,094 tradesmen or skilled artisans, 1,991 headmen, and 15,556 domestics. When combined together, there were 22,641 tradesmen, headmen, and domestics.[56] Another estimate was given by Stipendiary Magistrate Percy Fitzpatrick who reported that out of the 61,121 slaves, there were 6,201 artisans, 1,813 headmen, and 15,556 domestics. Fitzpatrick's report shows that there were 23,570 domestics, headmen, and skilled artisans.[57] They constituted between 37.1 and 38.6 per cent, or well over one-third, of the island's slave population.[58] Eugene Bernard had observed that many of the slaves who had been manumitted earned high wages. He described how a newly freed slave, who was a good carpenter, had refused a job for which he would have been paid 30 piasters or rix dollars per month.[59] A skilled slave, like a carpenter, could earn as much as 360 rix dollars for one year. Thus, it may be argued that the slaves who were skilled artisans and craftsmen were perhaps the most privileged slaves in the colony because they had the best access to financial resources and to purchase their freedom. In 1835, there were between 5,094 and 6,201 skilled slaves, and they made up between 8.3 to 10.1 per cent of the total slave population.[60] It is important to also state that when they were manumitted, they could also manumit their enslaved relatives.

In February 1835, the British officially abolished slavery in Mauritius, and after serving a four-year apprenticeship period, the island's more than 53,000 apprentices were freed on 31 March 1839. During the second half of the 1830s and after, thousands of Mauritian apprentices left their former owners and settled in different parts of the island. By the mid-1840s, Mauritius became the largest producer of sugar in the British Empire and surpassed even the older sugar plantation colonies in the Caribbean such as Jamaica. There was a need for a large supply of cheap and malleable labour to work on the Mauritian sugar estates in order to deal with the rapid expansion of sugar production and the labour shortage caused by a declining slave population.[61]

Local sugar planters began to import Indian labourers to supplement and eventually to replace the apprentice labourers to work in the island's sugar cane fields, in their homes, and in Port Louis. The establishment of the Apprenticeship System in Mauritius thus coincided with the gradual introduction of tens of thousands of indentured labourers who were paid wages and who in turn spent their money for the purchase of goods and services. Therefore, during this crucial decade of social and economic transition, the practice of wage labour and the use of money was gradually being introduced on several sugar estates in several of the island's rural districts and, to a lesser extent, in Port Louis.

Inevitably this had a direct impact on the way the apprentices viewed the value of their labour and they were able to earn some money for any additional work they performed for their masters or mistresses or anyone else who was ready to employ them. This was particularly the case of skilled artisans, semi-skilled workers and domestics on the sugar estates and in Port Louis. With access to capital, they were able to purchase their freedom as many others had done under slavery. At the same time, apprenticeship measures also made their manumission much easier when compared with preceding years.[62]

In 1905, the *Select Council of Government Committee on the History of Indian Immigration to Mauritius* chaired by Mr. Henri Leclezio, a Franco-Mauritian planter and politician, commented when it came to the transition from slave/apprentice labour to indentured labour that:

> As a result of Emancipation, a great number of apprentices left employment on the estates....and it soon became apparent that a very large portion of the land then in cane cultivation would become waste at the expiration of the apprentice system when it was exposed that the men employed in agriculture would almost wholly abandon that kind of work.... It was a question of existence for Colonial industry and agriculture; and the planters deeply impressed with a sense of the risks to which their properties would be exposed began to send recruiters to India to engage free labourers for them as an experimental measure.[63]

Between August 1834 and March 1839, a total of 26,028 contractual labourers, who included 24,837 adult males, 929 adult women, 177 young boys and 85 young girls, were brought to work mainly on the island's sugar estates and some in Port Louis.[64]

The Desire for Freedom during the Apprenticeship Period

Being disappointed with the fact that they had not been in reality freed, had been cheated of freedom and were 'half-slave, half-free', many apprentices chose to purchase their freedom. As under slavery, they did not wait for the ending of apprenticeship. In May 1840, while on a mission to London on behalf of Mauritian sugar planters, Charles Anderson, a former special magistrate, informed Lord John Russell, the Secretary for the State of the Colonies that from 1835 to 1837, around 600 apprentices had bought their freedom. By March 1839, around 9,000 apprentices had purchased their freedom. Therefore, between January 1837 and March 1839, most of these apprentices were able to manumit themselves and many gradually withdrew from the sugar estates and left their owners for good.[65] One of the key indicators that thousands of Mauritian apprentices had indeed bought their freedom was that the colony's apprentice population was shrinking rapidly.[66]

Table 4.3: Population of Mauritius, 1835–1838

Year	Free		Apprentices		Indian labourers		Total		
	Males	Females	Males	Females	Males	Females	Males	Females	Total
PORT LOUIS									
1835²	6,679	6,664	8,247	6,055	..	..	14,926	12,719	27,645
1836²	7,570	7,263	9,850	6,660	..	..	17,420	13,923	31,343
1837³	8,000	8,006	9,850	6,660	613	37	18,463	14,703	33,166
1838³	9,091	9,090	9,780	6,579	..	..	18,871	15,669	34,540
MAURITIUS									
1835⁴	15,282	14,330	36,527	24,518	..	..	51,809	38,848	90,657
1836	15,926	14,485	33,159	20,602	4,337		49,115²	35,085³	88,537
1837³	16,473	15,199	32,725	19,891	11,201	399	60,399	35,489	95,888
1838	19,504	18,361	34,994	18,236	23,520	339	78,018	36,986	115,004

Source: R. Kuczynski, A *Demographic Survey of the British Colonial Empire*: Volume II: Mauritius and its Dependencies, p. 774.

It should be noted that between 1834 and 1838, this segment of the colonial population declined from 64,331 to 53,230. This meant that in 1838, there were 11,101 fewer apprentices than in 1834, or a sharp reduction of 17.25 per cent in the colony's apprentice population in just over four short years.[67] It was reported that apprentices sought to effect their own emancipation prior to the end of the apprenticeship period and many did so."[68] The notarial record does confirm that apprentices secured their freedom before April 1839, but the extent of this activity is difficult to assess.[69]

Recent research at the Mauritius National Archives has shown that only 5,200 apprentices were manumitted, out of whom more than 80 per cent had purchased their freedom. Therefore, the figure advanced by Charles Anderson is questionable and needs to be revised.[70] However, there were other causes for the reduction in the apprentice population such as diseases, malnutrition, alcoholism, old age and maroonage.[71]

Furthermore, while testifying before the Immigrant Labour Committee of 1844, Brownrigg, a British planter and the representative of Cockrell & Co. of London in Mauritius, explained: 'After the apprenticeship system came into operation a gradual falling off of labour took place, this falling off was somewhat checked by the introduction of Indians...' Brownrigg was in a good position to give an accurate assessment of the labour situation in the colony because he arrived in Mauritius in 1835 and, ever since then, he had run four large sugar estates in the districts of Savanne, Plaines Wilhems, Black River and Pamplemousses.[72] During the second half of the 1830s, the gradual shrinking of the apprentice population also brought about a gradual reduction in the colony's apprentice labour force as they left the sugar estates.

During the apprenticeship period, many Mauritian apprentices did have access to financial resources.[73] As under slavery, many were skilled artisans and craftsmen; but there were also many unskilled apprentices who were able to generate revenue on their own when they worked in their spare time. According to North-Coombes, between 1835 and 1839, 'The apprentices seem to have been acutely aware of the existence of labour scarcity and of the high price their labour could command on a free market'. During this four-year period, the apprentices were obliged to work for at least 45 hours per week for their owners. In addition, if the apprentices performed any type of additional work, they had to be paid in cash for their labour.[74] Thus, it was quite common for the apprentices to be paid very small sums of money for the extra work they did for their former owners.

Slave-owners could no longer complain of manumission of apprentices as in August 1833, when the Act for the Abolition of Slavery was passed by the British Parliament, they, together with slave-owners of the Caribbean and Cape of Good Hope, were promised some £ 20 million in compensation. The Mauritian share was £ 2,112,632.[75] In May 1838, more than £1.5 million (71 per cent) of it had already reached the colony and more was on the way.[76] This meant that the ex-slave-owners were reimbursed for the cost of losing their slaves and could also afford to pay apprentices money for any type of extra work they did. In addition, the former slave-holders also made money from the common practice of hiring out their apprentices at high prices to other ex-slave-owners. The apprentices were hired out at a rate of $ 6-8 a month and they usually received $2 for their labour. Therefore, as the apprentices were being paid, 'The result was a spreading use of money amongst the former slaves, and a widening market for consumer goods'.[77]

In May 1838, Edward Baker, a Quaker missionary who spent several years in Mauritius, wrote: 'Many instances have come under my observation of apprentices purchasing an occasional month or week of freedom, and from ten to fifteen dollars a month have always been paid.'[78] For these apprentices, ten to fifteen dollars was a lot of money and this was the heavy price which they had to pay in order to secure either a few days or weeks of freedom in order to work for themselves and to visit their loved ones. At the same time, it becomes evident that many among the Mauritian apprentices did have access to money and were quickly learning how to use it. Baker also observed that during the apprenticeship period, the wages of the Free Coloureds as well as of the apprentices had risen steadily.[79]

In 1835, apprentices who were skilled artisans were paid eight to ten rix dollars and a field labourer around one dollar per month. But, just two years later, a skilled artisan could earn as much as 25 to 30 rix dollars and a field labourer around two dollars per month.[80] By 1839, *Le Mauricien*, a local pro-planter newspaper, reported that even an apprentice field labourer, who did extra work and carefully saved his money, could earn as much as between 30 to 40 rix dollars per year.[81] It is possible that over a four-year period, a hard-working and parsimonious apprentice labourer could save as much as 120 to 160 rix dollars.

It must be remembered that many among the Mauritian apprentices were skilled artisans and craftsmen and they could charge a high price for their precious labour in their spare time. In general, there were many skilled, semi-skilled, and unskilled apprentices who worked very hard in their spare time and saved their money in order to purchase their freedom. One good example would be the fact that between April 1837 and February 1839, in the district of Grand Port, around 138 apprentices were able to pay £1,736 and 8 shs to secure their freedom.[82]

Urban Apprentices

Between February 1835 and March 1839, about 5,200 apprentices obtained their freedom. These consisted of 2,860 apprentice women and girls (55 per cent) and 2,080 apprentice men and young boys (45 per cent). Of these manumissions, around 63 per cent of the apprentices occurred in Port Louis where around 25 per cent of the island's apprentices lived. Apprentice manumissions were thus concentrated in Port Louis and could be considered as an urban phenomenon.[83] However, this trend was also reflected earlier in the last years of slavery.

Orlando Patterson points out that in almost all slave societies, there was a strong correlation between urban residence and manumission.[84] During the late 1820s and early 1830s, this fact strongly applied to Port-Louis, a large and vibrant Indian Ocean port town. In Mauritius, Jean de la Battie, the local French consul and who had a good eye for details, reported that between 1825 and 1830, there were 283 manumissions in Port-Louis that included more than 14,000 slaves. Yet, at the same time, there were only 209 manumissions in the rural districts.[85] During the late 1820s, almost a quarter of the island's total slave population was found in Port Louis and 75 per cent of the colony's slaves were located in the rural districts, mostly on the sugar estates.[86] It must be pointed out that between 1825 and 1830 roughly around 1,525 slaves were manumitted. Therefore, the figures provided by de la Battie represent less than one-third of all the slaves who were freed during this period. Therefore, his figures might be seen as representing an accurate sample of the urban and rural slaves who were manumitted during the second half of the 1820s.[87]

De la Battie's sample indicates that, during this period, 57.6 per cent of the slaves who were manumitted were from Port-Louis and 42.4 per cent were from the rural districts.[88] Furthermore, he estimated that, between 1835 and 1839, almost 70 per cent of the apprentices who were freed were from Port-Louis and less than 30 per cent were from the rural districts.[89] These figures show that between 1825 and 1839, the number of urban slaves and urban apprentices being manumitted was increasing while, at the same time, the number of rural slaves and rural apprentices being freed was declining. This does not come as a surprise because there was a high mortality rate on the sugar estates and the price of slave was increasing. Equally important is the fact that there was a labour shortage and the Mauritian planters needed more and more slaves to cultivate their land in the rural districts.

For the period from 1831 to 1834, at the current stage of this research, no accurate manumission data has been uncovered for Port-Louis and the rural districts. But, de la Battie's figures may give an indication into rural and urban manumission trend during the early 1830s. At this point, it is necessary to make an average of the percentage of de la Battie's figures for the number of urban and rural slaves who were manumitted from 1825 to 1830 and from 1835 to 1839. This average may give us an idea of the number of slaves who were freed in Port-Louis and in the rural districts during the early 1830s. This proposed average yields a figure of 60 per cent for Port-Louis and 40 per cent for the rural districts.[90] Between 1831 and 1834, de la Battie had estimated that around 3,403 slaves were manumitted in the colony and the majority among them in Port Louis and they were skilled and semi-skilled artisans and domestics.

The imperative question is why many more slaves were manumitted in Port Louis than in the rural districts of Mauritius? Furthermore, what were the key factors which increased the chances of the urban slaves to obtain their freedom, through manumission, than their rural counterparts on the sugar plantations? Frederick Douglass once explained: '*A city slave is almost a freeman, compared with a slave on the plantation. He is much better fed and clothed, and enjoys privileges altogether unknown to the slave on the plantation.*'[91]

Furthermore, as Orlando Patterson explains, in many slave societies: 'The critical factor at work here was the fact that the urban areas offered more plentiful opportunities for slaves either to acquire skills or to exercise some control, if not marginal, over the disposal of their earnings or both,'[92] In 1833, a distinction was made 'in the Abolition Act between praedials and non-praedials urban and domestic slaves' in all the British slave colonies, with the exception of St. Lucia, an island in the Caribbean.[93] According to the *Abstract of District Returns of Slaves in Mauritius at the time of Emancipation* of 1835, there were around 3,237 non-praedials, head tradesmen and inferior head tradesmen, 929 non-praedial slaves, and also thousands of domestics.[94] Without a doubt, many of these non-praedial slaves were found in Port-Louis and they formed part of a large urban class of skilled, semi-skilled, and unskilled slaves which continued to exist during the early post-emancipation period.

Gender and Manumission

Between 1835 and 1839, the overwhelming majority of the male apprentices who purchased their freedom in Port Louis and on the sugar estates in the rural districts were headmen, *commandeurs* or overseers, estate workshop supervisors, stone masons, blacksmiths, mechanics, tailors, cart makers, cart drivers, house servants, carpenters and other skilled and semi-skilled workers. Female apprentices who bought their freedom were domestics, washerwomen, seamstresses, mid-wives, dyers, sugar bag makers, bakers, cooks and others engaged in skilled and semi-skilled work. The majority of apprentices who bought their freedom and were being manumitted by their masters and mistresses were apprentice females.[95]

Table 4.4: The Different Categories of Apprentices Manumitted in Mauritius, 1835–1839

Categories of Apprentices	Number & percentage of Apprentices
Apprentice Women and Girls	2,860 (55%)
Apprentice Men and Boys	2,340 (45%)
Total	5,200 (100%)

Source: Calculated from MNA/IE 42 to IE 45, Register of Manumission Acts of Apprentices between February 1835 to December 1836; MNA/IF 1 to IF 41 Certificates of Liberation from Apprenticeship or Enfranchisements 1835-1839.

The tendency towards a greater number of women seeking manumission was a feature of both slavery and apprenticeship. Gender played an immense role in influencing a slave's access to freedom.[96] Furthermore, Robert Shell once noted that 'the process of manumission favoured adult female slaves and their children' which was common in many slave societies including Mauritius.[97] Between 1768 and 1789, in Mauritius, out of 785 manumitted slaves, around 479 (or 61 per cent) were females and 306 (or 39 per cent) were males.[98] The result of having so many females being manumitted was that it caused a great imbalance in the sex ratio in the colony's free population of colour. In 1788, among the Free Coloureds, there were 725 females and only 435 males. By 1806, the Free Coloured females outnumbered the males by two to one in the colony and three to one in Port-Louis.[99] This demographic trend continued well into the early nineteenth century.

Between 1821 and 1826, around 433 slaves were manumitted, of whom 65.6 per cent were females and 34.4 per cent were males.100 Between 1829 and 1830, out of 612 slaves who were manumitted, around 45 per cent were males and 55 per cent were females.101 Between 1826 and 1832, female slaves consisted 38 per cent to 39 per cent of the slave population when compared with 62 per cent to 61 per cent for their male counterparts.[102] In Mauritius, the percentage for the manumission of female slaves remained almost the same between 1768 and 1825. But after 1829, or during the last years of slavery, the gap in the number of manumissions between the male and female slaves gradually increased.

These facts and figures are reinforced by Jean de la Battie, who observed that during the late 1820s and throughout the 1830s, those who were generally manumitted were young women and their children.1[03] According to the manumission records of the Protector of Slaves, between 1829 and 1831, more than 70 per cent of those who were freed were women and children. In addition, between 1829 and 1830, around 500 domestics, or 40 per cent of all the slaves who were freed, were manumitted.[104]

Many manumissions were the result of liaisons forged by the slave women with Free Coloured men. The Mauritian archival record gives numerous examples of this. In June 1816, Dimanche Terreux, a manumitted Malagasy slave, purchased the freedom of his common law wife, Raboude, a 28-year-old Malagasy female slave.[105]

In 1828, the Commissioners of Eastern Inquiry were critical of the island's colonial officials for not paying enough attention to the female government slaves in Port-Louis because: 'No notice having been taken in the Matricule establishment of the connections formed by the women in town'. They went on to observe that 'in no case does it appear that any of the women are married, although several have declared their willingness to marry the individuals with whom they have connected themselves'.[106] The observations by the Commissioners give a clear indication that there were many female government slaves in Port Louis who were intimately connected with a number of Free Coloured men. There were even fugitive female slaves who cohabited with Free Coloured males. In 1831, Symdaker, an Indian convict, was arrested along with Euphrasie. When questioned by the police, Symdaker stated that Euphrasie was his wife and, upon further investigation, it was discovered that she was a maroon slave.[107]

Apart from the Free Coloured men, the female slaves also had intimate but illicit relationships with the white male colonists. In Port Louis, these women usually lived with white male artisans and soldiers and those termed *petits blancs* (poor whites).[108] Some among the female slaves also bore children with these white colonists. This can be seen in the case of Anne and Julien. In July 1832, Julien, the son of Anne, an Indian female slave, and of an unknown white colonist, was baptized as a Catholic only eight days after his birth. Julien was recorded as a mulatto, but it seems that the father did not acknowledge the child.[109]

In 1828, the Commissioners of Eastern Enquiry had recommended that the Matricule Department, which had been created to take care and supervise the government slaves, had to be abolished because of the amount of money the local colonial government spent to maintain it.[110] The commissioners recommended that, for the female government slaves, 'The persons connected with the negresses, who are resident in Port Louis, should be required either to marry, or to give security to provide for them'.[111] Thus, in the event that the Matricule Department would be abolished, the royal commissioners strongly recommended that the free men, mostly Free Coloureds and a few white colonists who had formed intimate connections with these female slaves must either marry or provide for them.

In order for commissioners Colebrooke and Blair to make such a recommendation, these intimate relationships between the female government slaves and Free Coloured males were quite common. But, at the same time, it must be made abundantly clear that these female slaves were not simply the victims of sexual exploitation by their male lovers, because some of them willingly got involved into this type of relationship as a means of survival. In other words, they also stood to gain from such a relationship. The commissioners observed that the colony's Matricule Department,

> till lately did not possess any information regarding the connections of the female slaves, who, when not living with any of the Government Negroes, have resided in the town, attending from time to time to receive clothing and rations for themselves and the children they might have.[112]

Therefore, some of these female slaves were able to use the intimate relations which they had formed with the Free men in order to live with them in Port Louis, instead of with the other government slaves. These relationships forged in the town allowed these government-owned slaves to obtain clothes and rations for themselves and their children. Through these men, they also secured their freedom.

In June 1831, Charlotte Gentille, a female government slave who worked at the Royal College in Port Louis, paid £ 60 in order to get herself and her two children manumitted. Charlotte stated that over several years, she had saved her money and she had also developed an intimate relationship with a Free Coloured man who resided in Port Louis. She also mentioned that in some ways, this Free Coloured man helped her to obtain her freedom and to procure the clothing and food for herself and their children. It seemed therefore that Charlotte was the man's partner and that the two children were the result of their relationship.[113]

These relationships between the female slaves and the Free men of colour and white colonists did not end with the abolition of slavery, but continued during the apprenticeship period. Some 80 per cent (4,200) of all registered manumissions were through self-purchase. In addition, a careful analysis of the IE and IF series shows that 2,520 apprentice females (60 per cent) and 1,680 apprentice men (40 per cent) were manumitted through self-purchase. The high rate of female apprentice manumission during this period can be partially seen through the fact that the number of apprentice women in the colony decreased from 24,518 in 1835 to 18,236 in 1838 – a reduction of more than 25 per cent. It is interesting to note that even after 1838, there were several apprentice women who put forward large amounts of money in order to pay for their freedom. This went on even during the last weeks and days of the Apprenticeship System in Mauritius.

Table 4.5: Categories of Apprentices Manumitted through self-purchase in Mauritius, 1835–1839

Categories of Apprentices	Number & Percentage of Apprentices
Apprentice Females	2,520 (60 %)
Apprentice Males	1,680 (40 %)
Total	**4,200 (100 %)**

Source: Calculated from MNA/IE 42 to IE 45, and MNA/IF 1 to IF 41.

Between February 1835 and January 1837, more than 600 manumission acts were issued; however, from January 1837 to March 1839, more than 4,600 acts of manumission were granted with more than 4,000 of them (86 per cent) being through self-purchase. Therefore, the majority of the manumissions during the apprenticeship period were secured between January 1837 and March 1839. Over a period of 27 months, 148 apprentice manumissions on average were granted mainly through self-purchase. At the same time, between January 1837 and March 1839, about 2,500 apprentices (62 per cent) of those who bought their own freedom were apprentice women and young girls. Recent research shows that the female apprentices were determined to be free, and they had access to a certain amount of capital. The apprentice men and women were able to save their money and managed to secure their freedom.

The World View of the Apprentices

Some of the key questions which need to be addressed include the following: Why did so many apprentices, especially the female apprentices, struggle to purchase their freedom? What was their worldview? How did they perceive freedom and the apprenticeship system? It is essential to understand their ethos, perceptions and worldviews which help to dictate and shape the actions of the apprentice men and women. Some of the historical records of the 1830s provide some of the answers to the above questions.

In May 1838, Baker observed: 'A fundamental error of the apprenticeship system is that it has caused the Emancipation Act itself to be regarded as a reluctant concession, rather than as a just right or boon. However received in

England, the blacks themselves have never regarded, and to the last hour of their apprenticeship will regard it as a grievous continuation of slavery.' He also reported: 'Almost daily the apprentices are purchasing their freedom at enormous prices, just as if no act of emancipation existed. Thus the dignity and grandeur of the Act of Emancipation is utterly lost for the present black.'[114]

In his report for the month of June 1838, Special Magistrate Percy Fitzpatrick of the Savanne district observed: 'There is a great and general desire for the purchase of discharge from apprenticeship, an idea prevalent among the apprentices that the enfranchisement (or manumission) to be granted when the time of service expires will not be a secure state of liberty. They also think that liberty by purchase is more credible than freedom given by Parliament.'[115] Satteeanund Peerthum describes that during the apprenticeship period, the British Parliament or 'the mother of parliaments was a discredited institution in the eyes of the apprentices in Mauritius' and 'that the gift of freedom from above could only be spurious'.[116]

The thirst of these apprentices for freedom is given even greater credibility because between 1837 and 1838, the special magistrates from Savanne, Grand Port, Flacq, Rivière du Rempart, and the other rural districts reported that large numbers of apprentices were purchasing their freedom.[117] It must be remembered that, most of the apprentices had done so through self-purchase.[118] Therefore, it would not be an exaggeration to state that these Mauritian apprentices had a strong desire for freedom.

Their determination to be free was fuelled by the fact that in 1835 they had realised that they had been cheated out of their long-awaited freedom. Many of the apprentices, especially the females, desired to bring about their freedom through their own efforts rather than being freed by the British government. In their eyes, freedom from below was desired and seen as being honourable, while they rejected freedom from above or freedom being bestowed upon them by the British imperial government. This would certainly explain why there were hundreds of Mauritian apprentices, the majority of them apprentice women, like Pamela Bellehumeur, Marie Louise, Franchette, Coralie and Therese Batterie, who spent a big amount of money to secure their freedom during the last weeks and days of the Apprenticeship System in Mauritius in 1839.

In early February 1839, Pamela Bellehumeur, the female apprentice and domestic of Mr. Bouffe of Black River district, purchased her freedom from her owner which was officialised by the district's special magistrate. On the same day, Marie Louise, the female apprentice of Mr. Lionnet of Port Louis, was manumitted through self-purchase. Three days later, Franchette, the female apprentice of Mr. Robert of Black River district, secured her freedom. On the same day and in the same district, Coralie, the female apprentice and domestic of Mr. Bullen, purchased the rest of her time of service under the apprenticeship system which was sanctioned once again by the district's special magistrate. Even more dramatic

was the action of Therese Batterie, the apprentice of Mr. Aristide Buttie of the
district of Black River. During the first week of March 1839, Therese was able
to purchase her freedom, and of her two children, from her master barely three
weeks before final emancipation on 1 April 1839.[119]

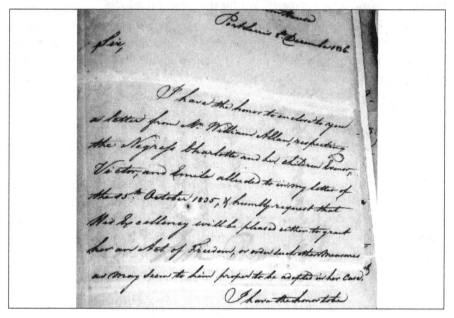

Photo 4.1: The manumission of a female apprentice and her children in
Mauritius, 1836

Source: Mauritius National Archives

Many of apprentices were able to work in their spare time; they were paid wages
and saved their money. Thus, Mauritian apprentices had access to financial
resources which proved to be the key to their freedom, especially between 1837
and 1839. Without a doubt, their determination to purchase their freedom
was fuelled by the realisation that they had been cheated of their long-awaited
freedom and they considered the apprenticeship system as a prolongation of
slavery. Therefore, during the second half of the 1830s, the apprentices gradually
bought their freedom and left their owners in order to carve an economic life of
their own as a free people in Port Louis and the rural districts of Mauritius.

Conclusion

One of the major objectives of this chapter has been to fill one of the glaring gaps in
Mauritian slave historiography by focusing on slave and apprentice manumission
between 1829 and 1839. This chapter has shown that there was a strong desire
on the part of the slaves and apprentices to purchase their freedom before the

abolition of slavery and the termination of the Apprenticeship Period. There were thousands of slaves and apprentices who were able to buy their freedom, especially the skilled and semi-skilled workers. Their desire to purchase their freedom was intimately linked with their worldview. Central to this was the determination to end their conditions of servility, attain some type of individual independence, and leave the perimeters of the sugar estate and the employment of their masters or mistresses in Port Louis. It has been highlighted that manumission through self-purchase might be viewed as an act of passive resistance where the slave or apprentice was able to end his or her condition of servility.

This chapter has also shown that despite restrictive manumission laws, a large number of slaves persevered and were freed. When they could not, they marooned. It is important to note, however, that between 1829 and 1839, the number of slaves and apprentices who were manumitted never surpassed more than 10 per cent of the total Mauritian slave and apprentice population. However, when compared with other British slave colonies, during the same period, such as Jamaica in the Caribbean and the Cape Colony in South Africa, British Mauritius had much higher manumission rates for its slaves and apprentices.[120] Furthermore, these high manumission rates highlight the human agency of thousands of these slaves and apprentices during this period of social and economic transition in Mauritian history. They did not wait for their owners and the British colonial authorities to free them, but they were able earn enough money through their wages, mostly as skilled and semi-skilled slaves and apprentices, to secure their freedom.

The arrival of indentured Indian workers brought with it the widespread use of money through the payment of wages which had a direct influence, to a certain extent, on some of the apprentices. During the 1830s, many of the female slaves and apprentices were gradually learning that access to finance and wages offered them a direct avenue of achieving their long-cherished dream of freedom, as they showed that they were fit for freedom.

This chapter has also highlighted the role of women slaves in ameliorating their status. This is similar to Zanzibar where another form of upgrading of status occurred when slaves became *suria* (see Chapter 4). When slavery was abolished, they struggled to retain their rights acquired during slavery.

Notes

1. Quotation and idea derived from John E. Mason, '"Fit for Freedom"': The Slaves, Slavery, and Emancipation in the Cape Colony, South Africa, 1806 to 1842' (PhD thesis, Yale University, 1992).
2. Herbert Aptheker, *American Negro Slave Revolts: Nat Turner, Denmark Vesey, Gabriel and Others*, New York, USA, International Publishers, 1974, Reprint of the 1943 original Edition, p.140.

3. Eric Williams, *Capitalism and Slavery*, Andre Deutsch Ltd, London, UK, 1964, p.204/205.

4. Christopher Saunders, 'Free Yet Slaves': Prize Negroes at the Cape Revisited' in Nigel Worden and Clifton Crais, eds, *Breaking the Chains: Slavery and its Legacy in the Nineteenth-Century Cape Colony* Witwatersrand University Press, Johannesburg, South Africa, 1994, p.114.

5. Allen, *Slaves, Freedmen*, p.83.

6. MNA/ID 2/No.3, Return of the Numbers of Manumissions effected by Purchase, Bequest, or Otherwise from 1st January 1821 to June 1826; Rene Kuczynski, *Demographic Survey*, Vol II, Part 4: *Mauritius and Seychelles*, London, 1949, p. 762-763; Allen, *Slaves, Freedmen*, p.83. For the Cape Colony See Bank, *The Decline of Urban Slavery at the Cape, 1806 To 1843*, Centre for African Studies, University of Cape Town, Communications, No.22 (1991), pp.173/178-179.

7. Eugene Bernard, 'Les Africains de L'Ile Maurice: Essai sur les Nouveaux Affranchis de l'Ile Maurice' in Archives Coloniales, Vol II (Port-Louis, Imprimerie de Maurice, 1890) (Reprint), p.530.

8. Allen, *Slaves, Freedmen*, p.83.

9. Statement showing the Number of Slaves Emancipated in each year since 1814 to the end of 1826, Enclosure E in Despatch No.3 of Governor Sir Lowry Cole to Lord Viscount Goderich, Mauritius, twentieth October, 1827, *BPP*, 1828, XXVII, p.367.

10. Statement showing the Number of Slaves Emancipated in each year since 1814 to the end of 1826, BPP, 1828, XXVII, p.367.

11. *Observations of the Commissioners of Inquiry upon the proposed Ordinance in Council, for improving of the Slave Population in Mauritius*, Enclosure 2 (a) in Despatch No.2 from Commissioners W.M.E. Colebrooke and W. Blair to the Right Honourable William Huskisson, Mauritius, nineteenth May 1828, BPP, 1829, XXV (338), p.23.

12. Author's Analysis; For impact of Manumission on the growth of Mauritian free coloured population see Kuczynski, Demographic Survey, p.760-763; Bernard, 'Les Africains', p.530; Bolton's Mauritius Almanac & Official Directory for 1851, (Mauritius, 1851), p.405; BPP, 1823, XVIII (89), p.125; MNA/ID 2/No.3, Return of the Numbers of Manumissions.

13. Teelock, *Bitter Sugar*, pp.220-221; Statement showing Number of Slaves Emancipated since 1814 to 1826, *BPP*, 1828, p.367.

14. Allen, *Slaves, Freedmen'*, p.41/45-46; Teelock, *Bitter Sugar*, pp.62-64/82-85/219-220; Barker, *Slavery and Antislavery in Mauritius, 1810-1833*, pp.73/74-78/119-125; For details on the extent of maroonage and maroonage statistics see MNA/IB 6, Return of Slaves and Prize Negroes Declared Maroons (1st January 1820-15th December 1826) in Correspondence and Returns Relating to Marron Branch of the Police Department at Mauritius.

15. Author's Analysis; See Barker, *Slavery and Antislavery in Mauritius*, pp.4-6; Teelock, *Bitter Sugar*, pp.220-221.

16. Barker, *Slavery and Antislavery in Mauritius*, pp.73.

17. Teelock, *Bitter Sugar*, pp.220-221; VijayaTeelock, 'Breaking the Wall of Silence: The History of the Afro-Malagasy Mauritians in the Nineteenth Century', *Journal of Mauritian Studies*, Vol.3, No.2 (1990), pp.5-6.

18. MNA/SA 16, Despatch from Lord Goderich to Governor Colville, Downing Street, London, 27 July 1831.

19. Return of Enfranchisements confirmed by HE the Governor of Mauritius, between the twentieth June 1828 and the twentieth June 1829, G.A. Barry, Chief Secretary to the Government, Chief Secretary's Office, Port-Louis, 1st July 1829, Enclosure No.2 in the *Report of the Protector and Guardian of Slaves from twentieth March to 24th June 1829*, Enclosed in Despatch No.1, from Sir Charles Colville, to Secretary Sir George Murray, Mauritius, 3 September 1829, BPP, 1830-1831, XV (262), p.57.

20. Despatch No.1, Governor Sir Lowry Cole to Earl Bathurst, Mauritius, 8th February, 1827, BPP, 1828, XXVII, p.275; *Ordinance of His Excellency the Governor in Council, Given at Port Louis, in the Island of Mauritius, 27th January 1827*, & *Proclamation, R.T. Farquhar*, Port-Louis, 30th December 1814, both Enclosed in Despatch No.1, pp.275-280.

21. Despatch No.2, BPP, 1828, XXVII, p.280-281; See also Governor Cole's Manumission Ordinance of January 1827, BPP, 1828, XXVII, pp.276-279.

22 Despatch No.2.

23. Despatch No.54, Extract of Despatch from Lowry Cole to Huskisson, Mauritius, seventeenth May 1828, BPP, XXV (333), p.98.

24. Statement showing Number of Slaves Emancipated since 1814, p.367; Despatch No.54, BPP, XXV (333), p.98.

25. *Observations of Commissioners* Encl. 2 (a), Despatch No.2, p.23.

26. Despatch No.2, pp.280-281.

27. BPP, 1829, XXV (338), p.23.

28. This very important theme has hardly been covered in the last twenty five years in the major academic studies on Mauritian slavery during the British period such as M.D.North-Coombes, 'Labour Problems'; Sadasivam Reddi, 'Aspects of Slavery; Nwulia, The History of Slavery; Barker, Slavery and Antislavery; VijayaTeelock, Bitter Sugar; Scarr, Slaving and Slavery; Richard Allen, *Slaves, Freedmen'*.

29. *Report of the Protector to Colville, from twentieth March to 24th June 1829*, Enclosed in Despatch No.1, p.4.

30. BPP, 1830-1831, XV (262), p.4; Thomas to Colville, Port-Louis, 28 December 1829, *Report of the Protector for the half year ending 24th December 1829*, Enclosed in Despatch No.4, 25th January, 1830, BPP, 1830-1831, XV (262), p.104.

31. BPP, 1830-1831, XV (262), p.6.

32. Robert Shell, *Children of Bondage: A Social History of the Slave Society at the Cape of Good Hope, 1652-1838*, (Johannesburg, Witswatersrand University Press, 1994), p.47.

33. *BPP*, 1830-1831, XV (262), p.104.

34. Teelock, *Bitter Sugar*, p. 99-100.

35. BPP, 1830-1831, XV (262), p.104.

36. Return of Enfranchisements between the twentieth June 1828 and the twentieth June 1829, 1st July 1829, Enclosure No.2 in the *Report of the Protector twentieth March to 24th June 1829*, Enclosed in Despatch No.1, p.57.

37. Calculated from Kuczynski, *Demographic Survey* , p.763.

38. Calculated from Ibid, p.763;

39. Calculated from MNA/IE 8-10, 12-16, 37-40, 42, 63-84, Affranchissements or Manumissions for January 1829-January 1835

40. Ibid, p. 763.

41. Calculated from Kuczynski, *Demographic Survey*, p.763; For the Slave Population See Kuczynski, *Demographic Survey* Table 15: Population by Sex & Race, Mauritius, 1822-8, p.770; MA/Mauritius Blue Book for 1835, p.322-323; See also Reddi, 'Aspects of Slavery during British Administration', p.108.

42. Reddi, 'Aspects of Slavery', p.119.

43. Aptheker, *American Negro Slave Revolts: Nat Turner, Denmark Vesey, Gabriel, and Others*, p.140.

44. Teelock, Bitter Sugar, p. 221.

45. Idea derived from Ibid, p.221

46. Shell, *Children of Bondage*, p.xlii

47. Ibid, p. 371-372.

48. Patterson, *Slavery and Social Death*, p.98; In this part of his academic study on slave societies, Patterson is discussing and analysing the ideas of Hegel on the slaves, the German philosopher from the late eighteenth century.

49. Eric Foner, *Nothing But Freedom*, Baton Rouge, Louisiana University Press, 1983. p.6.

50. John E. Mason, 'Social Death and Resurrection: Conversion, Resistance, and the Ambiguities of Islam in Bahia and the Cape', Seminar Paper presented at the University of the Witswatersrand Institute for Advanced Social Research, 14 August 1995.p.47.

51. Teelock, *Bitter Sugar*, p.220; Mason, "*Fit for Freedom*": *The Slaves, Slavery, and Emancipation in the Cape Colony, South Africa, 1806 to 1842*', pp.506-516.

52. *Observations of the Commissioners of Inquiry*, 19 May 1828, BPP, 1829, XXV (338), p.23.

53. Clause 29: Allowing a slave to purchase his freedom invito Domino, *Observations on the Order in Council of the 10th March 1824, with respect to the possibility of its adoption in the Island of Mauritius, the advantages and inconveniences resulting from it, and the means of conciliating its clauses with the Colonial interests, without violence or danger, Extract from the Deliberation of the 31st May 1827*, Enclosed as Appendix I in Despatch No.3, Governor Sir Lowry Cole to the Right Hon. Lord Viscount Goderich, Mauritius, twentieth October, 1827, BPP, 1828, XXVII, p.349.

54. Scarr, *Slaving and Slavery in the Indian Ocean*, p.63.

55. Teelock, *Bitter Sugar*, pp.220-221.

56. MNA/HA 73, Appendix G, No.163/No.8, Abstract of District Returns of Slaves in Mauritius at the Time of the Emancipation in the Year 1835 in Report of the Immigration Labour Committee in *Reports of the Immigrant Labour Committee for 1845*.

57. MNA/RA 833, Report of Percy Fitzpatrick, Stipendiary Magistrate of Port-Louis, Colonel George F, Dick, Colonial Secretary, 10th February, 1846; MA/HA 73.

58. MNA/RA 833, Report of Percy Fitzpatrick, Stipendiary Magistrate of Port-Louis, Colonel George F, Dick, Colonial Secretary, 10th February, 1846; MA/HA 73; Bernard, 'Les Africains, p.562-563.

59. Bernard, 'Les Africains, p.562; MA/HA 73.

60. MNA/RA 833, Report of Percy Fitzpatrick, Stipendiary Magistrate of Port-Louis, Colonel George F, Dick, Colonial Secretary, 10ᵗʰ February, 1846; MA/HA 73.

61. Huguette Ly Tio Fane Pineo, *Lured Away: The Life History of Cane Workers in Mauritius*, (MGI Press, MGI, Moka, pp.17-47; M.D. North Coombes, 'From Slavery to Indenture: Forced Labour in the Political Economy of Mauritius, 1834-1867', in M.D North-Coombes (Compiled and Edited by W. M Freund), *Studies in the Political Economy of Mauritius* (Moka, Mauritius, Mahatma Gandhi Press, 2000), p.78-88; Sadasivam J. Reddi, 'The Establishment of the Indian Indenture System, 1834-1842', in Bissoondoyal (Ed.), *Indians Overseas*, pp.3-12; David Northrup, *Indentured Labour in the Age of Imperialism, 1834-1922,* Cambridge, New York and Melbourne, 1995, p.31.

62. Edward Baker, '*Observations on the Apprenticeship System in Mauritius*' in Appendix to Letters of James Backhouse when engaged in a Religious Visit on the island of Mauritius, Sixth Part (London, Harvey &Darton, 1839), pp.74-75; Jean de la Battie, Rapport sur les résultats de l'émancipation a Maurice, pp.400-405; North-Coombes, '*From Slavery to Indenture*', pp.22-25;Satteeanund Peerthum, 'Obsessed with Freedom', Paper presented at the Conference Commemorating the 160ᵗʰ Anniversary of the End of the Apprenticeship & Post-Emancipation Mauritius, 1839-1911, Mahatma Gandhi Institute, Moka, 23-26ᵗʰ June, 1999, pp.1-5.

63. MNA/B1B/Henri Leclezio&Ors., Précis showing the different phases through which Immigration to Mauritius from the East Indies has passed before it assumed its present form (1905), p.1, paragraph 4.

64. MNA/ B1B/ 'Mauritius: Indian Immigration, Arrivals, Births, Departures and Deaths from 1834 to 1ˢᵗ January 1853' Enclosed in *Annual Report of the Immigration Department for 1859*; Reddi, Establishment of the Indian Indenture, in Bissoondoyal, pp.1-20; Pineo, Lured Away: Mauritius, 1984), p.26-29; See also Marina Carter & Raymond d'Unienville, *Unshackling the Slaves: Liberation and Adaptation of Ex-Apprentices* (Pink Pigeon Press, London, 2002), introduction and p.1-20.

65. Letter of Charles Anderson, Esq. To Lord John Russell, London, May 1ˢᵗ 1840, BPP, 1840, XXXVII (331), p.194; Charles Anderson was sent to London and his trip was paid by Franco-Mauritian sugar planters and local British merchants through the Mauritius Free Labour Association; "In 1840, he was sent to England to urge upon the government the expediency of allowing immigration into the Colony", Extract from MNA /HA 73/72, Evidence of Mr. Charles Anderson, 10ᵗʰ November 1838-30ᵗʰ November 1844.

66. Allen, *Slaves, Freedmen*', p.110.

67. The figure for the Slave Population for 1834 obtained from Kuczynski, Demographic Survey, See Footnote 2 below Table 19, p.773; The figure for the Apprentice Population for 1838 derived from Mauritius Archives/Mauritius Blue Book for 1838, pp.147-148.

68. Richard Blair Allen, 'Creoles, Indians Immigrants, and the Restructuring of Society and Economy in Mauritius, 1767-1885', Ph.D. thesis, University of Illinois, 1983, p.160.

69. Allen, *Slaves, Freedmen*', p.110.

70. MNA/IE 42 to IE 45, Register of Manumission Acts February 1835 to December 1836; MNA/IF 1 to IF 41 Certificates of Liberation from Apprenticeship or Affranchissements for the period between February 1835 to March 1839.

71. See Kuczynski, Demographic Survey, p.773-775; See Carter & d'Unienville, *Unshackling Slaves*; Moses F. Nwulia, *The History of Slavery in Mauritius and the Seychelles, 1810-1875;* M.D. North-Coombes, 'From Slavery to Indenture: Forced Labour in the Political Economy of Mauritius, 1834-1867'.

72. MNA/HA 73/Appendix B, Answers of Proprietors and Planters to First Series of Queries, No.6, Answers of Mr.Brownrigg, *Report of the Labour Committee of 1844*, 10th November 1838-30th November 1844.

73. Allen, *Slaves, Freedmen*, p.124; See also M.D. North-Coombes, 'From Slavery to Indenture: Forced Labour in the Political Economy of Mauritius, 1834-1867', in M.D. North-Coombes, Compiled and Edited by W.M. Freund, *Studies in the Political Economy of Mauritius* (Moka, Mauritius, MGI Press, 2000), p.25.

74. North-Coombes, 'From Slavery to Indenture', p.25.

75 Ibid, p.22.

76. Edward Baker, 'Observations on the Apprenticeship System in Mauritius', p.74; Highlighted Part Author's Emphasis.

77. North-Coombes, 'From Slavery to Indenture', p.25.

78. Baker, 'Observations on the Apprenticeship System in Mauritius', p.75.

79. Ibid, p.74.

80. James Blyth quoted in P.J. Barnwell, Visits and Despatches, Mauritius, 1589-1948 (Port-Louis, Standard Printing, 1948), p.248; See also Baker, 'Observations on the Apprenticeship System in Mauritius', p.75.

81. *Le Mauricien*, 24th April 1839

82. MNA/SD 28, Report of J. Davidson, Stipendiary Magistrate of Grand Port, to the Right Honourable the Colonial Secretary, Mahebourg, Grand Port, twentieth December 1845, Enclosed in Governor Sir William Gomm's despatch to the Secretary of State for the Colonies, January 1846; See also Nwulia, The History of Slavery, p.158; Allen, *Slaves, Freedmen'*, p.124.

83. Calculated from MNA/IE 42 to IE 45; MNA/IF 1 to IF 41 Certificates of Liberation; Jean de la Battie, Rapport sur les résultats ', pp.401-403; Kuczynski, Demographic Survey, p.773-774.

84. Orlando Patterson, Slavery and Social Death, (Cambridge, Harvard University Press, 1982).p.269; See Frederick P. Bowser, while studying Latin American societies during the late sixteenth and first half of the seventeenth centuries, explained "that manumission, in an age when few questioned the morality of slavery, was largely an urban phenomenon", See Bowser, 'The Free Person of Color in Mexico City and Lima: Manumission and Opportunity, 1580-1650' in in Stanley L. Engerman and Eugene D. Genovese (eds), Race and Slavery in the Western Hemisphere: Quantitative Studies (Stanford, California, Center for Advanced Study in the Behavioral Sciences, 1975), p.334.

85. Jean De la Battie, Rapport sur les résultats', in Abolition de l'esclavage dans les colonies britanniques: Rapports recueillis par le departement de la marine et les colonies, Tome II (Paris, Imprimerie Royal, 1842), pp.401-403.

86. Calculated from Kuczynski, Demographic Survey , p.773; Teelock, *Bitter Sugar*, p.100-101.

87. Calculated from Kuczynski, Demographic Survey , Manumission Table, p.763.

88. De la Battie, Rapport sur les résultats , pp.401-403.

89. Ibid, pp.402-403.

90. See Jean De la Battie, Rapport sur les resultats, pp.401-403 ; See also Teelock, Bitter Sugar', p.96-101.

91. Frederick Douglass, The Education of Frederick Douglass: Extract from Narrative of the Life of *Frederick Douglass, an American Slave*, Penguin Classic Books, New York 1999, p.43.

92. Patterson, Slavery and Social Death, p.269.

93. Worden, 'Between Slavery and Freedom: The Apprenticeship Period, 1834 to 1838', in Nigel Worden and Clifton Crais, eds, *Breaking the Chains: Slavery and its Legacy in the Nineteenth Century Cape Colony*, Johannesburg, Witwatersrand University Press, 1994. p.24.

94. MNA/HA 73.

95. Calculated from MNA/IE 42 to IE 45, Register of Manumission Acts; MNA/IF 1 to IF 41 Certificates of Liberation; Jean de la Battie, Rapport sur les resultants', pp.401-403; Kuczynski, Demographic Survey, p773-774; See Letter of Charles Anderson, Russell, BPP, 1840, XXXVII (331), p.194; Allen*, Slaves, Freedmen*', p.124.

96. Bank, The Decline of Urban Slavery at the Cape, 1806 To 1843, p.185.

97. Shell, Children of Bondage, p.xlii.

98. Jumeer, 'Les affranchissements et les libres a l'ile de France a la fin de l'ancien regime (1768-1789)', ' (MA thesis, Faculté des Sciences Humaines, Université de Poitiers, 1979), p.33.

99. Allen, 'Economic Marginality and the Rise of the Free Coloured Population of Colour in Mauritius, 1767-1835', Slavery and Abolition, Vol 10, No.2 (1989), p.131.

100. MNA/ID 2/No.3, Return of the Numbers of Manumissions 1ˢᵗ January 1821 to June 1826.

101. Calculated from No.4, List of Slaves who have presented their Acts of Enfranchisement to the Protector of Slaves for Registration from the 25ᵗʰ June to the 24ᵗʰ December 1829, inclusive, BPP, 1830-1831, XV (262), p.186-192; No.4, List of Confirmative Acts of Enfranchisement registered in the Protector' Office between the 24ᵗʰ December 1829 and the 24ᵗʰ June 1830 inclusive, BPP, 1830-1831, XV (262), p.310-321.

102. Calculated from Table 15: Population by Sex and Race, Mauritius 1822-8, p.770 & Table 19: Slave Population by Sex, Mauritius 1830 and 1832, Kuczynski, Demographic Survey, p.773.

103. De la Battie, Rapport sur les resultats ', p. 403.

104. Teelock, *Bitter Sugar*, p.100.

105. MNA/IE 26, Manumission of Raboude, June 1816.

106. Extract of that part of the *Report of the Commissioners of Inquiry, dated 15ᵗʰ December 1828, upon the Finances and Establishments of Mauritius, which relates to the Condition of the Slaves in that Colony*, Mauritius, 15ᵗʰ December 1828, No.3, BPP, 1829, XXV (338), p.28.

107. MNA/RA 457, Police Report, 21st-22nd November 1831
108. Carter, 'Founding an Island Society: Inter-Ethnic Relationships in the Isle de France', in Marina Carter (ed), Colouring the Rainbow: Mauritian Society in the Making (Port Louis, Mauritius, Alfran Co. Ltd, 1998), p.10-12/28-29/5/1-2.
109. Ibid, pp.5-6/3.
110. Extract of *Report of the Commissioners of Inquiry, Finances and Establishments of Mauritius*, BPP, 1829, XXV (338), p.27.
111. Ibid, p.29.
112. BPP, 1829, XXV (338), p.28.
113. MNA/RA 518/315, Letter of Charlotte Gentille, December 1831.
114. Baker, 'Observations on the Apprenticeship System in Mauritius', p.73.
115. MNA/RD 16, Report of Special Magistrate Percy Fitzpatrick for June 1838.
116. Satteeanund Peerthum, 'Obsessed with Freedom', Paper presented on Post-Emancipation Mauritius, 1839-1911', p.3.
117. Observations on the apprentices, manumission and their desire for freedom from different districts mentioned in several Letters and Reports submitted by the Special Magistrates in MNA/RD 12, RD 13 and RD 14 for 1837 and MNA/RD 15 and 16 for 1838; See also Peerthum, 'Obsessed with Freedom', p.5.
118. See MNA/IF 6 to IF 41 Certificates of Liberation.
119. MNA/IF 40, the Manumissions of Pamela Bellehumeur, Marie Louise, Franchette, Coralie and Therese Batterie for February and March 1839; Peerthum, 'Obsessed with Freedom', p.3-4; See Karishma Bundhooa, 'Female Apprentices in Mauritius, 1835-1839', B.A Hons thesis, University of Mauritius, March 2010, pp. 20-22.
120. Satyendra Peerthum, 'Determined to be Free: A Comparative Study of Manumission, the Slaves and the Free Coloureds in the Slave Societies of Mauritius, the Cape Colony and Jamaica, 1767-1848', B.A (Hons) thesis, Historical Studies Department, University of Cape Town, South Africa, pp.42-63/140-143.

5

Suria: Its Relevance to Slavery in Zanzibar in the Nineteenth Century

Saada Omar Wahab

Although much research has been undertaken on slavery in the Indian Ocean, Africa, the Americas and elsewhere, few studies have been produced on the history of female slavery. A major problem has been the lack of written sources, compared to those available for male slaves who were traded and required for labour and are therefore more fully documented in written sources. A gendered approach to the study of slavery reveals that much of their lives were not documented because it centred on personal relationships, family life and activities centred in or around the home. Even cultural practices maintained largely by women, were not documented when it was not publicly exhibited. Slave-owners, travellers, colonial officials during the time of slavery rarely ventured into slave camps nor questioned slaves about family affairs. There were few maroon women, few involved in criminal cases, and few with economic activities which entered financial records. Although to attempt to study a topic that is not well documented is to step on hazardous ground, two chapters in this project are devoted to making the first steps in reconstructing the lives of a group of women who did enter the historical record through their association with men, slave and free. This chapter will examine the particular and unique role of the *suria*, a particular Islamic institution in slavery as practiced in Zanzibar and the post-emancipation experience.

The *suria* are slaves and 'secondary wives' and must be distinguished from the term 'concubine' which has often been used in existing literature to describe them. The system itself had a long history as far as the system of slavery is concerned. The *suria* was part of the Arab social and family life system that was accepted in Islam in a modified form. In Zanzibar and elsewhere in East Africa where Muslim Arabs penetrated, the institution of the *suria* was also practiced as part of the family system. In the nineteenth century, it clashed with European perceptions of freedom, and the emancipation of *suria* as proclaimed by the British disturbed the family system of the Arabs and Muslims who owned slaves in Zanzibar.

The term *suria*, rather than the term 'concubine', is used in this project as there is difference between the two. While 'concubine' refers to extra-legal wives who were possessed by a man of high social status only, the *suria* refers to women who were bought, acquired as a gift, captured in war, or domestic slaves, and who established cohabitation with the slave masters as secondary wives with certain legal rights and social status.

The word *suria* originates from Arabic language and is believed to be related to the word *ajnab* (meaning 'a stranger in the community'). In Islam, this term was used to identify a female slave who established cohabitation with her owner and bore his children. However, a female slave became a *suria* only when her owner recognised the child.

The study of *suria* becomes important and relevant for this comparative study of slavery in Mauritius and Zanzibar, as it shows the extent of the Arab and Islamic influence on slavery in Zanzibar. In comparison with Mauritius, this institution in Zanzibar provides an insight into the process of ascending mobility of some female slaves and their offspring who shifted from a lower social position to a higher one as they were integrated with the free people of the community by becoming a *suria*. In Mauritius, this institution did not exist as a legal practice because until 1810, only Roman Catholicism was allowed on the island and most slave owners were Europeans and Christians. Although relationships did develop between female slaves and their owners, these were illicit relationships as the law forbade any sort of relationships, marital or otherwise, between slave and free, or between white and non-white inhabitants.

The Historical Context of the *Suria*

The *suria* as part of the Arab social system had it history long before the seventh century AD when Prophet Muhammad proclaimed Islam. It is believed that different Arab communities were engaged in capturing and developing relationships with female captives whose legal status was uncertain. However, the advent of Islam modified this practice. Islam like other social organisations regarded slaves as property that the owner possessed. This is referred to in the Qur'an as '*ma malakat aymanukum*' or 'what your right hand possesses'.[1] Due to this right of ownership, it became lawful for the owner of a slave girl to have intercourse with her. Consequently, *surias* were women who were available to their masters, but not formally married to them. A man could have as many *surias* as he could afford. However, there were some restrictions on the owner: he would not co-habit with a female slave belonging to his wife, and he could not have relations with a female slave if she was co-owned, or already married.[2]

The *suria* system as proclaimed by Islam has some 'benefits' for both slaves and owners. If the slave girl gave birth to her owner's child, her status immediately improved, notably as she became '*umm walad*' or 'mother of the child'.[3] She could not thereafter be sold, pawned, or given away, and when her owner died she automatically became free. This meant that the *suria* system as practiced by Islam had its own way of emancipating the slave women gradually. It started after she gave birth, and then completed after the death of her owner. In this sense, the status of the *suria* was different from that of other slaves.

Moreover, this system enabled the *suria* to bear children who were legitimate and free as they issued from her owner. They would therefore inherit property from their fathers as any other children from the other legal wives. In other words, the *suria* system gave female slaves relative security, and a chance to rise socially, and even gain power through their sons. It also provided a measure of economic security for the woman involved, although she did not acquire inheritance rights from her owner/husband except through her children.

This system also enabled the slave-owners to enjoy sexual relations with many women without being accused of harassing girl slaves or *zinaa*, or violating the Islamic *sharia*. It also enabled them to have children with other women apart from their wives; and these women were accepted by the Islamic *Sharia* and were not treated as illegitimate.

It is a fact that under Islam a *suria* enjoyed many privileges that other normal slaves, whether within or outside Muslim communities, could never imagine. At the same time, in comparison with other cultures, Islam tried to modify the condition of slaves, recognised the social reality of cohabitation with slave women, and went on to explicitly acknowledge their status and rights and those of their offspring.

In protecting *suria* from being a prostitute, the *Sharia* put it clearly that she could have sex only with her master/owner, and anyone else who had sex with her was guilty of adultery. A *suria* was not given any kind of payment for her services. Her status in a man's life was that of a wife. If she was owned by the father of the house, then his brothers or sons had absolutely no rights toward her.

However, the *Sharia* did not prescribe equality of time and sustenance between wives and *suria*. This means a man was not forced to share his time equally between his *surias* and his wives.[4] This distinguished a *suria* from a wife of the owner: she was a secondary slave wife whose rights were defined by the *Sharia*.

The *suria* lived in a *harem*. This was a private part of any Muslim household where the *suria* was required to live together with the family of her owner. The *suria* rarely lived in a separate harem from the owner's wife/ wives. But *surias* were treated far better than other female slaves.

From the rise of Islam in the seventh century AD, *surias*, as other groups of slaves, were obtained through different ways. But the most common one was through *jihad*, a religious war with those who were unbelievers in the mission of Muhammad. The war captives were used in different ways such as becoming *surias*. Prophet Muhammad declared it a sin to kidnap any free man, woman or child and make them slaves unless they had warred against the Muslims. After a war, he used to exchange prisoners of war if the warring parties agreed to it. If not, the captives were set free by taking a ransom, and if they could not afford the ransom, he showed generosity and released them without condition. If the captives had nowhere to return to, they were made slaves, and all efforts were made to socialise them into the existing Islamic society. Other *surias* were acquired as gifts which some Muslims received from their fellow Muslims or foreign rulers.

In general, seventh century Islam banned the ill-treatment of slaves, especially the slave girls. Prophet Muhammad taught that slaves were to be regarded as human beings with dignity and rights and not just as property, and that freeing slaves was a virtuous thing to do. This created a culture in which slaves became much more assimilated into the Islamic community.

The *Suria* System and the Reality of Zanzibar Slavery

As noted earlier, the *suria* was part of a social and family practice of Arab and Muslim communities in different parts of the world. It is not known exactly when this system was practiced in Zanzibar, but it flourished in the nineteenth century in Zanzibar and other city states of East Africa. There are different factors that explain why this practice developed during that time. From 1744, the Omani ruler had installed his governor in Zanzibar, but the local ruler, the *Mwinyi Mkuu*, remained as the chief of the native subjects. This gradually affected not only the political setup, but also the social and economic system.[5] The situation changed drastically in 1840 when Sultan Said transferred his capital from Muscat to Zanzibar.[6] This was the starting point of the Omani Arab Sultanate in Zanzibar, which was characterised by the opening up of large clove and coconut plantations. It resulted in a large inflow of Arabs from the Arabian world who came to establish their settlement in Zanzibar.[7] When they moved to East Africa and Zanzibar, they came in with their own family system as they had practiced it at home.

Secondly, in the nineteenth century slave trade and slavery became a lucrative and essential feature of Zanzibar's social and economic structure. Following the prosperity of the slave trade and the plantation economy, many businessmen and planters accumulated enough profits from these two sectors. At that time, local slaves in Zanzibar were very cheap, ranging from as little as $10 to $20.8 As a result of this, upper and middle-class Arabs, Indians as well as Swahili Muslims, were in a position to own slaves, including *surias*.

In addition, the Zanzibari commercial system of the nineteenth century facilitated the development of slavery and slave trade. Slaves were considered by Arabs and Swahilis as property that could be bought and sold. Although pawning a slave was forbidden by the *Sharia*, it operated as a local practice among Arab and Indian slave-owners. By traditional usage, a person who was heavily indebted or in urgent need of cash was allowed to make a pledge and put his slaves in a pawn to pay his debts or obtain cash.[9] However, the slaves were not allowed to be pawned for more than one month.

The *suria* were required to be healthy and energetic to serve the sexual desires of their owners as well as reproduce. If a master found anything suspicious, he would withdraw his offer, and the slave would continue to serve as *mjakazi* (a female domestic slave) instead of a *suria*. An example was Maryam binti Abdallah who was a slave from Abyssinia. She had been raped by a Nubian slave dealer who brought her to Zanzibar when she was only 12 or 13 years old. She suffered internal injuries that made it impossible for her to bear children. She was bought by the Sultan as she was very beautiful. The Sultan intended to make her one of his *surias*, but her injuries made this impossible.[10] Therefore she became one of the hand-maidens of Seyyid Ali bin Said bin Sultan, living in the palace along with other slave girls. Although one cannot generalise using only one example, this case showed that in this family system, the problem was not in her social status but what she could bring in terms of family. The owners expected to have children with their *surias* who could take on the family name and supervise their business in the future.

Another important theme is the ethnic origin of Zanzibar *surias*. There were local *surias* who came from East and Central Africa, as well as foreign *surias*. It is hard to establish the total number of *surias* who came from the different tribes. Sheriff's study on the social composition of Zanzibar slaves (1860-61) shows that many slaves who were used in Zanzibar were coming from the southern tribes in eastern Africa, including the Yao, Nyasa, Ngindo and others who constituted 68 per cent of the slave population in Zanzibar. The northern tribes included the Sagara, Mrima, and the Nyamwezi who contributed 18 per cent of the slave population (see Figure 3, p. 30). The remaining slaves included *vizalia* (born slaves).[11] This study, however, cannot be reliable in explaining the *suria* population of Zanzibar as many *surias* were not registered to obtain freedom. Generally speaking, these were the cheapest, and were owned by the middle as well as upper classes.

Apart from local *surias* there were also 'foreign *surias*'. They included Galla, Habshi (Ethiopians), Indian, and Circassian slaves from south-eastern Europe. The latter were the most expensive, with prices ranging between $50 and $250. For example, Ethiopian slaves sold for 50 to 150 German Crowns, 'the females being higher', and a 'superior Abyssinian female may sell at 300 Crowns in 1830'. In 1847, Kemball reported the price of between $60 and 200 for 'Habshi females'.[12] From Hejaz, girls ranged from $60 to $150.[13] Burton, as quoted by Sheriff, says Ethiopian slaves were 'exceedingly addicted to intrigue', but they were favourites with men, 'and, it is said, with Arab women'. Rigby reported in 1859 that an Indian had purchased a Galla slave woman for $159, while in 1871 a young Iranian had offered $250 for a Pathan (Indian) slave woman Fatima or Mariam.[14] White slave women were exceedingly rare and expensive, and were confined to the *harems* of the rulers and the upper class.

The *suria* in nineteenth century Zanzibar constituted the highest rank among domestic female slaves. At the beginning of the process, a man would buy a woman slave when her status would be that of *mjakazi* (woman slave) and keep her at home as a *suria*.[15] In some instances, a man would buy a *kijakazi* (young slave girl) and bring her home to be taught the customary housework. When the girl reached puberty, she was separated from other female slaves and was given a room for herself. She thus became a *suria* and was not allowed to go out alone. She then commanded the same respect from other slaves as the wife of the master did.[16]

There were two types of harem in Zanzibar. The first was a shared harem, where the *surias* shared a house with the wife (wives) of their owners. This was a common practice among sultans of Zanzibar and other slave-owners; a good example being the Royal Harem of Sultan Said bin Sultan. In this context, however, the *surias* did not have any say in the presence of the owner's wife.[17] The owner's wife/ wives ruled over everyone and everything within her reach in the harem. Bibi Azze, Sayyed Said's wife was feared by young and old, high and low, but liked by no one.[18] As the wife of the owner, she controlled everyone including her husband. The second type of harem was rare where only *surias* lived within it especially if the owner was single or widower. Under this type, some *surias* were said to have a greater say than the others. A woman's status depended on attracting the eye of her royal master. A study by Martin concluded that 'in most harems, important positions were held largely by women who came from other important families'.[19] These included white slaves (European) who were said to be expensive compared to black slaves.

Age was also an important factor in shaping a *suria*'s life within the harem. The number of years one served the system led to being considered experienced. Furthermore, older *surias* who had older children were more influential than new *surias* with younger children.

Nevertheless, the two types of harems shared the whole idea of social dissimilarity which is sharply noticeable in both. This classification was done not only between the *surias* on one side and the owner's family on the other, but also among *surias* themselves. In the shared harem, though *surias* had good opportunities and better position compared to other slaves, it seems that they could not share the same meal with the owner's wife and children (even those born by *surias* themselves). Sayyida Salme, one of the Sultan's daughters, who wrote the first surviving autobiography by a Zanzibari on life within royal harem, explained that all her older brothers came in from their houses to take their breakfast jointly with the father. No *suria* was permitted to take meals with the father; no matter how favoured she might be over others in other respects. Only his wife, Azze bint Seif, and his sister, Aashe, sat at his table.[20]

Skin colour among *surias* was also a differentiating factor. The white slaves such as Circassians, Persians and Turks thought of themselves as beautiful and expensive, hence they did not want to share anything with other slaves, even to take meals jointly with black slaves such as Abyssinians, or others from East and Central Africa.[21] While the price for a local slave ranged between $10 and $20, the foreign slave's price was between $50 and $250.[22] With this price variation, social distinctions existed within the harem, as the expensive (foreign) *surias* were treated far better than the local African *surias*.

Another kind of classification in the harem was observed among the *surias'* offspring. This classification was based on the ethnic origin of their mothers. As Salme stated in her book that, 'We, the children of the Circassian women, were usually called 'cats' ... because some of us had the misfortune of possessing blue eyes. Derisively, they called us "Highness", a proof of how annoyed they were about us having been born with lighter skin.'[23] However, this classification was not shared by their father. He treated them equally, with no colour distinction.

Socialisation of the *surias* was present in the harem. They were forced to adapt to the one or two common cultures accepted by their owners. When they came into the harem, they adapted to the new culture and maintained some of the elements of their original culture such as language, dress and food. In the royal harem, for instance, Sayyida Salme, explained:

> For us children the Babel of languages in this society was particularly diverting. In fact only Arabic should have been spoken and in my father's presence this order was strictly followed. But no sooner had he turned his back, than a kind of babel-like confusion of tongues prevailed. Persian, Turkish, Circassian, Swahili, Nubian and Abyssinian were heard promiscuously next to Arabic, not to mention the various dialects of these languages...

> As for the kitchen ... meals were cooked in the Arabic as well as in the Persian and Turkish fashion. In both houses [Mtoni and the town palaces] the various races were indeed living together and the most fascinating beauties as well as their opposites were abundantly represented. But among us only the Arabic fashion was permitted, and among the negroes the Swahili one. When a Circassian woman arrived in her clothes of ample shirts, or an Abyssinian woman in her fantastic attire, within three days she had to lay aside everything and to wear the Arabic clothes assigned to her. ... Immediately after she had been purchased, a newly arrived *suria* also received the necessary jewels as a present; at the same time the chief eunuch assigned her servants to her.[24]

Information provided by Salme explaining what was going on in the Royal Harem in Zanzibar was most probably experienced in many other ordinary harems. Another important fact observed from Salme's statements was that in the harem, tolerance seemed to prevail.

As a secondary slave wife, a *suria* was required to face *edda* following the death of her owner just like the wives did in Islam. *Edda* was a special religious mourning period that lasted four months that all the wives of the deceased had to submit to. Salme wrote that 'all the wives of the deceased without exception, the legitimate female slaves as well as the purchased ones, have to submit to special religious mourning, which last a full four months. They have to mourn their husbands or masters in a dark room; they are not allowed to step out intentionally into the brightness of the day... If [she] has to leave, she must throw a thick, black cloak over her mask, and cover self in such a manner that she is just able to see her way.'[25]

Concerning inheritance, Islam stated clearly that legal wives were entitled to inherit a quarter of the owner's wealth if the husband did not leave any child or grandchild, and if he did, the wife/wives inherited only one-eighth (*thumni*). However, the *surias* were not entitled to inherit the wealth of their masters unless they were identified in his *wasia* (will) out of the one-third that the person was allowed to allocate any way he wished.[26] Because of this law, there was hardly any *suria* who inherited from her owner directly, but archival records show *surias* received payments and civil allowances as allotted by their owners after their death.

In one instance, four *surias* who identified themselves as *surias* of Seyyid Ali bin Said, namely Sayaran bint Yussuf, Norein bint Abdallah, Fatma bint Yussuf and Rasha bint Abdullah, approached the British Resident to increase their monthly allowances.[27] In their letter they claimed that 'since the death of the Late Seyyid Ali bin Said, we have been left here under the hands of the Zanzibar government and Rs.15 each per month cost of our maintenance have been granted to us until about a year ago when it was increased to Rs.17.40 each.'[28] However they claimed that since the cost of living had greatly increased, they begged the government to increase their allowance. In response, the British resident approved that the allowance paid to one among them, Fatma bint Yussuf, who had died in August 1923, to be distributed equally amongst the surviving three wives from the total allowance of Rs.69.[29]

When one of them, Rasha binti Abdullah, passed away, the surviving *surias* placed another application in July 1929 in which Sayara binti Yussuf and Noreen binti Abdullah claimed that 'now one of the beneficiaries...Rasha binti Abdulla, who was drawing 1/3rd of the amount allotted to us, unfortunately through a motor accident she met her death..' They therefore requested that 'this amount be divided amongst us proportionately the two surviving beneficiaries'.[30] This was approved and the government distributed Rs.34 (Shs.51.50) equally among the surviving two *surias* from the date of Rasha's death.

Thirteen years later Sayara binti Yusuf submitted a similar request. She was now alone and seventy years of age as her fellow *suria* Nurein binti Abdallah had died. In her request, she asked that the pension of her fellow *suria* and friend be either wholly or partially amalgamated with hers, as she had lived with her departed friend all these past years and they had always pooled their resources together. As her friend had passed away, her life would be difficult without the extra allowance and that with only her pension, she could barely cook one meal a day.[31] In response, the Chief Secretary stated that Sayara who was 76, and the last survivor of the five *surias* of the Late Sayyed Ali bin Said, 'petitions that she be allowed to take the allowances of all the *surias* who have predeceased her'.[32]

The above observation portrayed an important theme that even after the decree for the abolition of slavery, the *suria* owners still felt that they had a responsibility to maintain their ex-*surias*, as they had to supply their basic needs although in this case it was the British colonial authorities had to decide on this, but they were probably following existing custom. This shows there were very special bonds that existed between the *surias* and their owners even after the death of the owners. Many *surias* maintained their relation with their owners and their families, as they regarded themselves as part of the owners' families.

Emancipation of the Suria in Zanzibar

The emancipation of *suria* started far back when this system was introduced. They obtained their freedom as a matter of course following the death of their owners, although this was at an individual level. The suppression of the slave trade between 1822 and 1873 and the slavery emancipation decree of 1897 did not disturb this aspect of social and family system of the Arabs and Swahili Muslims. The slavery emancipation decree intended to give the slaves the right to claim their freedom whenever they needed it. Article 5 of this decree stated clearly that, 'Concubines shall be regarded as inmates of the Harem in the sense as wives, and shall remain in their present relation unless they should demand their dissolution on the ground of cruelty, in which case the District Court shall grant it if the alleged cruelty has been proved to its satisfaction.'[33] The implication of this article was that the British who led these campaigns against slavery and slave trade were very much aware of the fact that the *suria* was part of Afro-Arab life and culture, and to abolish it meant to disrupt Muslim/Arab family structure and break the bond between the *suria* and her children who may stay with the father. Britain assured the Sultan that this decree would not interfere with the family life of the *suria* owners, but they soon realised that it would inevitably do so.

Shortly afterwards, in 1909, the Slavery Decree No. 11 was imposed in Zanzibar. This time the decree focused mainly on giving the *suria* their freedom and maintaining their rights over their children. This led to the emergence of a colossal contradiction between *suria*-owners on one side, and the British government on the other. The British now regarded *suria* as a category of slavery practiced within Zanzibar. They were in no position to let this practice continue as it had been a long-standing source of grievance with the British public that there still existed a form of slavery on the coast of Africa.

The *suria*-owners viewed the situation differently, as this was part of their social setup. Because of this, the *suria*-owners did not see the need to emancipate the *suria*s as this would disturb their family structure. To ask slave owners to grant freedom to their *suria*s was against their religion and it was referred to with great indignation among them. They argued that it would lead to a great increase in prostitution. Thus when the Sultan was asked to sign this decree, he replied that he had not understood how the British government could expect him to sign this in view of its former promises not to interfere with the family life of the Arabs.[34]

The following day the Sultan discussed the matter with his First Minister, General Lloyd Mathews, and legal member of the Protectorate Council, and he informed them that he was not going to sign the decree. The main argument for this objection was the fact that the owners would not wish that their *suria* leave, and went on to discuss the question of their rights to take away their children.[35]

The *suria* themselves stated that it would be difficult for them to ask for their freedom, and live outside their *harem*. As they argued, if freedom meant that they had to leave their children behind and go outside looking for their livelihood, they would prefer to stay as slaves for the rest of their lives.[36]

Under Islam a woman could claim the children's custody only if she did not marry again, and that if it was proved that she was leading an immoral life, she would sacrifice her rights. In this respect, the rights of custody would revert to the father in most cases. The sharia varied according to the sects. According to the *Ibadhi* law, the father had the right of custody of his sons, and the mother of the daughters only. So if this decree was implemented the *suria* would be allowed to have custody of their daughters only. According to the Sunnis, however, a free woman would have the right of custody of her children of both sexes.[37] The *Sharia* put it clearly that whether the mother or the father became custodian of the children, their inheritance rights from both of their parents remained.

However, regardless of the Sunni or *Ibadhi* point of view, the *suria* were in a position to take with them their children if they wanted to. But, again, it is important to consider their economic wellbeing. Were they in an economic position to sustain their children? The answer was that they were not in a position to maintain even themselves, even less their children. It was obvious that the decree would result in the disintegration of Arab families.

Moreover, under the *Sharia* no Muslim was allowed to hold a free woman as a *suria*. The owners would, after the issue of the decree, be compelled to either turn out their *suria*s or to marry them. But this posed a problem: how could they marry more than what Islam allowed? A man was allowed to marry up to four wives while he could own as many *suria*s as he could afford. The decree was thus adapted to accommodate the social structure of the Arabs.

Conclusion

Enslaved women's experiences in the two areas studied differed. In Zanzibar, the *suria* practice signified the upward mobility of some women slaves and their offspring from a lower social class to an upper level that was comparable to that of free men. In Mauritius, the French and later the British slave laws did not allow slave women to marry their owners nor could their children inherit from a white father. In Mauritius, female slaves and their children always experienced a descending mobility, unless they were freed and they married non-white freed persons.

In the earlier anti-slavery campaigns in Zanzibar, the British conceded the *suria* system as a social institution in Arab and Muslim lives. It was a family structure that had nothing to do with economic profits to the owners. Hence they had promised not to abolish it, as they believed abolition would disturb family structure of the Muslim slave-owners. This promise, however, did not last long; in early twentieth century, the *suria* system was abolished.

The abolition of the *suria* system in Zanzibar did not disturb the economic wellbeing of the Zanzibaris but rather the social setup. Arabs regarded this process as a breach of faith on the part of the British government against Zanzibaris after having given a definite assurance that they would not interfere with the family life of the Arabs.

Under Islamic laws, a *suria* was entitled to food and clothing so long as she remained with her master. She also had certain rights of inheritance through her children. Thus if she gave birth to her master's child and her master then died, the child inherited; and if the child then died, the mother inherited through that child. These rights were articulated by the Sharia based on the Qur-an.

Nevertheless, one cannot deny the fact that viewed from a modern perspective, the *suria* was an institution within slavery which breached human rights, exploited women, including selling and buying them as commodities, and sometimes involving them in non-consensual sex (rape in today's life), which made women live with less or limited freedom. and suffer many other social limitations, all of which deny them their freedom and rights, regardless whether one is discussing Islamic or any other system of slavery.

Notes

1. Yussuf Ali Trns. AL-Baqra http://www.harunyahya.com/Quran_translation/Quran_translation_index.php.
2. Ibid.
3. Interview with Sheikh A. Moh'd, November 2011, Bububu, Zanzibar.
4. Question and Answer in Islamic forum, http://www.Islamicforum.com.
5. Abdul Sheriff, *Slaves, Spice and Ivory in Zanzibar: Integration of an East African Commercial Empire into the World Economy, 1770-1873,* London, James Currey, 1987, p. 26.

6. Ibrahim F. Shao, *The Political Economy of Zanzibar: Before and After Revolution,* Dar-es-Salaam, Dar- es-Salaam University Press, 1992, p. 6.

7. Saada Wahab, 'Nationalization and Re-Distribution of Land in Zanzibar: The Case Study of Western District, 1965-2008', M.A Thesis; University of Dar-es- Salaam, 2010, p.10.

8. A. Sheriff, '*suria*: Concubine or Secondary Slave Wife? The case of Zanzibar in the nineteenth century' UB.

9. A.Y. Lodhi, *Institution of Slavery in Zanzibar and Pemba,* Research Report No. 16, Uppsala; Scandinavian Institute of African Studies, 1973, p. 10.

10. Maryam binti Abdallah to British Resident, 1921.ZNA AB10/116,*surias* of the Late Sd. Ali bin Said (i) Ajab [is it Rasha?] bint Abdullah (ii) Sayara bint. Yussuf, p. 18.

11. Sheriff, A. 'Localization and Social Composition of the East Africa Slave Trade, 1858-1873', in William Gervase Clarence-Smith, *The Economics of the Indian Ocean Slave Trade in the Nineteenth Century,* London: Frank Cass,1989, p.141.

12. A. Sheriff, *suria,* op.cit.

13. Ibid.

14. Ibid.

15. Lodhi, Ibid.

16. Ibid.

17. Sayyida Salme / Emily Ruete, *An Arabian Princess Between Two Worlds,* E. van Donzel, ed., Leiden, Brill, 1993, p.174.

18. Ibid., p.154.

19. Martin A. Klein, ' Sex, Power and Family Life in the Harem; A Comparative study', in Gwyn Campbell, et al., ed., *Women and Slavery: Africa, the Indian Ocean World, and the Medieval North Atlantic,* Athens: Ohio University Press. 2007, p. 65.

20. Salme, Ibid.

21. Ibid.

22. A. Sheriff in *suria,* op. cit. ; Wilson to Norris Bushire 28.1.1831, MAPD:1830-2/1/385 p.18-21. Kemball's Report, 12.11.1847, PRO:FO 84/692/15.

23. Salme, p.154.

24. Salme, pp. 175, 156-57.

25. Salme, p. 239.

26. Yusuff Ali, Ibid.

27. ZNA.AB/10/116, Sayara bint Yussuf, Norein bint Abdallah and Rasha bint Abdullah to British Resident. September, 1923, *suria* of the Late Seyyid Ali B. Said

28. Ibid.

29. Ibid., p. 15

30. ZNA.AB/10/116, Sayara bint Yussuf and Norein bint Abadallah to British Resident, July 1929, p.18.

31. Sayara bint Yusuf to British Resident, December 1944.ZNA AB.10/166, p.76

32. Chief Secretary to Sayara Yussuf January 1945.ZNA AB/10/166/ 77

33. Foreign Office Despatches: Inward. ZNA AC 5/1-

34. The Slavery Decree No. 11 of 1909.ZNA. AB 71/1-

35. Ibid.

36. ZNA. AB 10/ 108, Rosuna bint Tamimu ex-Sultan's Concubine.

37. Ibn 'Abd al-Barr, *al-Kaafi* (1/296); al-Mughni (8/194).www.online translation, Qur-an, 30.11.2011.

6

'Making a Life of their Own'[1]: Ex-apprentices in Early Post-emancipation Period, 1839–1872

Satyendra Peerthum

You ask me…why I will not work in that field, I will tell you: In that field my father worked as a slave, and was lashed as a slave, and do you think that I would work upon a spot that I cannot think of without pain?[2]

There can be no doubt of the fact that the ex-apprentices withdrew from cane cultivation more suddenly and entirely in Mauritius than in any of the West Indian colonies.[3]

From what had been gauged of slave behaviour between 1815 and 1835, it would seem that the idea of freedom in the slaves' mind was intimately linked to the idea of independence. The post-emancipation events and decisions of the ex-slaves also seem to bear out this view.[4]

Introduction

The objective of this chapter is to analyse the exodus of the ex-apprentices from the sugar estates, their desire to obtain land, the *petit morcellement* movement (or subdivisions of land which were sold to the ex-apprentices), and the rise of a Mauritian ex-apprentice peasantry or small landowners during the early post-emancipation period. It looks at the emergence of an important group of sharecroppers or *metayers* and squatters from within the island's ex-apprentice community between 1839 and 1872. It explores the worldview and ethos of the ex-apprentices as they struggled to make their concept of freedom a reality which entailed controlling their labour, mobility in the colony, rejection of estate labour, owning their own plot of land and working their land at their own pace. At the same time, it also looks at the situation of some of the ex-apprentices who continued to work and live on the sugar estates after the advent of final freedom in 1839.

This section of the study argues that the ex-apprentices are excellent examples of human agency in Mauritian history as they left estate labour, bought or settled legally or illegally on a plot of land, settled with their families there and grew their own vegetables and reared their farm animals. It demonstrates how they resorted to different strategies of survival such as collaborating with the Free Coloureds who employed them and even rented and sold them portions of land. In the process, the Free Coloureds offered them a viable alternative of permanently escaping estate labour. It argues that thousands of ex-apprentice property owners, sharecroppers and squatters emerged in all of the eight rural districts of Mauritius.

This chapter also shows that the former apprentices had access to capital and with their savings, which were large amounts of money, they purchased a sizeable piece of land during what has been called the *petit morcellement* between 1839 and 1851. It shows that ex-apprentice independent proprietors, as agriculturalists and farmers, were able to successfully integrate the non-plantation sector of the island's economy. It highlights the fact that they became a major supplier of garden produce and farm animals, and filled the gap which had been left ever since the 1830s by the Free Coloureds small estate owners.

This section of the study carries out an in-depth discussion and analysis of the dynamics of the *petit morcellement* movement and its significance for the colony during the 1840s. It also draws attention to the new social position of the ex-apprentices in early post-emancipation Mauritius, and the class division which was taking place within the island ex-apprentice community. It argues that they tried to make a life of their own beyond the perimeters and control of the sugar estates and their former owners between the late 1840s until the 1870s and even after.

The Exodus of the Ex-apprentices from the Sugar Estates and its Aftermath

Who was an ex-apprentice or a former apprentice in Mauritius during the post-emancipation era? The answer to this important question was provided, in February 1847, by the Commissioners of the Mauritius Census of 1847 who explained:

> the ex-apprentices are enumerated as such upon their own declaration, and therefore this class may be supposed to comprise only those who belonged to it at the expiration of the apprenticeship in March 1839, omitting those who obtained their freedom between the date and the Act of Emancipation in February 1835.[5]

Thus, an ex-apprentice, or former apprentice, was an individual who was given his or her freedom in 1839 by the local British colonial authorities. In fact, these apprentices were unable to purchase their freedom, unlike thousands of their fellow apprentices who had between 1835 and 1839.

On 31 March 1839, with the ending of the Apprenticeship System in Mauritius, 53,000 apprentices were given their freedom.[6] During the same month, the newspaper *Le Mauricien* reported that most of the ex-apprentices were leaving the sugar estates and their former owners.[7] Barely one month after the conclusion of the apprenticeship period, more than 26,000 apprentices had deserted the sugar plantations.[8] This figure is significant because by the time the apprenticeship system was abolished, around 30,000 apprentices had been involved in the production of sugar, and they had consisted of around 55 per cent of the island's agricultural labour force.[9]

In May 1839, Governor Nicolay reported, with a tone of despair that, 'a great number of the large sugar estates have been wholly abandoned by the former apprentices...'[10] During their first few weeks as free people, the ex-apprentices celebrated their freedom through feasts, they visited their relatives and friends, they travelled to different parts of the island, and wore what had been denied to them under slavery, shoes.[11] Pierre Gueyraud considers the liberation of the ex-apprentices in 1839 and after to be 'a real revolution in the life of the colony'.[12]

At the same time it is important to note that in May 1839, the British government of India passed the Indian Act XIV of 1839 which disallowed and almost brought to a halt the exportation of Indian labourers overseas.[13] This was the third major problem which plagued the sugar plantocracy and the island's colonial administrators. Brenda Howell explains:

> It can be imagined with what dismay they learned early in 1839 of the suspension of immigration and the decision to bring negro apprenticeship to a premature end. The planters were well aware that if they persisted in their programme of expansion, wages must inevitably rise. In the absence of fresh labour supplies, the ex-apprentices would certainly exploit fully the planters' need for labour.[14]

More than a decade ago, in a booklet on Indian immigration in Mauritius, it was emphasised that:

> By 1840 and 1841, the shortage of labour was felt by sugar planters: contracts of both ex-apprentices and immigrant labourers were reaching termination. Wages began to rise as well as discontent from those still bound under contract with lower wages. A labour crisis was imminent.[15]

It becomes evident that with the abolition of the apprenticeship system and the suspension of the importation of Indian labourers, it was clear that the planters would face a labour shortage.[16] However, at the same time, the planters and colonial administrators did dramatise the situation and seriousness of the problem because what the planters wanted was a large quantity of cheap labour in order to keep wages extremely low at all times.[17] Thus, between May 1839 and December 1842, the sugar planters and colonial administrators were mostly preoccupied with overturning the prohibition on Indian immigration and dealing with the labour shortage.[18]

However, despite the mass exodus, not all apprentices left the sugar estates and their former owners. In May and June 1839, the stipendiary magistrates sent returns of the working population in their districts to the colonial secretary in Port Louis which highlighted this important fact. In the Mauritius Archives, only the returns of the working population for the districts of the Savanne, Grand Port, Flacq, and Rivière du Rempart are available. Therefore, these returns represent only samples of the total working population of these four important sugar-growing districts. They show that, in March 1839, there were 5,977 apprentices who worked on the white-owned sugar estates and on the small free coloured estates.

In May and June of the same year, only around 2,021 former apprentices were engaged for a period of one year. Thus, the samples from these four rural districts clearly indicate that around 34 per cent of the ex-apprentices (who worked there in March 1839) had engaged themselves for one year, mostly with the sugar planters and also with some of the small free coloured landowners. Around 66 per cent of these former apprentices had refused to make any type of contract. Without a doubt, the withdrawal of these labourers brought about a major labour crisis for the island's sugar barons, between 1839 and the early 1840s, as Mauritius was gradually becoming the premier sugar-producing colony in the British Empire.[19]

In May 1840, John Russell, the Secretary of State for the Colonies, was informed that overall in Mauritius, between 1839 and 1840, around 4,000 to 5,000 ex-apprentices had re-engaged themselves as estate labourers for a period of one year. But, he placed a great deal of stress on the fact that these unfortunate labourers took on this engagement because of a number of reasons, such as not having anywhere else to go and being tricked or forced to sign contracts by certain local magistrates.[20] In addition, in April 1839, Le Mauricien reported, almost with prophetic accuracy that, ' it has been shown that 5,000 other individuals will again next year abandon the sugar estates to purchase ground and set up themselves...' Therefore, it definitely did not come as a surprise to the Mauritian sugar planters that, most of the ex-apprentices, who had re-engaged themselves, did not do so again in 1840.[21]

During that same year, Governor Lionel Smith informed John Russell that, in general, the ex-apprentices were filled with a 'spirit of animosity against the planters' of the colony, and as a result, many who had signed a labour contract in 1839 refused to do so the following year.[22] Six years later, Percy Fitzpatrick, the Stipendiary Magistrate of Port Louis, sent a lengthy report to Governor Gomm, in which he explained that the source of this hatred for the planters was directly linked with the reasons the former apprentices withdrew from the sugar estates. Fitzpatrick placed a lot of emphasis on the fact that the apprentices had been treated in a very cruel manner, and they had been overworked by their former owners. Furthermore, during the apprenticeship period, it was a common practice among the ex-slave owners, either to delay in paying their apprentices for the extra work they did, or not paying them at all.[23]

All these trials and tribulations left a great deal of bitterness in the hearts and minds of the ex-apprentices and it gave rise to what was termed as their spirit or attitude of animosity against the planters. It also propelled the overwhelming majority of the former apprentices not to sign any contracts with the planters and to abandon the sugar plantations. In order to give meaning to their newfound freedom, most of the ex-apprentices sought a better life beyond the perimeter of the sugar estates, and they tried to carve an economic life of their own away from their former owners.[24]

The Spatial Distribution of the Ex-apprentices: Urban Migration and Internal Rural Migration

Apart from settling on the coast, on some of small free coloured estates, and squatting on unoccupied Crown land, there were hundreds of ex-apprentices who were skilled artisans, semi-skilled workers and domestics and they settled in Port Louis. According to the *Abstract of District Returns of Slaves in Mauritius at the time of Emancipation* of 1835, there were around 3,237 non-praedial head tradesmen and inferior head tradesmen, 929 non-praedial slaves, and also thousands of domestics.[25] Without doubt, many of these non-praedial slaves were found in Port-Louis, and they formed part of a large urban class of skilled, semi-skilled slaves who continued to exist during the early post-emancipation period.[26] An 1846 census of the colony shows that in Port-Louis, there were over 2,816 urban ex-apprentices who were involved in commerce, trade, and the manufacturing sector. This group of former apprentices also included hundreds carpenters, carters, wheelwrights, tailors, masons, seamstresses, domestics, dyers, washerwomen, cooks and bakers.

In 1846, in his report on the ex-apprentices in Port-Louis, Stipendiary Magistrate Fitzpatrick pointed out that there was a large and thriving class of urban ex-apprentices, and many among them were skilled artisans and craftsmen. The other former apprentices who formed part of this urban underclass were cooks, grooms, sailors, boatmen, shopkeepers, traders, hawkers, domestics and seamstresses. The majority among these ex-apprentices had either lived for many years or had spent most of their lives in Port Louis. In addition, they continued doing the same work that they did as urban slaves, and they even taught their trade to their children.

During the early 1830s, many of these urban slaves, especially the skilled artisans and craftsmen, were able to earn high wages and were financially better off than most of the rural slaves.[27] Thus, what can be concluded is that during the late 1820s and early 1830s, a large class of skilled, semi-skilled, and unskilled urban slaves had emerged in Port-Louis. Most of them remained in Port Louis, and their ranks were supplemented during the late 1830s and 1840s as hundreds of skilled and semi-skilled apprentices and ex-apprentices settled in Port Louis. Furthermore, these urban slaves and apprentices, especially the skilled ones, had access to financial resources, and could set themselves up in trade and commerce, work for themselves and employ other ex-apprentices and ex-indentured immigrants.[28]

During the mid-1850s, Patrick Beaton, a British missionary who lived in Mauritius for five years, wrote that when the ex-apprentices:

> found themselves their own masters, the former slaves preferred supporting them-selves by cultivating small patches of land in the highland of Moka and Vacoas, than to labouring on the land of their former masters. If they had acted otherwise, they would have shown themselves unworthy of liberty; it would have been like a galley slave resuming the oar, when told that he was free.[29]

During the early post-emancipation period, the former apprentices and their children were criticised and condemned by the sugar planters and the colonial administrators for their dislike of working as agricultural labourers on the sugar estates. Beaton believed that such an attitude was unreasonable and that the ex-apprentices and their descendants had to be understood. In order to make his point, the British missionary related his conversation with a Mauritian creole (whose father and mother had been slaves) who said:

> You ask me…why I will not work in that field, I will tell you: In that field my father worked as a slave, and was lashed as a slave, and do you think that I would work upon a spot that I cannot think of without pain?[30]

Without a doubt, it was Reverend Beaton's interaction with the former apprentices and their descendants which led him to observe:

> The remembrance of the horrors of slavery is engraven upon their memories with a pen of iron and no lapse of time will ever erase it. Labour in the fields will ever be regarded by them as a mark of degradation on account of the painful associations and memories which it awakens.[31]

Many years after the abolition of the apprenticeship system, the former apprentices used to refer to the days of their enslavement, in Mauritian creole, as 'temps *margoze'* or bitter days. This gives an idea of how the ex-apprentices viewed the period when they were still held under the shackles of forced servitude.[32]

Gradually, it became clear why many Mauritian slaves and apprentices tried, at all costs, to secure their freedom, through manumission during the last years of slavery and the apprenticeship period. In 1846, in his report on the condition of the Mauritian ex-apprentices, Percy Fitzpatrick, the liberal-minded Irish Stipendiary Magistrate of Port Louis, explained that the apprentices deserted the plantations because of three major reasons: '(1) The love of independence, (2) The want of confidence in the magistrates, (3) the intemperate conduct of the masters'.[33]

Vijaya Teelock observes that:

> from what had been gauged of slave behaviour between 1815 and 1835, it would seem that the idea of freedom in the slaves' mind was intimately linked to the idea of independence. The post-emancipation events and decisions of the ex-slaves also seem to bear out this view.[34]

It is evident that during the apprenticeship period and after its termination, the abandonment of the sugar estates en masse by the Mauritian apprentices is 'best seen, not as a symptom of weary despair, but as a continuation of the dogged resilience they had displayed in bondage'.[35]

Collaboration between the Ex-apprentices and the Free Coloured Landowners

Between 1829 and 1835, or during the last years of slavery in Mauritius, many of the rural slaves who were manumitted remained in the rural districts.[36] In 1834, Bernard observed that many slaves who had been manumitted between 1827 and 1833, began to occupy very small plots of land in the rural districts such as Grand Port, Plaines Wilhems, Black River and Moka. They usually settled on a small plot of land of around half an acre or more, and upon which they erected a small hut and cultivated vegetables. Some of these rural manumitted slaves even owned one or two slaves.[37]

Ex-apprentices who earned high wages saved their money and purchased their freedom. In addition, they were able to rent land from other free coloureds, make some type of informal sharecropping arrangements with them, and some of the ex-apprentices even purchased small plots of land. It is possible to see that during the late 1820s and the 1830s, these manumitted slaves and some of the former apprentices formed the lowest and smallest group among the island's rural free coloured landholders.

By 1830, a large group of free coloured property owners owned around 566 small rural estates in Mauritius. In Savanne district alone, there were 44 small estates which were owned by the free coloureds, compared with 63 large estates owned by the Franco-Mauritians. It should be noted that between 1825 and 1830, more than 40 per cent, or 226 of the 566 free coloured small estates, which ranged in size from 10 to 45 acres, were brought under sugar cane cultivation. The remaining 60 per cent, or 340 free coloured small estates, which ranged in size from one to nine acres, grew mostly garden produce and reared domesticated farm animals to be sold in Port Louis and the local district markets.[38] Gradually, during the 1820s and 1830s, a number of Free Coloured individuals were accumulating wealth, property, and some of the rich families were able to educate their children.[39]

Between 1806 and 1830, the amount of land owned by them increased from 15,877 to 36,419 acres, or more than doubled. The number of livestock owned by the free coloureds increased by more than eight times, and between 1825 and 1830, the number of carts, carioles, and carriages increased by more than three-fold.[40] By 1830, it was estimated that this segment of the local population controlled around 20 per cent of the island's wealth, owned between 20 per cent to 23 per cent of the colony's slaves, and over 13 per cent of all the colony's inventoried land.[41] Therefore, by the 1830s, many among the colony's rural free population of colour owned a substantial amount of land and many slaves, which was a clear indication of their prosperity.[42] Thus, the Free Coloureds of Mauritius were wedged 'between the propertied and propertyless classes of plantation society'. In that colony, the propertied class was dominated by the slave-owning white sugar barons and the slaves were the propertyless.[43]

The Free Coloureds still had enough social and economic power, which they had developed during the 1820s and 1830s, to help frustrate the attempts of the Mauritian sugar barons from forcing their former slaves back onto the sugar estates. In April 1839, *Le Mauricien*, a local pro-planter newspaper reported that those:

> individuals who have abandoned the sugar estates, a considerable number have entered into the service of those who supply the bazaar with vegetables, fruits, and poultry, who cut and sell timber, who rear and speculate in cattle. Others became house servants and some have engaged with certain small proprietors on condition of receiving a proportionate part of their revenue. [44]

The last observation clearly hints at some type of sharecropping arrangement between the Free Coloured small proprietors and the ex-apprentices who were in their employment.

Between May and June 1839, the stipendiary magistrates from the rural districts provided George F. Dick, the Colonial Secretary, with a return of the colony's working population which showed the number of Indian labourers and ex-apprentices who worked on the sugar estates and with small proprietors. The small landholders were also mentioned as being '*vieux affranchis*' or manumitted slaves and as '*gens de couleurs libres*' or Free Coloureds. The returns for the districts of Flacq, Savanne, Grand Port, and Rivière du Rempart clearly show that many small Free Coloured proprietors had employed anywhere from two to ten ex-apprentice labourers to work on their land, mostly for a one-month period.[45]

For the district of Savanne, there were hundreds of ex-apprentices who were employed on 16 small estates which did not grow sugar, and most of them were employed for one month, which was renewed on a monthly basis. For example, twelve ex-apprentices worked for Mr. D. Constantin, sixteen ex-apprentices worked for Mr. M. Mamet, both small Free Coloured estate owners, and they did not employ any indentured immigrants unlike the large estates.[46] Thus, some among the former apprentices went to work for the colony's landowning free coloureds as hired labourers, house servants, and even made sharecropping arrangements with them.[47] It becomes evident that the Free Coloureds used this as a strategy to attract ex-apprentice labour to their estates.[48]

In April 1840, Captain John Lloyd, the surveyor-general of the colony, provided some indications that there was close collaboration between the ex-apprentices with the Free Coloureds and ex-slaves on the smaller estates. Some type of sharecropping arrangements gradually arose with the Free Coloureds. This trend existed in almost all the rural districts.[49] Allen observes: '…some landowners responded by leasing land in question or entering into informal share-cropping agreements'.[50] In 1839, Civil Commissioner Hugnin reported that near the settlement of Vacoas and several other parts of Plaines Wilhems district, ex-apprentices left their owners and readily found employment with Free Coloured small estate owners. Mr Fortenay explained that sixty-two out of ninety-two ex-apprentices left his sugar estate during the months of April and May 1839 and went to work for nearby free coloured landowners. At the same time, Widow Senneville indicated that fifty-four out of sixty former apprentices obtained employment with Free Coloured cultivators.[51] Thus, it becomes evident that the free coloured cultivators and landowners offered many of the ex-apprentices a viable alternative to working on the sugar estates during the early post-emancipation period which continued well into the 1840s. After all, in December 1845, Civil Commissioner Hugnin reported that there were four areas in Plaines Wilhems district where the former apprentices were found 'on the premises of these small proprietors where their means of subsistence is precarious'.[52]

In June 1840, just over a year after the final emancipation of the ex-apprentices, Acting Governor J. Power declared:

> I believe that I am within bounds in saying that not more than a third of the island is under cultivation whilst all of it may be made productive. There is also ample employment more than enough for the lately liberated population without returning to the sugar estates, in the cultivation of provisions, vegetables, and in

rearing of minor stocks such as fowls, pigs, etc...which they fully understand....
the prices of the majority of these articles are now nearly double what they were
ten years ago.[53]

Shortly after his arrival in Mauritius in 1840, Governor Lionel Smith was able to
visit some of the rural districts in order to gauge the social and economic impact
of emancipation on the colony. In August of the same year, he wrote to Russell
to inform him that:

> I find very few of the emancipated population have returned to sugar cultivation,
> but it is not true as was represented to me in England, that they were in a state
> of vagrancy and idleness, committing thefts throughout the island. They labour
> sufficiently either for themselves or others for subsistence and are a quiet, and
> content people.[54]

Small-scale Sharecropping or *Metayage* during the 1840s

How many individuals may have been involved in the practice of sharecropping
between 1839 and 1846? A rough indication is provided by the Mauritius Census
of 1847 which was carried out in August 1846. The census Commissioners
explained that there were 4,826 ex-apprentices (4,805 males and 21 females) who
were involved in agricultural activities, and 4,841 ex-apprentices (3,491 males
and 1,350 females) were classified as being labourers. Thus, there were a total of
9,667 ex-apprentices who did not work on the sugar estates, and they did not
form part of the group of ex-apprentice independent landowning cultivators.
Furthermore, they consisted more than 36 per cent of the active ex-apprentice
population of 26,243 individuals, and 56 per cent of the ex-apprentices ranged
between fifteen and fifty years of age or those who were fit for work.[55]

A careful reading of several letters from the civil commissioners and stipendiary
magistrates located in the eight rural districts, to the Colonial Secretary in Port
Louis between 1839 and 1846, show that these apprentices, who were listed
as being involved in agricultural activities, and consisted of two distinct and
important groups emanating from within the island's ex-apprentice community.
Firstly, they consisted of squatters who ever since 1839 and the early 1840s, lived
and grew vegetable produce, fruits, livestock and poultry illegally on government
and private lands. Secondly, they were *metayers* or sharecroppers who operated
within the bounds of the law, and leased land from the other landowning ex-
apprentices, some Franco-Mauritians, and mostly from the Free Coloureds.

Ever since 1839 and during the 1840s, they shared their agricultural produce,
fruits and domesticated farm animals with their landlords. They resided mostly
in the rural districts of Grand Port, Plaines Wilhems, Moka, Savanne, Black
River, Flacq, Pamplemousses, and on the outskirts of Port Louis.[56] In 1845, the
Colonial Office in London required Governor Gomm to submit a detailed report

about the social and economic conditions of the ex-apprentice population in the colony. The British governor, through the colonial secretary, instructed the island's civil commissioners and stipendiary magistrates to report on the condition of the former apprentices in their districts. An analysis of these important reports, which were submitted between November and December 1845, shows that the practice of *metayage* or sharecropping was widespread, and involved thousands of ex-apprentices in all the eight rural districts.[57]

While oral or informal agreements were a common feature of Mauritian rural life during the 1840s, it is important to highlight that the Notarial Records contain several written sharecropping agreements in the form of land leases. During the first half of the 1840s, they were made between ex-apprentices who rented land as *metayers* or sharecroppers from other landowning ex-apprentices, Free Coloureds and even some Franco-Mauritians who did not own sugar estates.

On 15 April 1842, Henri Pierre, who was described as being a '*ci-devant apprenti*' or former apprentice and cultivator, leased one arpent of land for three years from Mr Descroches, a small Franco-Mauritian landowner, near the village of Mesnil in Plaines Wilhems district. He used this land to grow vegetables, and was required to provide half of his produce to Mr. Descroches at the end of each month, and he was allowed to live on the land.[58] Another interesting case-study is that of Louise LaVictoire, who was also an ex-apprentice, a seamstress and the mother of three young children. On 30 June 1843, she leased half an arpent of land at Vallee des Pretres, to the north of Port Louis, from Madame Marguerite Labonne, a small free coloured landowner. Louise rented the land for five years and had to provide one quarter of her garden produce and some of the livestock which was reared on that land at the end of each month to Mrs Marguerite. She was also allowed to live on the land with her children and some of her other ex-apprentice relatives.[59]

On 10 July 1843, Jacques Colas, a former apprentice and cultivator, rented three arpents of land from Thomas Francois and his mother, Widow Francois in Moka district for six years in order to cultivate vegetables and rear some cattle and poultry to feed his family and sell the surplus at the local market in the villages of Moka and Quartier Militaire. At the end of every two months, he had to provide one-third of his agricultural produce to his landlords. He was allowed to erect a hut on the land.[60]

It is important to note that the land which was provided to these three ex-apprentices was in fact marginal and unused land which they had to clear, water and make fertile. These ex-apprentices had to procure their own tools, fertilizer and seeds, and they did not have access to any type of credit and received no help from their landlords. As a result, they had to pay for the means of production which was stipulated in their sharecropping or land lease agreements. It becomes evident that during the 1840s, hundreds of such ex-apprentice *metayers* or sharecroppers led a complicated and difficult life of toil from dawn to dusk. Thus, during the early post-emancipation period, life on and off the sugar estates was a hard lot for the former apprentices, as they engaged in a daily arduous struggle to make a life of their own.[61]

On 193 large sugar estates, there were 3,725 ex-male apprentices who were mostly skilled and semi-skilled artisans, and did not automatically work in the sugar cane fields. There were also 6,309 women and children who were mostly ex-apprentices. In Savanne district, there were 21 estates which employed 2,649 Indian indentured workers and 430 ex-apprentices with 259 women and children who were mostly ex-apprentices. Even more interesting was the fact that on 237 small estates there were 1,197 ex-male apprentices with 1,234 ex-apprentice women and children. For Savanne district, there were 35 estates where 425 Indian immigrants and 165 ex-apprentices were employed with 157 women and children who were mostly ex-apprentices. On the majority of the small estates, sugar cane was not cultivated and vegetables were being grown and domesticated farm animals were being reared.[62]

The reports of civil commissioners Peter Heyliger and Armand Hugnin from December 1845 made it obvious that, 'On the eve of the 1846 census, district authorities reported that many ex-apprentices continued to find employment with these small farmers.'[63] This fact is not surprising because towards the end of 1845, several reports were filed by the civil commissioners and stipendiary magistrates who were based in the rural districts on the ex-apprentices. Some of them indicated that even during the mid-1840s, sharecropping arrangements were a common practice between some of the Free Coloureds and the ex-apprentices in the districts of the Savanne, Moka, Plaines Wilhems, Pamplemousses, Flacq, Grand Port and Black River.[64]

This can clearly be seen in the observations of stipendiary magistrates Davidson, Self and Regnard from three different rural districts. In December 1845, J. Davidson wrote that in his district, Grand Port, an important number of former apprentices were 'cultivating small portions of land, the produce of which they divide with the proprietors for the use of the land'.[65] During the previous month, H.M. Self reported that there were many ex-apprentices in Pamplemousses district who were involved in sharecropping agreements where they had to provide half of the vegetable produce to their landlord for the privilege of using their land. [66] In December of the same year, Stipendiary Magistrate J. Regnard reported that it was a common practice among many ex-apprentices to rent a small portion of land where they built a hut and settled with their families. In return for the use of the land, they provided a certain percentage of their agricultural produce and livestock to their landlords.[67] It is important to note that Grand Port, Pamplemousses and Flacq contained almost 40 per cent of the colony's ex-apprentice population in 1846.[68]

In December 1845, Regard made a similar observation that when it came to the sharecroppers in the district of Flacq: 'They seldom follow for any length of time the same employment or remain long in the service of the same person.'[69] This observation can also be applied to the other rural district where many the ex-apprentices who were involved in such arrangements remained usually three to five years in the employment of any one particular Free Coloured estate owner. After all, they cherished their independence which was a direct consequence of many years of forced servitude under slavery and the Apprenticeship System.[70]

The Practice of Squatting in Mauritius

The Rural Districts

One way the ex-apprentices wanted this great desire of independence was by occupying or squatting on plots of land which did not belong to them. In 1840, John Lloyd, the surveyor-general, reported that the most significant category among the ex-apprentices were the squatters who resided illegally on government and private lands.[71] These were former apprentices who could not afford to purchase land, and without official authorisation settled or squatted on properties belonging to the colonial government and individuals. They settled their families on these lands and engaged in agricultural activities such as growing of vegetables and rearing livestock and poultry. Immediately after final emancipation, some of these ex-apprentice squatters settled in the vicinity of sugar estates and were considered a threat to law and order by the local planters.[72]

Between April and May 1839, several planters in the districts of Plaines Wilhems complained of the presence of hundreds of ex-apprentices who were illegally settled close to their estates and whom they suspected of theft and other illicit activities. Governor Nicolay directed commissioners Hugnin of Plaines Wilhems and Beaugendre of Moka to investigate. Shortly after, the two civil commissioners played down the threat which these former apprentices posed to the planters in their districts. They reported that these rural squatters were only concerned with growing their agricultural produce and livestock in order to provide for their families.[73] In 1839 and 1840, there were a few other cases in each of the eight rural districts, of planters complaining of the presence of ex-apprentice squatters in their districts. These complaints were investigated by the civil commissioners and local police, but were never taken seriously by the local colonial authorities since they never posed a serious law and order problem, as long as they did not engage in illegal activities such as theft.[74]

In May 1839, Stipendiary Magistrate F. Thatcher wrote to Governor Nicolay and addressed two specific questions to him with regard to a Royal-Order-in-Council of Queen Victoria dealing with squatting and long-established squatters in the rural districts:

I also beg to be informed of the spirit of that part of Her Majesty's order in council relative to the illegal possession of lands running through the *Pas Geometriques* [government land]. If individuals have been in peaceable possession of lands for several years but cannot produce any lawful title, can they be dispossessed of them, and if so by whom is it to be carried into effect?

A few days later, the colonial secretary, responded to these queries on behalf of the British governor and explained:

This seems to the Governor a very unfortunate difficulty for under the Order in Council it would seem that the signature or mark of each of the contracting parties was required to the agreement to make it legal...With respect to the *Pas Geometriques* His Excellency has no intention at present at disturbing any well disposed person settled there.[75]

This statement is extremely important because it seems evident that the colonial authorities, including the governor himself, did not want to start the eviction of squatters who occupied plots of land for several years which they knew would cause social instability in the colony, since it involved hundreds of individuals throughout the island's eight districts. This could also be applied, to a certain extent, to the newly freed apprentices who established themselves illegally on government and private lands. However, there were several cases in the rural districts where squatters were evicted by the local colonial authorities such as in Plaines Wilhems district during the early 1840s.

In June 1840, Jonathan Coeur was arrested by a constable of the Plaines Wilhems police on suspicion of theft on the estate of Mr William S. Saunders. It turned out that Jonathan was an ex-apprentice of Mr Saunders, and with his family he was squatting on a small plot of land belonging to the government near the estate of Saunders. They were growing vegetables and rearing some livestock on the land which they occupied. Jonathan was released from police custody and under the orders of Civil Commissioner Hugnin, the local police proceeded to evict him and his family from where they resided.[76]

More than a year later, in August 1841, Ernest Philip and Marguerite Vieux, two former apprentices, who were suspected of trespassing on the property of Widow de Senneville, were arrested by the local police. They were married and living with their children illegally on a plot of land which belonged to the widow where they grew vegetables for their subsistence. The police released them and they were evicted from Senneville's property who refused to make a lease agreement with them.[77]

While some of the ex-apprentice squatters were being evicted from the marginal land which was owned by the sugar estate owners of Plaines Wilhems, there were other Mauritian planters who offered some of the squatters a chance to regularise their precarious situation in the colonial society. In May 1847, William Wade

West, the owner of Vale Sugar Estate and one of the most important planters in Pamplemousses district, put a notice in a local colonial newspaper in which he offered the former apprentices a deal. He offered them a small plot of ground to grow some vegetables and keep some farm animals, a place to live, fuel to cook their food, medical care and medicines. West even offered to send their children to a school in Grand Bay village at his expense. The former apprentices would be required to live and work on Vale Sugar Estate, near Grand Bay, and share some of their garden produce and farm animals with Mr West. However, none of the ex-apprentices who resided near Vale Sugar Estate and Grand Bay village responded to his offer.[78]

Despite this negative response by the ex-apprentices, there were other planters in that part of Mauritius who made similar offers. Napoleon Savy was a free coloured sugar estate owner, a well known barrister in the colony and originally from the Seychelles. During the 1840s, he acquired Petite Rosalie Sugar Estate as well as other properties in Pamplemousses district. He was also a member of a very small group of influential Mauritian planters which included individuals such as Evenor Dupont and Ernest d'Unienville, planter in the Savanne district, who were promoting the *metayage* or sharecropping system in the rural districts.[79]

Mr Savy was ready to put 150 *arpents* of arable land at the disposal of mainly the ex-apprentices and some of the Indian indentured workers in the south Pamplemousses area. He wanted to establish a 'system of partnership' or system of sharecropping or *metayage* in order to grow sugar cane, corn and roots. However, he reported that all his efforts, during late April and early May 1847, to get ex-apprentices living in the Long Mountain and La Nicoliere area, in the remote areas of Pamplemousses district, to work for him failed.

As a result of this difficult situation, he sent a letter, through the colonial secretary, to Governor Gomm. Napoleon Savy explained to the British administrator with regard to the ex-apprentices:

> I shall be happy to supply them with fertile land, advance them the necessary seed, and the wood and thatch to build their dwellings, on the terms which I have already alluded. I will, besides, make arrangements with the assistance and under the control of Government, to have their children educated.[80]

Within less than ten days of receiving his letter, Governor Gomm, through the colonial secretary, informed Savy that:

> as the object which you have in view, can alone be brought about by the operation of a mutual confidence between the parties themselves, His Excellency does not consider that he can interfere in the manner you propose.

The response of Governor Gomm underscores a paradox which existed in British Mauritius during the 1840s and after. Ever since 1839, the British colonial authorities encouraged the Mauritian planters to devise strategies for the ex-apprentices to return to field labour. However, when West, Savy and others requested the colonial administrators for some support in introducing and encouraging this type of proposal, the British governor gave a negative response. After all, Governor Gomm was extremely reluctant to interfere in such matters since he saw it as a master-servant issue and he could not interfere.[81]

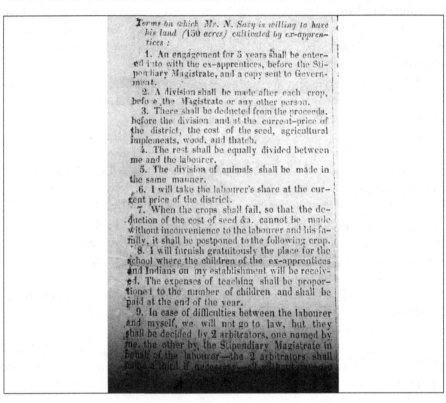

Photo 6.1: The terms and conditions of Napoleon Savy's 'the system of partnership' or sharecropping (or *metayage*)
Source: *Le Cerneen*, Friday, 21 May 1847

In 1845, an important segment of the ex-apprentice community in Flacq district continued to squat on government lands which bordered several sugar estates.[82] In July 1847, in the report of the Council of Government on the state of the 'Emancipated Population' in the colony, which was forwarded to the Colonial Office, it was mentioned that the ex-apprentices: 'squatted in bands in remote places, and in the forests beyond the reach and influence of the planters, and obtained a meagre and often insufficient subsistence from small and ill-cultivated patches of land'. Almost a decade after final emancipation in 1839, a large number of the former apprentices continued to squat on government and private lands throughout the eight districts. At the same time, their numbers surpassed the number of ex-apprentices who were property-owners and who still worked and lived on the sugar estates.[83]

The Urban Setting: Port Louis

During the post-emancipation period, the rural districts were not the only places where squatting took place and became a matter of concern for colonial authorities. Between 1835 and 1839, there was an influx of the apprentices into Port Louis, and they settled in areas such as *Camp des Noirs Libres* or Black Town, the slopes of Signal Mountain, the other mountain slopes located to the south of the town and some in remote areas such as present-day Tranquebar (located on the western edge of Port Louis).

During the late 1830s and early 1840s, the overcrowding and squatting by the new arrivals was a source of concern for the colony's chief medical officer. In June 1839, he described the new settlements, where hundreds of former apprentices resided in the south of Port Louis, as being unsanitary and could breed diseases. As a result, these illegal settlements posed a health problem to the town and the entire colony. The chief medical officer believed that the settlements should be destroyed and the squatters relocated elsewhere. However, his recommendations to Governor Nicolay fell on deaf ears and it would take three decades before the local authorities took action.[84]

From the 1840s to the late 1860s, the practice of squatting by the former apprentices and their descendants continued unchecked in Port Louis. In the aftermath of the catastrophic Malaria Epidemic of 1867 to 1869, and also due to the fact that they did not pay their ground rent for many years, in 1869 and 1870s, the British colonial authorities, specifically the Board of Health, decided to take action against the ex-apprentice squatters. In 1869, a group of squatters were removed from parts of the slopes Signal Mountain and the other mountains located to the south of Port Louis town. [85] During the following year, a total of 97 out of 523 huts were pulled down. The residents of the remaining huts were required to pay ground rent and to improve the sanitary conditions of their living quarters or face eviction. Another group of ex-apprentices, who were residing illegally on land belonging to the War Department, were forced out by members of the British military.[86]

Despite these evictions, the squatter problem remained a prominent issue during the early 1870s in Port Louis and also in the rural districts. In 1872, J. Duncan, the surveyor-general, while testifying before colony's Crown Land Commission, explained that there were ex-apprentice squatters all over the island, especially near the sea shores. There were some squatters who were authorised by the local authorities to reside on a plot of land which they had occupied for more than 10 years. Between the 1850s and early 1870s, some portions of government land or Crown Land had been set aside near existing villages where these squatters were offered an opportunity to reside within the bounds of the law. The lands earmarked were divided into lots and the squatters were able to purchase or lease these lots.

There were many squatters who purchased these village lots and became the legal owners of their own land. Some of these lots were sold near the villages of Souillac, Mahebourg, Poudre d'Or, Pointe des Lascars and Trou aux Biches. However, there were many other ex-apprentice squatters and their families who refused any type of land sale or leases. Surveyor-General Duncan highlighted another important issue that Crown Lands which were leased to private individuals, who wanted to develop their newly acquired land, but faced the problem of squatters present on that particular plot of land. Evidently, it was a daunting task to evict them. He recommended that all unoccupied government lands needed to be leased as a way for the local British government to generate some revenue.[87]

Another important testimony was given before the Crown Land Commission of 1872 by W. Thies, a sergeant major and forest ranger, who had wide experience dealing with squatters in the region of Port Louis and elsewhere on the island. Thies explained that sometime between 1869 and 1870, he was sent by the surveyor-general to convince the ex-apprentice squatters, who resided on the slopes of Signal Mountain and its surroundings, to abandon the land they occupied. He told them that they would be given another plot of land elsewhere which would be provided by the local colonial government.

However, they all refused because they did not have the means to move their belongings. Thies revealed that the squatters mentioned to him that they were ex-apprentices and ex-slaves who had been imported, presumably from East Africa and Madagascar. Ever since final emancipation in 1839, or for more than 30 years, they had lived and worked in Port Louis and desired to spend their remaining days there. They were aware that the land where they squatted belonged to the colonial government and would leave if asked to do so. Eventually, a large delegation of former apprentices went to see Governor Gordon who forwarded the matter to Surveyor–General J. Duncan, who in turn asked Sergeant Major Thies to drop the matter. The forest ranger concluded by saying that the squatters were very poor individuals who most of the time could not afford to pay lease fees which were very high.[88] It is interesting to note that between April 1839 and March 1840, as many as 200 thatched huts were erected by ex-apprentices on the slopes of Signal Mountain and its surroundings who came mostly from the rural districts to settle in Port Louis.[89]

How many recorded squatters were there in Port Louis and in the eight rural districts? A detailed return which was provided by Duncan to the Crown Land Commission Report of 1872 indicated that between 1860 and 1872, there were only 1,097 squatters. The majority of these squatters lived with their families which consisted of four to five individuals or even more. Thus, it is possible to estimate that during this period, island-wide there were between 4,300 and 5,200 individuals on government lands in Port Louis and the eight rural districts. The majority among the squatters, around 590 or 54 per cent, were located in Port Louis, and 507 or 46 per cent were located in the rural districts, with Flacq, Black River and Riviere du Rempart sheltering the bulk of these individuals.

Between 1860 and 1872, the majority (94 per cent of the squatters) paid their rent on time and regularly. This underscores the fact that during this period, there was a general willingness among most of the squatters, who were mostly ex-apprentices, their children and grandchildren, to regularise their situation by paying the annual rent of one shilling to the local colonial administration. They wanted to operate in accordance with the law and not get evicted from the land they occupied for many years. At the same time, in Port Louis and the rural districts, there were thousands of squatters who were not recorded by the local colonial government, and they settled on government lands and private properties and did not pay any rent.[90] Between the 1850s and early 1870s, there were many ex-apprentice squatters who tried to purchase or lease plots of land in order to remain within the bounds of the law.[91]

'The General Desire of these People is to Possess Land'[92]: The *Petit Morcellement* Movement between 1839 and 1851

While there were thousands of ex-apprentices in the rural districts who were squatters and involved in sharecropping arrangements with the free coloureds, during that same period there were hundreds among them who were also purchasing land and becoming independent proprietors. Richard Allen has termed this economic and social process the '*petit morcellement*', or literally the small sub-division of land, which took place during the early post-emancipation period. The term petit morcellement refers specifically to the land which the ex-apprentices and some Free Coloureds bought and formed part of much larger plots of marginal land or small estates which were being sub-divided.

The *petit morcellement* took place immediately after the former apprentices left the sugar estates in 1839 and lasted until around the time the census of 1851. It was different from the "*grand morcellement*" which took place between the 1860s and early 1900s when thousands of the ex-indentured labourers, their descendants and some non-indentured Indian immigrants spent tens of millions of rupees for the purchase of tens of thousands of acres of land throughout the eight rural districts of Mauritius.[93]

In September 1846, Sir William Gomm reported to Lord Gladstone, the secretary of state for the colonies, that by the mid-1840s, it was not only the free coloureds who had acquired land, but the ex-apprentices:

have taken up new ground for themselves, benefiting the community while they work for their own advantage, holding a station intermediate between that of the field-labourer on the estates and the smaller property-owners. They have purchased small plots of ground and cultivate vegetables to daily increasing extent, for the supply of the markets, many of them engage an Indian or more, to assist them in their occupation and the latter is the salaried servant of the small Black proprietor.[94]

It is important to take a brief look at the situation in the colony during the 1840s or the early post-emancipation period which served as a backdrop to the *petit morcellement* movement. In 1846, around 75 per cent of the former apprentices lived and worked in the eight rural districts and only 25 per cent lived and worked in Port Louis. The ex-apprentice community formed around 31 per cent of the local population with 49,365 individuals. In the rural districts, the majority of the former apprentices were concentrated in Pamplemousses, Flacq, Plaines Wilhems and Grand Port.[95] It is important to note that between 1839 and 1850, Port Louis experienced a decline of almost 33 per cent of its ex-apprentice population who emigrated to the rural districts. Thus, they emigrated by the hundreds to the rural districts in search of better life and new economic opportunities as Port Louis rapidly became overcrowded, and good and stable jobs were scarce during the early post-emancipation period.[96]

What may have brought about the *petit morcellement* movement? The first half of the 1840s was a time of economic crisis in the colony and economic hardships for the Franco-Mauritian and some Free Coloured sugar planters. After all, they had to deal with a labour shortage that was caused by the abolition of the apprenticeship system which brought in its wake the exodus of the ex-apprentices who worked on the sugar cane fields. At the same time, another cause of the labour shortage was the suspension of the export of indentured labour from India until 1843.

The planters also had to deal with the rise in the wages of labourers, the cost of importing tens of thousands of indentured workers and increases in the cost of sugar production which was gradually expanding each year. As a result, large landowners sought different ways to raise money in order to meet the ever-growing expenses of running their plantations and small estates and they did not hesitate to capitalise on the desire and the ability of some former apprentices to purchase land. Furthermore, this gave them a good opportunity to sell some of their undeveloped and marginal land located on the perimeter of their properties. As mentioned earlier, they sold this marginal and unused land at high prices and made profits of 200 to 300 per cent.

A careful analysis of some of the notarial records of the 1840s show, to a certain extent, that this move by some of the Franco-Mauritian and free coloured planters and estate owners was part of a conscious strategy to restructure local socio-economic relationships so as to facilitate the reconstitution of an agricultural work force at a time when their ability to coerce labourers was circumscribed.

In effect, the planters, by renting and selling land to the former apprentices encouraged, although in a limited way, the creation of a reserve pool of workers on the perimeters of their estates who could be employed. Despite the fact that these ex-apprentices cherished their freedom and independence, they were offered good wages, not required to sign any contract and work for the planters for only a period of several weeks during the sugar cane harvest period. The Franco-Mauritian and Free Coloured property-owners wanted 'to establish as stable a work force as local conditions would allow'. After all, they also wanted to retain some of the skilled and semi-skilled artisans whose labour was in high demand during this period.[97]

At this stage, it is crucial to address the question of why some of the former apprentices spent their hard earned savings in order to acquire land. What was their worldview and ethos which propelled them to take such an important endeavour? What were the sources of their income which allowed them to achieve their objective? The answer was partially provided in 1845, in the short reports which the stipendiary magistrates and civil commissioners submitted to Governor Gomm which provide important insight into the social and economic conditions of the ex-apprentices between 1839 and 1845.

In December 1845, E. Ravel, the Civil Commissary of Riviere du Rempart district, explained that the desire for the ownership of a plot of land among the former apprentices was almost like an obsession.[98] At the same time, on 24 December of the same month, P. A. Heylinger, the Stipendiary Magistrate of Pamplemousses, made the famous observation that: 'the general desire of these people is to possess land'. He also highlighted the fact that during the 1840s, the ex-apprentices had purchased parcels of land of between half an acre to three acres in different parts of his district, sometimes at high prices.[99]

During the early post-emancipation period in Mauritius, like elsewhere in the European colonial plantation world, as mentioned earlier, the majority of the former apprentices wanted to make a life of their own. They wanted to occupy or legally acquire a plot of land, settle with their families there and grow their own crops for their subsistence, and what remained would be sold in the local markets. They also wanted to have freedom of movement, earn their own income, and control their own labour. As a result, they did not want to sign any contract and were not interested in working for their former owners. These were some of the ways that the Mauritian former apprentices wanted to translate their concept of liberty into freedom which the Mauritian planters and the British colonial officials found difficult to understand and accept.[100]

The other reports from 1845 and the Mauritius Census of 1847 reflect some of these observations, to a certain extent, and contain interesting information on the emergence of this Mauritian ex-apprentice peasantry. In the district of Pamplemousses, there were a great number of ex-apprentices who had bought one to two *arpents* of land where they engaged in small-scale vegetable cultivation.[101] In the district of Flacq, the former apprentices had erected huts and settled with their families on the plots of land which they had recently acquired. They became 'farmers' since they planted vegetables, manioc, sweet potatoes and maize which were just enough to feed their families.[102] However, it is important to note that districts such as Riviere du Rempart, Pamplemousses and Flacq (the island's major sugar-growing districts) only contained a small number of ex-apprentice peasants and farmers. The majority of these individuals had bought land and resided in districts such as Grand Port, Moka, Plaines Wilhems, Savanne and Black River.[103]

In December 1845, J. B. Davidson, the Stipendiary Magistrate of Grand Port, provided the only estimate of the amount of land bought and the amount of money spent by the ex-apprentices in a particular district during the first half of the 1840s. Davidson mentioned that the ex-apprentices spent more than £1,391 for the purchase of 161 *arpents* of land in different parts of Grand Port. This meant that they spent more than £8 or more than 40 rix dollars per *arpent* and paid the notarial fees on time. Davidson highlighted that there were several ex-apprentice families in the village of Vieux Grand Port and elsewhere in the district who owned property and as many as 20 to 25 head of cattle.[104]

In the districts of Plaines Wilhems and Moka, a significant amount of land was sold to a large number of former apprentices who were mainly of African origin. In some areas in those two districts, the landowning ex-apprentices were able to form small settlements where they worked and lived side by side and which can be seen as a genesis of community life for them.[105] In Savanne district, Civil Commissioner F. Giblot mentioned that in his district there were 2,526 former apprentices out of whom 577 individuals (22.8 per cent) were landowners and cultivated their own land which may have varied between one half and three arpents in size.[106]

Around 81 per cent (1,928 of the 2,388 ex-apprentice independent proprietors) were located in the minor sugar-growing districts such as Grand Port, Plaines Wilhems, Moka, Black River and Savanne. In the sugar-growing districts such as Pamplemousses, Riviere du Rempart and Flacq, there were 460 ex-apprentice independent proprietors (19 per cent of the total number on the island). The district which was the focal point of the *petit morcellement* movement was Grand Port where there were 844 ex-apprentice independent proprietors (more than 35 per cent of the island's total number of landowners of this particular category).

The other district which experienced the full impact of this social and economic process was Plaines Wilhems with 712 ex-apprentice independent proprietors (almost 30 per cent). Together, these two districts contain almost two-thirds of the island's landowners of that category.[107] In general, in 1846, there were 4,121 independent proprietors in the colony, and the ex-apprentices consisted of 58 per cent of the class of individuals.[108] At the district level, in Grand Port, they consisted of 47 per cent or almost half of all the independent property-owners, in Plaines Wilhems around 23 per cent, in Moka more than 21 per cent, and in Savanne district less than 20 per cent.

This census data, along with the observations from the reports of the civil commissioners and stipendiary magistrates, clearly show that between 1839 and 1845, many of the former apprentices left the major sugar-growing districts and went to settle as individuals or with their families and purchased land in the minor-sugar growing districts. It was in those districts in the central, south-eastern, southern and western parts of the island, that the *petit morcellement* played an important role in the local micro-economies of those districts.[109]

With the advent of the *petit morcellement* movement what position did the ex-apprentice property-owners occupy in Mauritian colonial society during the 1840s? In September 1846, after having analysed the reports of the stipendiary magistrates and civil commissioners, Governor Gomm sent an important despatch to Lord Gladstone, the secretary of state for the colonies. He observed that:

> They have taken up new ground for themselves benefitting the community while they work for their own advantage: holding a station intermediate between that of the field labourer on estates and the smaller occupants [estate owners] of such.... They have purchased small plots of ground and cultivate vegetables to daily increasing extent, for the supply of the markets, many of them engage an Indian or more, to assist them in their occupation and the latter is the salaried servant of the small Black Proprietor.

Thus, during the early post-emancipation period, the former apprentice peasant and property-owner occupied a position between the indentured labourers who lived and worked on the sugar estates and the small Free Coloured estate owners.[110]

Some of the notarial records from the 1840s also show, although in a limited way, that other ex-apprentices and old immigrants also worked for the landowning former apprentices. On 20 April 1842, Thomas Sage, a former apprentice and carpenter, bought a plot of more than three *arpents* from Pierre Louis, a free coloured small estate owner, who resided near the present-day village of Moka. He paid cash for that plot of land, the registration of the land purchase and notarial fee which amounted to a total of more than £60 pounds sterling or 302 rix dollars. Ever since June 1839, or for almost three years, Sage had occupied that land and paid a monthly rent of three rix dollars which was to be paid three months in advance at the beginning of each quarter.

This amounted to 36 rix dollars or more than £7 per year. By April 1842, or after almost three years, Thomas Sage was able to save enough money to purchase the land which he occupied from Pierre Louis. By 1842, Sage was able to build a small wooden house, settled his family, his wife and three children, on that land and opened a small workshop. At the same time, he managed to employ two old immigrants whom he paid five rupees per month and who helped with the cultivation of his land and the rearing of cattle and poultry. With the help of his workers, he sold his surplus farm produce at the market of Moka.[111]

On 25 June 1843, Francois Bernard, another former apprentice who was a blacksmith, purchased a plot of land of five *arpents* from Paillotte Sugar Estate in the present-day town of Vacoas. What is interesting is that he was employed there as the chief of that estate's workshop and remained there even after the advent of final freedom in March 1839. Bernard's newly acquired land was located on the perimeter of Paillotte sugar estate and he paid £104 pounds or 520 rix dollars which included the registration of the land purchase and the notarial fees. He built a small house and settled there with his family, his concubine and five children. He grew maize, manioc, potatoes and other garden produce and he also reared some livestock. Bernard managed to employ four old immigrants who had served their indenture contracts on the sugar estates of Solferino and Bonne Terre.

He paid them six rupees per month and they were required to grow his vegetables and tend to his cattle. Bernard sold his surplus garden produce to Paillotte Sugar Estate and to a lesser extent, to Solferino and Bonne Terre. It seems that Bernard derived several advantages by continuing to work for Paillotte since he was paid a good wage, provided with food and a place to live. However, it reached a point when he wanted to own his plot of land, leave the estate camp and provide food for his family. Despite all the advantages he enjoyed, he began the long and arduous task and process of breaking the chains of dependency by leaving the estate camp and settling on his own land.[112]

On 7 July 1843, Anne Marie Marthe, a former apprentice and seamstress, bought a four-arpent plot of land near Mahebourg in Grand Port district. She paid more than £76 or 304 rix dollars for the land and other related expenses. Anne Marie settled on her newly acquired land with her three children, was able to build a small house there and continued to practice her trade there. She hired two former apprentices who were cultivators and two ex-indentured Indian labourers who were formerly employed on Beau Vallon Sugar Estate to work her land. She paid them five rupees per month and they grew maize, potatoes and other types of vegetables and also reared a large amount of poultry. Anne Marie was able to feed her family and the surplus vegetable produce which was sold at the market in Mahebourg. She continued to work as a seamstress and supplemented her income from the sale of vegetable produce and poultry.[113]

Sage, Bernard and Marthe are three excellent examples of former apprentices who achieved some type of social and economic mobility during the early post-emancipation period. As skilled workers, they were able to earn high wages, saved their money, and after three to four years, they were able to buy their own plot of land. They formed new elite among the ex-apprentices, especially among the landowning ones. They were able to build small houses on their properties and got their families settled there.

Sage, Bernard and Marthe grew vegetables and provided for their families and the surplus of their garden produce, livestock and poultry were sold at the local district markets or to neighbouring sugar estates. They generated sufficient income from their small-scale farm activities and their skilled trades to employ old immigrants and other ex-apprentices. Without doubt, they were among the former apprentices who were classified as independent proprietors in 1846 and showed that they made their concept of freedom, of being economically independent and their desire for land a reality. At the same time, ex-apprentices like Sage, Bernard and Marthe, made an important contribution in helping to produce and safeguard the island's food supply. It is evident that they were able to integrate successfully into the non-plantation section of the island's economy. [114]

Between 1843 and 1846, there was a gradual increase in the amount of agricultural produce which was being provided to the island's local markets by the ex-apprentice property-owners who engaged in such activity.[115] By 1845 and 1846, the ex-apprentice landowners, apart from the free coloured small estate owners, became some of the major suppliers of vegetables and fruits to the Port Louis Central Market which was the colony's largest market.[116] Gradually, the free coloured small estates were unable to satisfy the colony's food demands and the situation worsened with the influx of tens of thousands of indentured labourers between the mid-1830s and mid-1840s. As a result, during the 1840s, as the ex-apprentices bought land, especially those who were classified as independent proprietors, they tried to fill the economic gap left by the free coloureds as they became some of the island's major suppliers of maize, manioc, sweet potatoes, *brede*, rice, other garden produce, fruits, livestock, poultry and pigs.[117]

Most of the ex-apprentices who took part in the *petit morcellement* movement were skilled and semi-skilled artisans, such as Sage, Bernard and Marthe who, usually after three to four years, were able to save enough money to purchase plots of land of two to five arpents.[118] At the same time, there were also many unskilled ex-apprentices such as the former field labourers who were also able to buy smaller plots of land usually between a half and two arpents.[119] Almost all the reports of the stipendiary magistrates and the civil commissioners of November and December 1845 and the despatches of Governor Gomm in 1846 highlight the fact that there was a large number of skilled and semi-skilled ex-apprentice workers who lived and worked in the colony's eight rural districts. There was a great demand for their precious labour and they were paid good wages which allowed them to achieve some type of capital accumulation.[120] In 1845, in Moka district, a stone mason and carpenter was paid £4 per month for his labour and a domestic or servant earned £2 per month.[121]

At the same time, a skilled worker who worked hard could earn enough money in one week through his labour and live comfortably for one whole month.[122] In Grand Port district, a skilled apprentice, after several years of savings, bought a property of £120 in the village of Mahebourg. In 1845, a collection of funds was launched by the stipendiary magistrate of Grand Port for the construction of a district hospital in Mahebourg. The local ex-apprentices supported this initiative and 977 individuals of that particular community donated anywhere between one pound sterling and one shilling.[123] It should also be remembered that there were thousands of slaves and apprentices, who had purchased their freedom between 1829 and 1839, and they were mostly skilled and semi-skilled workers who had access to some kind of financial resource, such as wages, even before the abolition of slavery and the termination of the apprenticeship system.[124]

Some Aspects of the *Petit Morcellement* and its Decline

What were some of the major features of the *petit morcellement* movement of the period between 1839 and 1851? Around 60 per cent of individuals who took part in the *petit morcellement* movement were the ex-apprentices. The majority of the former apprentices who bought land were skilled and semi-skilled workers with some unskilled workers such as ex-field labourers. Many of them became independent proprietors who did not depend on wage labour or employment on the sugar estates, but could produce enough vegetables, other garden produce, livestock, poultry and pigs to feed their families and sell the surplus. In addition, many among them employed other ex-apprentices and some old immigrants whom they paid wages. Thus, they made profits from their farm activities and many among them established their workshops on their properties from which they also generated some income.

What was the price they paid for their plots of land? For an *arpent* of land in a remote part of the island, such as in Black River and Savanne districts, the price was £2. An *arpent* of uncleared and marginal land in areas such as Plaines Wilhems and Moka districts, the price was £20 per *arpent*. For an arpent of cultivated land in Grand Port and Pamplemousses, a purchaser could be expected to pay as much as £40. The geographical location and accessibility to a plot of land played a crucial role in its sale price and value. Therefore, it is not surprising that the ex-apprentices paid a lot of money for some of these plots of land since they did have access to capital.

The majority of the former apprentices who purchased land were adult males and couples. It was also extremely rare for an ex-apprentice to have bought land from his former master or mistress. Around 90 per cent of the former apprentices who bought plots of land paid in cash the day the land sale was finalised and this included the registration of the land transaction deed and the notarial fee. This compares with 65 per cent of the free coloureds between 1811 and 1830 when they bought land during the slavery era. More than two-thirds of the land which was sold was one to three *arpents* in size.[125]

However, a brief survey of land purchases in NA 80 to NA 85 and NA 66 for the 1840s, for Plaines Wilhems, Moka and Grand Port districts, hint at the fact that many of the former apprentices who had paid the full amount in cash had contracted a loan. They undertook this financial engagement with other former apprentices, Free Coloureds and some Franco-Mauritians in order to acquire the land they desired. At the same time, it is possible that the precarious way in which many of these properties were acquired may point to the massive land dispossession of many of these ex-apprentices, as they defaulted on the loan payment.[126]

Another striking feature of the *petit morcellement* is that the notarial records indicate that 'at least 75 per cent of those persons who purchased land during the *petit morcellement* resided in the same district in which the land they were buying was located'.[127] Lastly, unlike the small British Caribbean islands such as Barbados and Antigua, Mauritius had a lot of unused land which could have been converted into arable land. In 1830, it is estimated that only 74,839 *arpents* of the island's 272,022 inventoried *arpents* were under cultivation, mainly sugar cultivation which represents just over 27 per cent. By 1840, the amount of land on the island under cultivation surpassed 40 per cent, as the sugar cultivation continued to expand during this era of the Mauritian sugar revolution. At the same time, Mauritius became the most important exporter of sugar in the British Empire by the middle of the 1840s.[128]

The significance of the *petit morcellement* movement between 1839 and 1851, or in the early post-emancipation period, in Mauritius cannot be underestimated. It shows the human agency of this segment of the colonial population, as many of them had access to some financial resources, they were able to save their money and undergo a process of capital accumulation which permitted them to purchase land sometimes at very high prices. They were also able to achieve some type of social and economic mobility. The purchase of land by the former apprentices allowed them to become an integral part of the non-plantation sector of the island's economy.

As farmers and agriculturalists, more specifically as independent proprietors, they made an important contribution in safeguarding and production of the island's food supply and to the economy of the rural districts. It becomes evident that they were able to successfully integrate into the non-plantation section of the island's economy. During the 1820s and 1830s, the Free Coloureds dominated this sector of the colonial economy which was gradually taken over by the ex-apprentice agriculturalists during the 1840s and, to a lesser extent, the 1850s. As mentioned earlier, the ex-slaves and ex-apprentices collaborated closely and were employed by the free coloured small estate owners during the 1830s and 1840s.

This offered them a viable alternative to working for the sugar planters who resorted to the importation of tens of thousands of indentured Indian workers during this period.[129]

During the 1840s and early 1850s, a major social process took place and was intimately linked with the *petit morcellement* which brought about the gradual six-fold division of island's ex-apprentice community. Who comprised this six-fold division? They are listed as follows:

(1)   the independent proprietors, or landowning peasants and farmers, who were involved in agricultural activities and rearing of farm animals in order to satisfy their nutritional needs and supply the local markets and sugar estates, and also employed some labourers, and this group includes the other former apprentices who had bought plots of land, but who engaged in subsistence farming and agricultural activities;

(2)   ex-apprentices who paid a rent or entered into sharecropping arrangements or made lease agreements with other landowning apprentices, *Free* Coloureds and some Franco-Mauritian planters for the use of their land;

(3)   former apprentices who were squatters and illegally occupied government or Crown lands and private properties and they were unregistered by the colonial authorities;

(4)   ex-apprentices who continued to live and work on the sugar estates and depended on wage labour for their livelihood but were not bound by any labour contract;

(5)   ex-apprentices who owned property in Port Louis and lived and worked there;

(6)   and lastly, the former apprentices who rented a small hut, wooden building and plot of ground in Port Louis and others who were squatters on the slopes of Signal Mountain, on the other mountains and hills and on the perimeters of that colonial town.[130]

The *petit morcellement* shows that during the 1840s and after, the views and observations of British colonial officials and Franco-Mauritian planters, when it came to the former apprentices, were based on racism and prejudice. There were thousands of ex-apprentices who were landowners, sharecroppers or *metayers* and squatters, thus they were involved in agricultural activities. This proves that the former apprentices were not lazy and did not have an aversion to agriculture, but wanted to work on their own land and according to their own schedule. This enabled them to control their labour, freedom of movement on the island, safeguard their independence and their freedom.

The Mauritius Census of 1851 indicates that only 778 former apprentices (549 males and 229 females) were independent proprietors. This census data indicates that the number of independent proprietors, who were the elite and the most successful among the landowning former apprentices, decreased by almost 70 per cent as a class within the island's ex-apprentice community. In 1846, they consisted of around 5.3 per cent of the ex-apprentice working population and fell to just 2 per cent in 1851. The number of ex-apprentices who were classified as agricultural labourers but were not working on sugar estates decreased from 4,826 (4,805 males and 21 females) in 1846 to 2,561 (1,339 males and 1,222 females) in 1851. This represents a decline of more than 45 per cent; but what is even more striking is the massive increase in the number of female ex-apprentices who returned to work as agricultural labourers. In a period of just five years, their numbers increased from 21 to 1,222. In 1846, these labourers consisted of around 15.4 per cent of the ex-apprentice working population which fell to 13.1 per cent in 1851.

During this same period, there was an almost five-fold increase in the number of former apprentices who lived and worked on the island's major sugar estates. In 1846, there were only 486 ex-apprentices on the plantations and, barely five years later, their number rose to 2,170 with the overwhelming majority or more than 90 per cent being adult males. During the same period, there was also an increase in the number of former apprentices who were skilled and semi-skilled workers and small shopkeepers and traders from 8,409 (5,923 males and 2,486 females) in 1846 to 9,605 (6,367 males and 3,238 females) in 1851 or an increase of more than 12 per cent. Overall, within five years the active working ex-apprentice population decreased by more than 10 per cent. At the same time, in 1851, more than 39.3 per cent of the ex-apprentice population was unemployed, while only 60.7 per cent was employed, which was a very high unemployment rate for this segment of the colonial population. It should be noted that the unemployed included many women and young boys and girls.[131]

Despite the fact that there was a rapid decline in the number of ex-apprentices who were independent proprietors and non-plantation agricultural labourers, in 1851, the census commissioners observed that:

> the phenomena which they exhibit are consistent with the disposition evinced during this period by the ex-apprentices to migrate from the Town of Port Louis, in which they congregated immediately after the emancipation, and from the richer districts in the North of island, where they were serving at the period, to more wooded and less cultivated [and sparsely populated] districts of the island, in which they can purchase plots of ground at a cheap rate, or find it easier to occupy them without purchase.[132]

Between the late 1840s and early 1850s, there were still hundreds of former apprentices who were migrating from Port Louis and the large sugar districts to the minor sugar districts in the colony. For example, between 1846 and 1851, there was a decrease of three to two per cent of the ex-apprentice population in

Port Louis, Pamplemousses and Riviere du Rempart. During the same period, this same segment of the colonial population increased by two per cent in districts such as Moka, Grand Port and Flacq. They continued to purchase property, enter into lease agreements as sharecroppers and squat on government land and private properties but on a much lesser scale when compared with the period between 1839 and 1846.[133]

When looking at the census data from 1846 and 1851, it becomes evident that an important restructuring of the economic life and also major demographic changes were taking place among the former apprentices which forever altered the history of that community.[134] Before analysing the economic changes, what were some of the demographic changes? It should be noted that during this period, the number of ex-apprentices declined from 49,365 to 48,330, but in terms of their proportion, with regard to the colony's total population, their percentage dropped from 31 per cent to 26 per cent or more than 5 per cent as they became a minority. By 1851, in terms of numbers, they ranked behind the General Population, which consisted of the Franco-Mauritians and Free Coloureds, and the Indian indentured labourers. This fact is quite ironic because in 1839 they were the majority population and it underscores the demographic revolution which was underway ever since the 1830s and would reach its peak by the early 1860s.

In addition, between 1835 and 1846, the death rate among the apprentices and ex-apprentices was 3.5 per cent per year and a total of more than 7,000 apprentices and ex-apprentices passed away during that period. At the same time, the number of 'ex-apprentices born in Africa and Madagascar had diminished by 2,908' and 'their proportion to the total of their class is reduced from 25 to 20 percent'. This census data indicates that the number of former apprentices who were born outside of Mauritius and who were in their forties, fifties and sixties were rapidly disappearing while the Mauritian-born former apprentices were stabilising. The causes of their deaths were due to many reasons, diseases, malnutrition, alcoholism and lack of access to proper medical care.

The female and male ratio also was gradually stabilising, with 57 per cent of the ex-apprentice population being males and 43 per cent being females in 1846. Five years later, this number stabilised at 55 per cent for the males and 45 per cent for the females respectively.[135] By 1861, the ex-apprentices disappeared as a clearly distinguished segment of the colonial population. This can clearly be seen in the census of that particular year when they were classified as 'General Population', along with the Franco-Mauritians and Free Coloureds. The indentured and non-indentured Indian immigrants consisted of more than 60 per cent of the local population as the Mauritian demographic revolution reached its peak.[136]

The landowning ex-apprentices could not obtain financial credit from the local colonial banks which limited their access to capital. Droughts, floods, cyclones and crop failures were a regular feature of the Mauritian rural landscape, and when the crops of the former apprentices were destroyed it took them several months to recover.[137] Many did not recover and they sold their properties for cash. There were also many skilled and semi-skilled ex-apprentice workers who purchased land, and since they were not farmers and cultivators, they found it difficult to successfully initiate and manage vegetable cultivation and the rearing of farm animals. In fact, many among them who were unable to manage their newly-established farms and agricultural activities sold their land.[138]

Between 1846 and 1851, the number of proprietors within the general population increased from 1,728 to 2,213. Allen has argued that many of these new proprietors were in fact former apprentices who classified themselves as 'General Population' in order to enhance their social standing in the colonial society. This would partially account for the decrease in the number of independent proprietors within the ex-apprentice community.[139] Some of the archival records also hint at the fact that some of the former apprentices who returned to estate labour might have been unsuccessful independent proprietors and sharecroppers who were left with no other source of employment.

One of the major factors which greatly influenced the fortunes of this segment of the colonial population was the introduction of the Indian indentured labourers. Between 1848 and 1851, there were thousands of ex-indentured labourers who completed their five-year contracts and many among them did not return to work on the sugar estates. They preferred to take up employment as labourers, gardeners, house servants, hawkers, some engaged in skilled and semi-skilled work and a few even purchased property. The old immigrants became actively involved in commerce, trade and manufacturing, and they occupied jobs which were previously dominated by the former apprentices. This process was further consolidated by 1861 as the indentured and ex-indentured workers and their families formed the majority segment of the local colonial population.[140]

Between 1853 and 1858, Beaton had frequent contacts with the ex-apprentices and their children during his stay of five years on the island. He described them as hardworking and that the majority of them did not want to return to work on the sugar estates because of the bitter memories of the inhumane treatment they suffered. Beaton observed that many among the former apprentices still resided in some of the remote parts of the island as landowners, sharecroppers and squatters who were engaged in growing vegetables and rearing farm animals. They wanted to preserve their freedom and independence.[141]

In July 1866, Governor Sir Henry Barkly, provided one of the last detailed accounts on the social and economic situation of the ex-apprentices by a British colonial official. He explained that during the 1860s, there were many former apprentices who were still property owners, sharecroppers and squatters in all the island's rural districts. Many among them also joined government service and were skilled and semi-skilled workers. It shows that former apprentices still occupied an important and not entirely marginal position in the island's local economy.[142] The accounts of Duncan, Beaton and Barkly highlight the fact that although as landowners, sharecroppers and squatters, the importance of the ex-apprentice community declined in Mauritius between the late 1840s and early 1850s, they still formed an integral and visible part of Mauritian colonial society during the second half of the nineteenth century.

Conclusion

The objective of this chapter was to analyse the exodus of the ex-apprentices from the sugar estates, their desire to obtain land, the *petit morcellement* movement, and the rise of a Mauritian ex-apprentice peasantry or small landowners during the early post-emancipation period. It looked at the emergence of an important group of sharecroppers or *métayers* and squatters from within the island's ex-apprentice community between 1839 and 1851. It explored the worldview and ethos of the ex-apprentices as they struggled to make their concept of freedom a reality which entailed controlling their labour, mobility in the colony, rejection of estate labour, owning their own plot of land and working their land at their own pace. At the same time, it also looked at the situation of some of the ex-apprentices who continued to work and live on the sugar estates after the advent of final freedom in 1839.

This section of the study has argued that the ex-apprentices are excellent examples of human agency in Mauritian history as they left estate labour, bought or settled legally or illegally on a plot of land, settled with their families there and grew their own vegetables and reared their farm animals. It demonstrated how they resorted to different strategies of survival such as collaborating with the Free Coloureds who employed them and even rented and sold them portions of land. In the process, the Free Coloureds offered them a viable alternative of permanently escaping estate labour. It has argued that thousands of ex-apprentice property owners, sharecroppers and squatters emerged in all of the eight rural districts of Mauritius.

This chapter has shown that the former apprentices had access to capital and with their savings, which were large amounts of money, they purchased an impressive quantity of land during what has been called the *petit morcellement* between 1839 and 1851. It explained that the ex-apprentice independent proprietors, as agriculturalists and farmers, were able to successfully integrate the non-plantation sector of the island's economy. It highlights the fact that they became major suppliers of garden produce and farm animals and tried fill the gap which since the 1830s had been left by the Free Coloureds small estate owners who engaged in sugar cultivation. This chapter carried out an in-depth discussion and analysis of the dynamics of the *petit morcellement* movement and its significance for the colony during the 1840s. It also drew attention to the new social position of the ex-apprentices in early post-emancipation Mauritius and the sub-class divisions which were taking place within the island ex-apprentice community during this period.

This section of the study analysed the decline of the Mauritian ex-apprentice peasantry between 1846 and 1851 and its aftermath. It looked at the demographic changes and the economic restructuring which took place within the Mauritian ex-apprentice community during the late 1840s and early 1850s. It threw light on the social and economic position of the former apprentices between the 1850s and early 1870s. It attempted to explore the early post-emancipation era which is one of the least known and understood periods of the colonial Mauritian history. Furthermore, it tried to make a contribution to one of the research themes of modern Mauritian historiography, which until recently has been largely overlooked by scholars, namely: the social history of the ex-apprentices. It analysed the question of what happened to the ex-apprentices after 1839.

This chapter has shown that by voluntarily leaving the sugar estates, squatting, leasing and purchasing land, working at their own pace, choosing their occupations, getting married and having children, the ex-apprentices were able to make a life of their own. As a result, during the early post-indenture era, they were able, to a certain extent, to make their idea of freedom a reality by exerting control on their mobility, labour and lives, while operating in difficult legal, social and economic circumstances in a hierarchical and complex Mauritian colonial society.

Notes

1. Quotation and idea derived from Michael Craton, *Testing the Chains: Resistance to Slavery in the British West Indies,* Cornell University Press, Ithaca, USA, 1982, pp.44-51.
2. Reverend Patrick Beaton, *Creoles and Coolies, or, Five Years in Mauritius,* pp. 85. Reverend Beaton narrating the comments of the son of a Mauritian ex-apprentice almost two decades after the exodus of the apprentices from the sugar estates.
3. MNA/SD 85, Governor Sir Henry Barkly to Lord Caldwell, Secretary of State for the Colonies, 26th July 1866.
4. Vijaya Teelock, 'Bitter Sugar: Slavery and Emancipation in Nineteenth Century Mauritius', Ph.D thesis, University of London, 1994, p.332.
5. *Report of the Committee appointed to conduct and complete the census of the colony (1846): The Mauritius-Census of 1847,* Enclosed in Despatch No.47 from Governor Sir William Gomm to Earl Grey, Mauritius, sixteenth September, 1848, British BPP, 1849, XXXVII (280-II), p.194.
6. Teelock, 'Breaking the Wall of Silence', p.2.
7. *Le Mauricien,* 26th April, 1839.
8. *Le Mauricien,* 24th April, 1839.
9. Richard B. Allen, *Slaves, Freedmen,* p.120; Charles Anderson revealed that there were around 28,000 field workers who laboured on the sugar estates just before

the termination of the apprenticeship system, See Mauritius Archives/HA 73/72, Evidence of Mr. Charles Anderson, Protector of Immigrants, December 1844, Port Louis, before *the Immigrant Labour Committee of 1844*, p.65-66, in *Reports of the Immigrant Labour*

10. Mauritius Archives/SD 18/No.57, Despatch from Governor William Nicolay to Lord Gleneg, Mauritius, 4th May, 1839.

11. Pierre Gueyraud, 'The Integration of the Ex-Apprentices into Mauritian Society, 1839-1860' (M.A thesis, University of Sorbonne, Paris, 1985), p.16.

12. Ibid, p.15.

13. MNA/J/K3A, Report of the Royal Commission of 1875, p.47, paragraph 189/p.50, paragraph 199; Howell, 'Mauritius, 1832-1849; A Study of A Sugar Colony', Vol. I, p.160.

14. Howell, *Mauritius, 1832-1849; A Study of A Sugar Colony*, Vol. I, p.169.

15. Teelock & Deerpalsingh, *Labour Immigrants in Mauritius: A Pictorial Recollection*, p.29.

16. MNA/RC 27/3173, Transmitting the Report and Observations of Thomas Hugon on the State of the Indians in the Colony (29th July 1839), Enclosed in Letter of T. Hugon to George F. Dick, Colonial Secretary, Mauritius, 29th July 1839; Howell, *'Mauritius, 1832-1849; A Study of A Sugar Colony'*, Vol I, pp.161, 169-170, 173-175; Teelock, *Mauritian History*, pp. 225-231.

17. Howell, *Mauritius, 1832-1849; A Study of A Sugar Colony*, Vol. I, pp.161, 169-180/181-185; North-Coombes, *From Slavery to Indenture: Forced Labour in the Political Economy of Mauritius, 1834-1867*, pp.28-34; Carter & d'Unienville, *Unshackling Slaves*, pp.13-17; Teelock, *Mauritian History*, pp.225-231.

18. Calculated from MNA/RD 16, Return of the Working Population on the Estates in the District of Savanne by Stipendiary Magistrate Percy Fitzpatrick, 25th May 1839; RD 16, Return ... of the Estates in the District of Grand Port, No.2412, Enclosed in a Letter of Stipendiary Magistrate Davidson, to George F. Dick, Colonial Secretary, 2nd June 1839; RD 19, Return ... of District of Flacq, 14th May, 1839, by Stipendiary Magistrate S.M. Regnard; RD 19, Return ...on the Estates in the District of Riviere du Rempart, 1st Section, submitted by the Stipendiary Magistrate, 9th June 1839.

19. Letter of Charles Anderson, Esq. To Lord John Russell, London, May 1st 1840, British BPP, 1840, Vol XXXVII (No.331), p.195; According to Charles Anderson, there might have been some 3,000 ex-apprentices who remained on the sugar estates between 1839 and 1840, See MNA /HA 73/72, Evidence of Mr. Charles Anderson, December 1844, Port Louis, before the Immigrant Labour Committee of 1844, p.65-66, in Reports of the Immigrant Labour; Howell, *Mauritius, 1832-1849, A Study of A Sugar Colony*, Vol II, p.174.

20. *Le Mauricien*, 24th April, 1839.

21. MNA/SD 19, No.50, Letter of Governor Lionel Smith to Lord John Russell, Mauritius, 28th November 1840.

22. MNA/RA 833, Report of Fitzpatrick, Stipendiary Magistrate of Port-Louis to Colonel George F. Dick, Colonial Secretary, 10th February, 1846, Port-Louis.

23. MNA/SD 19, No.50, Letter of Governor Lionel Smith to Lord John Russell, Mauritius, 28th November 1840; MNA/RA 833, Report of Fitzpatrick, Stipendiary

Magistrate of Port-Louis to Colonel George F. Dick, Colonial Secretary, 10th February, 1846, Port-Louis.

24. MNA/HA 73, Appendix G, No.163/No.8, Abstract of District Returns of Slaves in Mauritius at the Time of the Emancipation in the Year 1835.

25. Author's Analysis.

26. Appendix 10: Statement, showing the Employment of the Persons enumerated in the Districts of Mauritius on 1st August 1846, in *Census of 1847*, p.212.

27. MNA/RA 833, Report of Percy Fitzpatrick, Stipendiary Magistrate of Port-Louis, Colonel George F, Dick, Colonial Secretary, 10th February, 1846.

28. Author's Analysis.

29. Beaton, *Creoles and Coolies*, p.85.

30. Ibid, pp. 85-86.

31. Ibid, p. 265.

32. P.J. Barnwell & Auguste Toussaint, *A Short History of Mauritius*, London, Longmann Green & Co, 1949, p.146.

33. MNA/RA 833, Report of Fitzpatrick, Stipendiary Magistrate of Port-Louis to Colonel George F. Dick, Colonial Secretary, 10th February, 1846, Port-Louis.

34. VijayaTeelock, 'Bitter Sugar', Ph.D thesis, 1994, p.332.

35. Barker, *Slavery and Antislavery*, p.167.

36. Peerthum, 'Determined to be Free', p. 80-81; Satyendra Peerthum, ' "Forging an Identity of their Own": The Social and Economic Relations Between the Free Coloureds, Slaves, Maroons, Apprentices, Ex-Apprentices and Indentured Labourers in Early British Mauritius, c.1811-1844', Paper presented at the 'Mauritius 1810: International Conference, October 2010, Mauritius), p.17-23.

37. Eugene Bernard, 'Les Africains'. pp. 550-551; Edward Baker, 'Observations on the Apprenticeship System in Mauritius', pp. 67-83.

38. See Allen, *Slaves, Freedmen*, p.113-120; Huguette Ly-Tio-Fane Pineo, 'Food Production and Plantation Economy of Mauritius', in U. Bissoondoyal & S. Servansingh, eds, *Slavery in the South West Indian Ocean*, Moka, Mauritius, MGI Press, 1989 pp. 210-225; Deryck Scarr, *Slaving and Slavery in the Indian Ocean*, London, MacMillan Press, 1998, pp.163-164.

39. Allen, *Creoles, Indians Immigrants*, p.190.

40. Richard B. Allen, *Slaves, Freedmen and Indentured Laborers in Colonial Mauritius*, Cambridge, Cambridge University Press, 1999, pp.104/100-101.

41. Allen, *Creoles, Indians Immigrants*, pp. 98-104.

42. Daniel North-Coombes, 'Race as Ideology: The Origin and Functions of Racism in the Plantation Settlement of Mauritius, 1790-1810', in M.D North-Coombes (Compiled and Edited by W. M Freund), *Studies in the Political Economy of Mauritius*, Moka, Mauritius, Mahatma Gandhi Press, 2000, p. 3; See also Allen, *Creoles, Indians Immigrants*, pp.140-150.

43. Allen, *Creoles, Indians Immigrants*, p.146.

44. *Le Mauricien*, 24th April 1839.

45. MNA/RD 19, Return of the Working Population on the Estates in the District of Savanne by Stipendiary Magistrate Percy Fitzpatrick, 25th May 1839; RD 19, Return of the Working Population of the Estates in the District of Grand Port,

No. 2412, Enclosed in a Letter of Stipendiary Magistrate Davidson, to George F. Dick, Colonial Secretary, 2nd June 1839; RD 19, Return of the Working Population of the District of Flacq, 14th May, 1839, by Stipendiary Magistrate S.M. Regnard; RD 19, Return of the Working Population on the Estates in the District of Riviere du Rempart, 1st Section, submitted by the Stipendiary Magistrate, 9th June 1839.

46. MNA/RD 19, Return of the Working Population on the Undermentioned Estates 25th May 1839.

47. Allen, *Slaves, Freedmen*, pp.112-115/120-121.

48. Ibid, p.121.

49. PRO/167/226-Letter of Captain Lloyd to John Irving, Mauritius, April 4th 1840, p.1-4.

50. Allen, *Slaves, Freedmen*, p.121.

51. MNA/HA 108, Civil Commissioner Armand Hugnin to the Colonial Secretary, 15th May 1839; See also in HA 108 letters sent by the Civil Commissioner to the Colonial Secretary and Chief Commissary of Police between May and December 1839.

52. MNA/104, Report of Civil Commissioner A. Hugnin to the Colonial Secretary, 1st December 1845.

53. MNA/SD 18, No.38, Miscellaneous, Despatch from Acting Governor J. Power to Lord John Russell, Mauritius, 22nd June 1840.

54. MNA/SD 18, No.5, Miscellaneous, Governor Lionel Smith to Lord John Russell, Mauritius, 8th August 1840, paragraph 4.

55. *Census of 1847*, pp.196-199; Chan Low, 'Les ex-apprentis dans la societe colonial: le recensement de 1846', p. 42-45.

56. See MNA/HA 100 to HA 111 and HA 111 to 116 and RA 613 to RA 883 which contain letters from the Stipendiary Magistrates to the Colonial Secretary which, on different occasions, mention the emergence of squatters, metayers or sharecroppers and small independent landholders within the island's ex-apprentice community in all the rural districts between 1839 and 1846 which still need to be fully studied and analysed; See also Chan Low, 'Les ex-apprentis dans la societe colonial: le recensement de 1846', pp.42-45.

57. For reports of the Stipendiary Magistrates see MNA/RA 833, HA 112 to 116 for Letters and Reports received from Stipendiary Magistrates by Colonial Secretary for 1845; For reports of Civil Commissioners 1845: HA 100 to HA 106 and HA 110 to HA 111.

58. MNA/NA 66, 15th April 1842 (MNA/NA 66, The Notarial Records of C.J. Montocchio for the period between 1822 to 1874)

59. MNA/NA 66, 30th June 1843.

60. MNA/NA 66, 10th July 1843.

61. See Allen, *Creoles, Indians Immigrants*, pp.168-170/196-197.

62. MNA/HA73/Appendix G/No.7/No.162/Statement of the Number of Indians and Ex-Apprentices with their families attached to the estates in Each District distinguishing Sugar from other Estates in the month of July 1844.

63. Allen, *Slaves, Freedmen*, pp.120/197.

64. For reports of the Stipendiary Magistrates see MNA/RA 833, HA 112 to 116 for Letters and Reports received from the Stipendiary Magistrates by the Colonial

Secretary for 1845; For the reports of the Civil Commissioners for 1845 See HA 100 to HA 106 and HA 110 to HA 111.

65. MNA/ RA 833/ Report of the J. Davidson, Stipendiary Magistrate of Grand Port to the Colonial Secretary, Mahebourg, twentieth December 1845.

66. MNA/ RA 833/ Report of the H.M. Self, Stipendiary Magistrate of Pamplemousses to the Colonial Secretary, Pamplemousses, 29th November 1845.

67. MNA/ RA 833/ Report of the J. Regnard, Stipendiary Magistrate of Flacq to the Colonial Secretary, Flacq, nineteenth December 1845.

68. Census of 1847, p.195.

69. MNA/ RA 833/ Report of the J. Regnard.

70. MNA/HA 111/No.567, Report of G. Ducray, Civil Commissioner of the Savanne to the Colonial Secretary, No.567, Savanne, 26th November 1845; MNA/RA 833/ Report of the J. Davidson, Stipendiary Magistrate of Grand Port to the Colonial Secretary, Mahebourg, twentieth December 1845; MNA/HA 103/No.254, Report D. Beaugendre, Civil Commissioner of Moka, to Colonial Secretary, Moka, nineteenth December 1845; MNA/HA 103/No.861, Report of E. Magon, Civil Commissioner of Pamplemousses, to the Colonial Secretary, Pamplemousses, twentieth December 1845; MNA/HA 100/No.185/Report of H.L. Lawns, Civil Commissioner of Black River to Secretary, Black River, 5th December 1845; See also L. Jocelyn Chan Low, 'Les ex-apprentisdans la societe colonial: le recensement de 1846' in Revi Kiltir Kreol(Nelson Mandela Centre for African Culture) (No.1, February 2002), p.40-50; Carter & d'Unienville, Unshackling Slaves, p.103-140.

71. PRO/167/226-Letter of Captain Lloyd to John Irving, Mauritius, April 4th 1840, p.1-4.

72. Allen, Creoles, Indians Immigrants, , pp.167-170/196-197.

73. MNA/HA 108, Letter of Civil Commissioner Hugnin to the Colonial Secretary, 15th May 1839; MNA/HA 103, Letter of Civil Commissioner Beaugendre to the Colonial Secretary, twentieth May 1839; See Teelock, Breaking the Wall of Silence, pp.12-13.

74. See MNA/HA 100 to HA 106 and HA 111 : Letters from Civil Commissaries to Chief Commissary of Police and Colonial Secretary for 1839 and 1840 on issue of squatting by ex-apprentices.

75. MNA/RC 27, Letter of F. Thatcher, Stipendiary Magistrate to the Colonial Secretary, 9 May 1839 with the Governor's Reply dated 13th May 1839.

76. MNA/HA 105, Letter from Civil Commissioner Hugnin to the Chief Commissary of Police John Finiss, seventeenth June 1840

77. MNA/HA 104, Letter from Civil Commissioner Hugnin to the Chief Commissary of Police John Finiss, 21st August 1841.

78. Le Mauricien, 3 May 1847; Le Mauricien, 10 May 1847.

79. 'Necrologie of Napoleon Savy', Le Mauricien, 13th July 1858; Hugh Tinker, A New System of Slavery: The Export of Indian Labour Overseas, 1830-1920 (Oxford University Press/Institute of Race Relations, Great Britain, 1974), p.239/398; Dr. Satteeanund Peerthum, 'Napoleon Savy: Protecteur inofficiel des immigrants indiens' (Unpublished research paper, 2001), p.1-4; K. Hazareesingh, History of Indians in Mauritius (Revised Edition), p.38.

80. Letter of Napoleon Savy to General Gomm, 4th May 1847, Reproduced in *Le Cerneen,* Friday, 21 May 1847, p.2.

81. *Le Cerneen,* Friday, 21 May 1847, p. 2; *Le Cerneen,* Friday, 23 May 1847, p. 2.

82. MNA/RA 833, Report of J. Regnard, Stipendiary Magistrate of Flacq to the Colonial Secretary, nineteenth December 1845.

83. MNA/SD 30, Report of the Committee appointed by the Council on the twentieth April for the purpose of drawing up and submitting to the Secretary of State the opinion of the Council with reference to the several suggestions contained in his Lordship's Despatch of the 31st December, 1846, No. 73, on the Subject of the Emancipated Population in the Colony, Enclosed in dispatch from Governor Gomm to Earl Grey, Mauritius, 12th July, 1847.

84. MNA/RA 592, Letter of the Chief Medical Officer to the Colonial Secretary, 21st June 1839.

85. MNA/RA 1980, Report of the Committee of the General Board of Health on Black Town, March 30th See Moses Nwulia, *The History of Slavery in Mauritius and the Seychelles, 1810 to 1875* (Farleigh Dickinson, New Jersey, Farleigh Dickinson Press, 1981), p.202.

86 MNA/RA 2144, Minutes of Proceedings of the General Board of Health July 10th 1873; See Nwulia, The History of Slavery in Mauritius and the Seychelles, 1810 to 1875, p.202.

87. Evidence of J. Duncan, Surveyor-General of Mauritius before the Crown Land Commission, 2nd February 1872 in MNA/B6, Minutes of Evidence of the Crown Land Commission of 1872, p.12-14; Carter & d'Unienville, *Unshackling Slaves,* pp.163-164.

88. Evidence of W. Thies, Sergeant Major of Forest Rangers before the Crown Land Commission, 5th February 1872 in MNA/B6, Minutes of Evidence of the Crown Land Commission of 1872, p.26-28; Carter and d'Unienville, *Unshackling Slaves,* pp.163-164.

89. PRO/167/226-Letter of Captain Lloyd to John Irving, Mauritius, April 4th 1840, p.4-5.

90. MNA/B6, The Crown Land Commission Report of 1872, Return showing Squatters and Rent Payments made between 1860 and 1872 submitted to Governor Gordon, 14th October 1872.

91. MNA/B6, Minutes of Evidence, Evidence of Duncan before Crown Land Commission, p.12-14.

92. Quotation from MNA/RA 833, Report of Stipendiary Magistrate P.A. Heylinger of Pamplemousses to the Colonial Secretary, 24th December 1845

93. Allen, *Creoles, Indians Immigrants,* pp.172-177; Allen, *Slaves, Freedmen,* pp.104-152/114/179-180; Chan Low, 'Les ex-apprentis', pp.54/40-50; Gueyraud, 'The Integration of Ex-Apprentices' pp.30-31.

94. MNA/SD 27, No.174, Governor Gomm to Gladstone, 7th September, 1846.

95. *Census of 1847,* pp.194-196.

96. Teelock, *Breaking the Wall of Silence,* p.13.

97. Allen, *Slaves, Freedmen,* p.121/120-122/112-115; See Allen, 'Creoles, Indians Immigrants,*, p.172-173/196-198.

98. MNA/HA 110, Report of E. Ravel, Civil Commissioner of Riviere du Rempart, to the Colonial Secretary, 4th December 1845.

99. MNA/833, P.A. Heylinger, Stipendiary Magistrate of Pamplemousses, to Colonial Secretary, 24th December 1845.

100. Allen, *Creoles, Indians Immigrants*, and, pp.168-178; Allen, *Slaves, Freedmen*, pp.108-115; Chan Low, 'Les ex-apprentis', pp. 42-43.

101. MNA/RA 833, H.M. Self, Stipendiary Magistrate of Pamplemousses, to the Colonial Secretary, 29th November 1845.

102. MNA/RA 833, Report of J. Regnard, nineteenth December 1845.

103. Appendix 10: 'Statement showing the Employment of the Persons enumerated in each district of Mauritius on 1st August 1846' in *Mauritius-Census of 1847* p.212-231; See Teelock, *Breaking the Wall of Silence*, pp.14-17.

104. MNA/RA 833, Report of the J. Davidson.

105. MNA/RA 833, Report of S. Seignette, the Stipendiary Magistrate of Plaines Wilhems to the Colonial Secretary, 3rd December 1845; MNA/HA 103/No.254, Report D. Beaugendre.

106. MNA/HA 111/No.567, Report of G. Ducray.

107. Appendix 10, *Census of 1847*, p.212-231; See Chan Low, 'Les ex-apprentis', p.43.

108. *Census of 1847*, p.197.

109. Appendix 10. p.212-231; See MNA/RA 833, Reports of the Stipendiary Magistrates for November and December 1845; See MNA/HA 100 to HA 111 Reports of Civil Commissioners for 1845; See also Teelock, *Breaking the Wall of Silence*, pp.14-17.

110. MNA/SD 27/No.174, Governor Gomm to Gladstone, Mauritius, 7th September 1846.

111. MNA/NA 66, twentieth April 1842.

112. MNA/NA 66, 25th June 1843.

113. MNA/NA 66, 7th July 1843.

114. See MNA/NA 66/12, twentieth April 1842; MNA/NA 66/14, 25th June 1843; MNA/NA 66/15, 7th July 1843; MNA/SD 27/No.174, Governor Gomm to Gladstone, 7th September 1846; See also MNA/SD 30, Report of the Committee, 1846, No,73, on Subject of Emancipated Population, Para. 5, Enclosed in a dispatch from Governor Gomm to Grey, 12th July, 1847; *Census of 1847*, p.212-231; See Allen, *Creoles, Indians Immigrants*, pp.178-179.

115. MNA/SD 27/No.174, Governor Gomm to Gladstone, 7th September 1846; See Allen, 'Creoles, Indians Immigrants, pp.178-179.

116. MNA/SD 27/No.5, Governor Sir William Gomm to Lord Stanley, 7th January 1846.

117. See Allen, *Slaves, Freedmen*, p.113-120; Allen, 'Creoles, Indians Immigrants, pp.170-180/189-194/196-200.

118. See MNA/NA 66/12, twentieth April 1842; MNA/NA 66/14, 25th June 1843; MNA/NA 66/15, 7th July 1843; See also Allen, *Creoles, Indians Immigrants*, pp.170-180/189-194/196-200; Allen, *Slaves, Freedmen*, pp.113-120.

119. Allen, *Creoles, Indians Immigrants*, pp.170-180/189-194/196-200; Allen, *Slaves, Freedmen*, pp.113-120.

120. MNA/RA 833, Reports of the Stipendiary Magistrates for November and December 1845; See MNA/HA 100 to HA 111 1845; MNA/SD 27/No.174, Governor Gomm

to Gladstone; MNA/SD 30, Report of the Committee, 1846, No,73, on Subject of Emancipated Population, Para.5.

121. MNA/RA 833, Report of Stipendiary Magistrate J.M. Randall to the Colonial Secretary, nineteenth December 1845.

122. MNA/SD 30, Report of the Committee, 1846, No,73, on Subject of Emancipated Population, Para.7.

123. MNA/RA 833/ Report of the J. Davidson.

124. See Chapter 3, pp.53-76, which deals with the manumission of slaves and apprentices through self-purchase etc.

125. Allen, *Slaves, Freedmen*, pp.112-129; Allen,*Creoles, Indians Immigrants*, pp.169-180.

126. See MNA/NA 66; MNA/NA 80, 81, 82, 83, 84 and 85 for the period between 1839 and 1851.

127. Allen, *Slaves, Freedmen*, p.118.

128 Ibid, pp.119/2-3.

129. Allen, *Slaves, Freedmen*, pp.105-135; Allen, *Creoles, Indians Immigrants*, pp.167-200; Chan Low, 'Les ex-apprentis', pp. 40-46; Sydney Selvon, *History of Mauritius: A Comprehensive History of Mauritius* (2001), pp.209-217; Teelock, *Breaking the Wall of Silence*, pp.12-14/18-19.

130. Allen, *Slaves, Freedmen*, pp. 105-135; Allen,*Creoles, Indians Immigrants*, pp.167-200; Chan Low, 'Les ex-apprentis', pp. 40-46; Selvon, *History of Mauritius*, pp .209-217; Teelock, *Breaking the Wall of Silence*, pp.12-14/18-19.

131. *Census of 1847*, p.197-199; MNA/KK 28, *Mauritius Census of 1851*, pp.7-9/2.

132. MNA/KK 28, *Mauritius Census of 1851*, p. 4.

133. Ibid, p.4-7.

134. Allen, *Slaves, Freedmen*, p.131.

135. MNA/KK 28, *Mauritius Census of 1851*, pp. 2-7.

136. Allen, '*Creoles, Indians Immigrants*', p.180; Allen, *Slaves, Freedmen*, pp.134-135.

137. Allen, *Slaves, Freedmen*, p.105-135; Allen,'*Creoles, Indians Immigrants*', p.165-194; Selvon, *History of Mauritius*, pp.209-235; Gueyraud, 'The Integration of Ex-Apprentices, p.30-50; Chan Low, 'Les ex-apprentis', p. 40-54; Peerthum, 'Forging an Identity', pp.17-25.

138. See MNA/NA 66/NA 80/NA 83/NA 84/NA 85, Notarial Records for the period between 1839 and 1851; See also Allen, *Slaves, Freedmen*, pp.105-135; Allen, '*Creoles, Indians Immigrants*', pp.165-194; Peerthum, 'Forging an Identity', pp.17-25.

139. Allen, *Slaves, Freedmen*, p.131.

140 MNA/KK 28, *Mauritius Census of 1851*, pp. 2-15; Allen, *Slaves, Freedmen*, p.105-135; Allen, *Creoles, Indians Immigrants*, pp.165-194; Selvon, *History of Mauritius*, pp. 209-235; Gueyraud, '*The Integration of Ex-Apprentices*, p.30-50; Chan Low, 'Les ex-apprentis', p.40-54; Peerthum, 'Forging an Identity', pp.17-25.

141. Beaton, *Creoles and Coolies*, pp. 84-86/264-267.

142. MNA/SD 85, Governor Sir Henry Barkly to Lord Caldwell, Secretary of State for the Colonies, 26th July 1866.

7

Conclusion

Abdul Sheriff and Vijayalakshmi Teelock

Although the two islands, Zanzibar and Mauritius, are of similar size and population, and both are located within the western Indian Ocean, they went through their experience of slavery and transition which were influenced by both the global hegemony of the capitalist mode of production under which both of them had developed during the eighteenth and nineteenth centuries, but they were also affected by the inherent and varying cultural milieux of the two islands which imprinted their differences. Zanzibar, which is only a few miles from the East African coast, was settled by humans almost thirty centuries ago, had been inducted into the Indian Ocean commercial system at least two millennia ago, and had been part of the Muslim world for at least a millennium. Mauritius, on the other hand, is in the middle of the Indian Ocean, and was not settled by humans until its discovery by the Europeans in the seventeenth century, bringing with them their European and Christian traditions. Despite these initial differences, both these islands developed their dependent slave modes of production from the eighteenth century when they came under the sway of capitalism and European colonialism which set the tone for their histories without erasing their cultural differences in some aspects of their slavery and emancipation.

Slavery was not a new phenomenon for Zanzibar, but that concept is a very broad one covering a whole range of servile relations that cannot be equated to the better known slavery in the Americas that had developed at a particular juncture with the rise of capitalism as a world system. The two islands of Lanjuya (Unguja) and Qanbalu (Pemba?) are mentioned by the Arab literati Al-Jahiz in the tenth century as having been enmeshed in the slave trade that supplied slaves to southern Iraq where a plantation economy based on slave labour had developed under a predominant tributary mode of production. However, the consequent Zanj Rebellion shook the foundation of the Abbasid Empire and brought to an end the massive slave trade, although trade on a smaller scale may have continued over the next many centuries. Side by side with the slave trade, there may also have been slavery on the East African coast itself, as indicated by the history of Kilwa, although the mainstay of the economy of the Swahili city states was oceanic trade in many other mundane commodities, including mangrove poles, foodstuffs, cloth and ivory, most of which were probably produced by free peasants.

When a plantation system based on slave labour did develop on these islands in the nineteenth century to produce cloves for export, the world was already under the dominance of capitalism that exercised a powerful influence on the slave system there. However, the underlying cultural matrix had varying impacts on the different sectors of slavery. In a culture long influenced by Islam, its conception of slavery was bound to put its imprint on the treatment of slaves and relations between owners and slaves. In Islam, slaves are not merely chattel but human beings with certain (though diminished) human rights and responsibilities. In classical slavery, slaves were supposed to be fed by their owners who had total control over their production; but in Zanzibar in the nineteenth century slaves were given plots to produce their own foodstuffs and sell the surplus in the market for their own benefit. Emancipation of a slave is a built-in feature of slavery in Islamic law, it being recommended in numerous circumstances that created a freed population in every Muslim society as a norm. One such example is the Persian Gulf at the beginning of the twentieth century before slaves were emancipated by the British as noted by Lorimer.

The influence of Islam is even more apparent in the domestic arena where some slaves were integrated even into the families of their owners. Cohabitation between slave owners and slaves is a universal phenomenon in slave societies, but according to Islamic law, offspring from such cohabitation is legitimate with equal rights to inheritance with children of free mothers, and the mother cannot thereafter be sold. This was not a rare occurrence but widespread to the extent that many of the Abbasid caliphs as well as sultans in Zanzibar and Oman had slave mothers. According to a recent genetic study, while 35 per cent of Zanzibaris traced the origin of their fathers from across the sea, 98 per cent of their mothers originated from sub-Saharan Africa, and their mother tongue is naturally Kiswahili.

On the other hand, Mauritius experienced slavery in circumstances similar to those in the West Indies at 'the rosy dawn of the capitalist mode of production'. For an island without a people, all labour had to be brought from abroad to establish a servile system from scratch to cut timber and grow food for passing ships, to experiment with cloves, before finally landing on its colonial monoculture of sugar. However, unlike the West Indies, slaves in Mauritius were multi-ethnic, including the Malagasy, those from India, as well as from Mozambique and the Swahili coast, while the slave owners were predominantly white, giving slavery there a distinct racial texture.

More crucial in maintaining the racial character of slavery in Mauritius was the legal and cultural superstructure that hindered the reintegration of society. Cohabitation between slave owners and their female slaves, of course, could not be prevented considering the gross gender imbalance in the planter society. However, Christian morality and monogamy and the prevailing legal system prevented the recognition of the reality of the social process that was going on. Thus, while the planter class struggled to maintain its lily white purity, the pigmentation of their offspring lightened with every generation, but they and their mothers remained slaves, and the racialised class division of the society was frozen to a much greater extent than in Zanzibar.

Both Mauritius and Zanzibar came under British colonial rule, the former in 1810 as a British colony, and the latter in 1890 as a British protectorate. Committed to the abolition of slavery so that capitalist imperialism could mature, Britain pushed for the dissolution of slavery in both islands in comparable steps, but again the underlying cultural differences introduced some contrasting results.

In Mauritius the abolition of slavery was part of an empire-wide movement that involved the payment of compensation to the slave owners of £20 million voted by the British Parliament in 1833, of which £2 million went to the slave-owners of Mauritius to help them make the transition to free labour. Moreover, to help them further make a soft landing, the colonial government introduced a so-called apprenticeship system whereby all slaves were 'apprenticed' to their former owners for the next five years. During this period, they remained in all senses bound to their former owners. Under the apprenticeship system, the apprentices were required to work 45 hours for their employers and, if they performed any type of additional work, they had to be remunerated in cash for their labour. At the same time, they could 'buy' their freedom for a certain amount of money – and as Peerthum shows – many scraped all their resources to buy their own freedom and that of their loved ones. Between February 1835 and March 1839, a total of 4,200 apprentices purchased their freedom with the majority being female apprentices. At the end of the 'apprenticeship', the remaining 53,000 apprentices were finally freed, and a vast majority moved away from the plantations of their former owners, preferring to work on the small plots of their own or those of the free Coloured rather than remain at the site of their former humiliation.

The Mauritian free population of colour partly consisted of non-whites who were local-born and shared a mixed European, African and Indian ancestry. Furthermore, the free Coloured were also composed of African, Indian and Malagasy slaves who had been manumitted or the *vieux affranchis* and of some free Indian and Malagasy immigrants who came to the island between the 1730s and early 1800s. Between 1767 and 1830, apart from a high birth rate and a low death rate among the free Coloured, it was the manumission of the slaves which was one of the major reasons for the rapid growth of the Mauritian free population of colour. During the early 1800s, free Coloured communities gradually emerged in Port Louis, Grand Port, Moka and Plaines Wilhems districts and other parts of Mauritius which were made up mostly free Coloured who were free-born and manumitted slaves. Between 1806 and 1830, they were active in commerce and trade in Port Louis and Grand Port. They saved their money, were able to achieve capital accumulation and purchased and established hundreds of small estates in the island's rural districts. By 1830, the free Coloured controlled one fifth of the island's wealth, owned almost a quarter of the slaves, and more than one-tenth of the island's inventoried arable land.

Between 1829 and 1839, there were more than 7,100 slaves and apprentices, the majority being female slaves and apprentices, who secured their freedom. They took full advantage of the liberal and flexible manumission laws during the amelioration period (1829-1834) and apprenticeship era (1835-1839), and purchased their freedom and that of their loved ones. They did not wait for 1 February 1835, when the slavery was abolished in Mauritius, and 31 March 1839, when the local British colonial government terminated the apprenticeship system. During the 1830s, there were thousands of female slaves and apprentices who wanted to secure their own freedom and that of their loved ones through their own efforts, and did not want freedom from above or for it to be bestowed on them by the British government.

Between the 1810s and 1830s, it was common for free Coloured males to have intimate relationships with slave women who were their companions or concubines and bore them several children. They even purchased the freedom of their enslaved companions, got married to them and legitimised their children. This was considered acceptable in Mauritian colonial society as well as under colonial law. Furthermore, it was a common practice and can clearly be seen in the archival records. However, during the early nineteenth century, this was not the same case when it came to intimate relationships between white colonists and female slaves. After all, it was not allowed under colonial law and frowned upon by the island's conservative slave-owning elite. Most of the time, these relationships were kept hidden from the public view, and the slave-owner did not recognise his slave children or give any rights to his slave concubine. Thus, it was difficult for the freed children to claim any inheritance from their slave-owner father who either did not recognise them or the law did not permit them to inherit anything from him. This practice continued even after December 1829 Royal-Order-in-Council, which otherwise removed the colour bar and outlawed social and legal discriminations against the free Coloured and ex-slaves by the island's white ruling elite.

It is not clear from the archival records that in cases where the slave-owner was manumitting his female slave and her children, if she was the concubine of her owner and the children were his offspring. There were some cases where manumitted slave women were given plots of land, money or even a small house to live in, but it is not clearly stated that she was the concubine or companion of her master. Therefore, most of the time, it can only be inferred and a matter of interpretation when it comes to the available Mauritian archival data.

In the case of Zanzibar, emancipation came in the wake of what has been dubbed 'the shortest war in history' in 1896 when Arab power was finally broken, and the British placed on the throne a pliant sultan who signed the emancipation decree the following year. In the ensuing decade a total of 11,837 slaves were emancipated through the courts, and compensation was paid to the owners amounting to nearly Rs.500,000 (£33,000) which, however, was paid not by the British Treasury as in the case of Mauritius, but out of the Zanzibar revenue – the price of British 'protection'. Cooper points out that 'the average compensation was about what slaves had cost when they were abundant, but was well under their cost in the 1890s and equivalent to less than five months' wages'.[1]

As in Mauritius, the British tried to provide for a smooth transition from slave to semi-free labour by trying to tie the freed slaves to the land to prevent the collapse of the clove economy of their new protectorate. They introduced the 'contract system' under which freed slaves were provided with a plot of about four acres to grow their food crops in return for three or four days' work a week for the former owners for free, reinforced by vagrancy laws if they failed to prove fixed domicile and means of support. This system diverged little from the preceding system of slavery, and 'there was no rush for freedom'.[2] However, such was the shortage of labour that the freed slaves refused to work for free and had to be paid the going wage, but they were obliged to work on their landowner's land first before moving on to other plantations during the clove-picking season, the price for keeping their plots. The number of such annual contracts declined rapidly, and by 1900 the system had been abandoned, to be replaced by the squatter system. However, as the number of freed slaves declined, they were supplemented by fresh free squatters from the mainland.

But the emancipation of these slaves through the courts was only half the story. The other half owes its origin to the persisting influence of Islam which had attached so much importance to emancipating slaves as a pious act. The process appears to have accelerated after the promulgation of the emancipation decree by owners who preferred heavenly rewards in the hereafter rather than accept paltry earthly compensation from the British hand. According to Mrs. Saada Wahab, between April 1897 and December 1901, out of a total of 13,264 slaves emancipated, 3,700 slaves or 28 per cent were emancipated by their owners without going through the British courts and obtaining compensation. A larger number of these slaves were probably domestic slaves who had developed more intimate relationships with their owners, rather than among the plantation slaves.

Even more poignant was the question of the *suria* (secondary slave wives or 'concubines'). They were considered inmates of the Arab Muslim households with the slave mothers occupying a special status, *umm al-walad* (mother of the child), and their children who enjoyed equal rights with their siblings of free mothers. To abolish concubinage was therefore considered direct interference in the social structure of an Arab family. It would have meant throwing the *suria* onto the street and separating her from her children who were her sole source of support. Therefore the emancipation decrees provided that they were to be treated as wives and were not to be freed except on the ground of cruelty, until 1911 when that article of the decree was repealed.[3]

The comparative study of slavery and the transition from it during the nineteenth century in Mauritius and Zanzibar, representing respectively the Atlantic and Indian Ocean tendencies, has thus been very instructive, bringing out similarities as well as differences, tracing the similarities from the hegemony exercised by the capitalist mode of production over both these islands in the Indian Ocean, and the differences from the different cultural environments in which they were reared. Such a nuanced exploration of slavery in the Indian Ocean is likely to be more informative than imposing the Atlantic model across the whole world and all times.

Notes

1.   F. Cooper, *From Slave to Squatters*, 1980, p.73.
2.   L.W. Hollingsworth, *Zanzibar under the Foreign Office 1890-1913*, 1953, p.145.
3.   Hollingsworth, *Zanzibar*, pp.137, 141, 157.

References

Primary Sources: Manuscript Sources

Mauritius National Archives (MNA), Coromandel, Mauritius

B1B/ 'Mauritius: Indian Immigration, Arrivals, Births, Departures and Deaths from 1834 to 1st January 1853, Enclosed in Annual Report of the Immigration Department for 1859.

E 8-10, 12-16, 37-40, 42, 63-84, Enfranchisements for January 1829-January 1835 (33 Volumes).

HA 73, Appendix G, No.163/No.8, Abstract of District Returns of Slaves in Mauritius at the Time of the Emancipation in the Year 1835 in Report of the Immigration Labour Committee in Reports of the Immigrant Labour Committee for 1845.

HA 73/72, Evidence of Mr. Charles Anderson, Protector of Immigrants, December 1844, Port Louis, before the Immigrant Labour Committee of 1844 in *Reports of the Immigrant Labour Committee for 1845.*

HA 73/Appendix B, Answers of Proprietors and Planters to First Series of Queries, No.6, Answers of Mr. Brownrigg, *Report of the Labour Committee of 1844*, 10th November 1838-30th November 1844.

IHA 100 to HA 116, Letters and Reports from the Civil Commissioners and Stipendiary Magistrates from the rural districts to the Colonial Secretary for the period between 1839 and 1845 (16 Volumes).

IB 6, Return of Slaves and Prize Negroes Declared Maroons (1st January 1820-15th December 1826) in Correspondence and Returns Relating to Maroon Branch of the Police Department at Mauritius.

ID 2/No.3, Return of the Numbers of Manumissions effected by Purchase, Bequest, or Otherwise from 1st January 1821 to June 1826.

IE 26, Manumission of Raboude, June 1816.

IE 42 to IE 45, Register of Manumission Acts of Apprentices for the period between February 1835 to December 1836 (4 Volumes).

IF 1 to IF 41 Certificates of Liberation from Apprenticeship for the period between February 1835 to March 1839 (41 Volumes).

KK 28, *Mauritius Census of 1851*.OA 109 (1769), dossier 4, ff 32.

NA 66, The Notarial Records of C.J. Montocchio for the period between 1842 and 1843.

NA 80 to 85 for the period between 1839 and 1851 (6 Volumes).

RA 457, Police Report, 21st-22nd November 1831.

RA 518/315, Letter of Charlotte Gentille, December 1831.

RA 592, Letter of the Chief Medical Officer to the Colonial Secretary, 21st June 1839.

RA 833, Letters and Reports of the Stipendiary Magistrates from the rural districts to the Colonial Secretary for the period between January and December 1845.

RA 1980, Report of the Committee of the General Board of Health on Black Town, March 30th 1869.

RA 2144, Minutes of Proceedings of the General Board of Health July 10th 1873.

RC 27/3173, Transmitting the Report and Observations of Thomas Hugon on the State of the Indians in the Colony (29th July 1839), Enclosed in Letter of T. Hugon to George F. Dick, Colonial Secretary, Mauritius, 29th July 1839.

RD 12 to 16 and RD 19, Letters and Reports from the Special Magistrates for the period between 1837 and 1839 (6 Volumes).

SA 16, Despatch from Lord Goderich to Governor Colville, Downing Street, London, 27th July 1831SD 18/No.57, Despatch from Governor William Nicolay to Lord Glenelg, Mauritius, 4th May, 1839.

SD 18, No.38, Miscellaneous, Despatch from Acting Governor J. Power to Lord John Russell, Mauritius, 22nd June 1840.

SD 18, No.5, Miscellaneous, Governor Lionel Smith to Lord John Russell, Mauritius, 8th August 1840.

SD 19, No.50, Letter of Governor Lionel Smith to Lord John Russell, Mauritius, 28th November 1840.

SD 27/No.5, Governor Sir William Gomm to Lord Stanley, 7th January 1846.

SD 27/No.174, Governor Gomm to Lord Gladstone, Mauritius, 7th September 1846.

SD 28, Report of J. Davidson, Stipendiary Magistrate of Grand Port, to the Right Honourable the Colonial Secretary, Mahebourg, Grand Port, twentieth December 1845, Enclosed in Governor Sir William Gomm's despatch to the Secretary of State for the Colonies, January 1846.

SD 30, Report of the Committee appointed by the Council on the twentieth April for the purpose of drawing up and submitting to the Secretary of State the opinion of the Council with reference to the several suggestions contained in his Lordship's Despatch of the 31st December, 1846, No.73, on the Subject of the Emancipated Population in the Colony, Enclosed in a dispatch from Governor Sir William Gomm to Earl Grey, Mauritius, 12th July 1847.

SD 85, Governor Sir Henry Barkly to Lord Caldwell, Secretary of State for the Colonies, 26th July 1866.

British National Archives, London (Ex-Public Record Office)
PRO: CO 167/16, Report of Dr. Burke to Kelso, 13 July 1813.

PRO: CO 167/16, Dr. Burke to Farquhar, 15 October 1813.

PRO: CO 167/118, Colebrooke and Blair to Lord Howick, 17 December 1828.

PRO/167/226-Letter of Captain Lloyd to John Irving, Mauritius, April 4th 1840.

Zanzibar National Archives (ZNA), Zanzibar, Tanzania
AA12/3, Register of Freed slaves,. Slave Relief Book.

AA 12/4, Reports on Slaves & Slave Owners in Pemba & MombasaAB71/1,The Slavery Decree No. 11 of 1909.

AB71/1.Colonial Office to Foreign office, January 9, 1910.

AB 71/1, Mr. Sinclair to Edwards Grey, Zanzibar. January 19, 1909.

AB10/116.Surias of the Late Sd. Ali bin Said (i) Ajab bint Abdullah (ii) Sayara bint. Yussuf.

AB 10/ 108, Rosuna bint Tamimu ex- Sultan's Concubine.

AC/8, Vice Consulate Pemba to Consul General of Zanzibar, 3rd August 1903.

AC 1/11, Cave to Landsdowne, 24, 9, 1902.

AC/1/11, Mr. Armitage to Consul Cave, Pemba, August 20, 1902.

AC1/11 Cave to Marquess of Salisbury (Received November) Zanzibar, October 26, 1897.

AC 5/4 Vice Consulate Mr. O' Sullivan to Foreign Office, May 15, 1900.

AC 5/ Vice Consulate Mr. O' Sullivan to Foreign Office, May 15, 1900.

DL/10/12, Mr. Farler to Cave. A slavery Report for 1901, January 1902.

DL/ 10/12, Mr. Cave to the Marquess of Lansdowne, Zanzibar, February 2, 1902.

DL/10/12, Mr Last to General Raikes Zanzibar, February 6, 1902.

DL 10/12. Mr Cave to the Marquess of Lansdowne, Zanzibar, February 21, 1902.

DL/10/12 Colonial office to Foreign Office. Received April 1902.

DL 10/12, Colonial to foreign Office, Zanzibar, Received April 20. 1902.

Printed Primary Sources

Mauritius National Archives

B6, *Report of the Crown Land Commission of 1872 of the Council of Government submitted to Governor Sir Hamilton Gordon on 14th October 1872.*

B6, *Minutes of Evidence of the Crown Land Commission of 1872.*

B1B/Henri Leclezio & Ors., *Précis showing the different phases through which Immigration to Mauritius from the East Indies has passed before it assumed its present form* (1905).

JK1/3, W.E. Frere &V.A.Williamson, *Report of the Royal Commissioners appointed to Inquire into the Treatment of Immigrants in Mauritius* (London, W. Clowes & Sons, 1875).

Newspapers: National Library of Mauritius (NL)

Le Mauricien, 24th April 1839

Le Mauricien, 26th April, 1839

Le Mauricien, 3rd May 1847

Le Mauricien, 10th May 1847

Centre for African Studies, University of Cape Town Libraries (South Africa): British Parliamentary Papers (BPP)

Statement showing the Number of Slaves Emancipated in each year since 1814 to the end of 1826, Enclosure E in Despatch No.3 of Governor Sir Lowry Cole to Lord Viscount Goderich, Mauritius, twentieth October, 1827, BPP, 1828, XXVII.

Observations of the Commissioners of Inquiry upon the proposed Ordinance in Council, for improving of the Slave Population in Mauritius, Enclosure 2 (a) in Despatch No.2 from Commissioners W.M.E. Colebrooke and W. Blair to the Right Honourable William Huskisson, Mauritius, nineteenth May 1828, BPP, 1829, XXV (338).

Return of Enfranchisements confirmed by HE the Governor of Mauritius, between the twentieth June 1828 and the twentieth June 1829, G.A. Barry, Chief Secretary to the Government, Chief Secretary's Office, Port-Louis, 1st July 1829, Enclosure No.2 in the *Report of the Protector and Guardian of Slaves from twentieth March to 24th June 1829*, Enclosed in Despatch No.1, from Sir Charles Colville, to Secretary Sir George Murray, Mauritius, 3rd September 1829, BPP, 1830-1831, XV (262).

Despatch No.1, Governor Sir Lowry Cole to Earl Bathurst, Mauritius, 8th February, 1827, BPP, 1828, XXVII & *Ordinance of His Excellency the Governor in Council, Given at Port Louis, in the Island of Mauritius, 27th January 1827*, & *Proclamation, R.T. Farquhar*, Port-Louis, 30th December 1814, both Enclosed in Despatch No.1, p.275-280 BPP, 1828, XXVII.

Despatch No.2, Secretary W. Huskisson to Governor Sir Lowry Cole, Downing Street, 10th October, 1828, BPP, 1828, XXVII.Despatch No.54, Extract of Despatch from Lowry Cole to Huskisson, Mauritius, seventeenth May 1828, BPP, XXV (333).

Report of the Commissioners of Inquiry, dated 15th December 1828, upon the Finances and Establishments of Mauritius, which relates to the Condition of the Slaves in that Colony, Mauritius, 15th December 1828, No.3, BPP, 1829, XXV (338) British Parliamentary Papers, 1829, XXV (338).

No.4, List of Slaves who have presented their Acts of Enfranchisement to the Protector of Slaves for Registration from the 25th June to the 24th December 1829, inclusive, BPP, 1830-1831, XV (262) No.4.

List of Confirmative Acts of Enfranchisement registered in the Protector' Office between the 24th December 1829 and the 24th June 1830 inclusive, BPP, 1830-1831, XV (262)

Thomas to Colville, Port-Louis, 28th December 1829, *Report of the Protector for the half year ending 24th December 1829*, Enclosed in Despatch No.4, 25th January, 1830, BPP, 1830-1831, XV (262).

Clause 29: Allowing a slave to purchase his freedom invito Domino, *Observations on the Order in Council of the 10th March 1824, with respect to the possibility of its adoption in the Island of Mauritius, the advantages and inconveniences resulting from it, and the means of conciliating its clauses with the Colonial interests, without violence or danger, Extract from the Deliberation of the 31st May 1827*, Enclosed as Appendix I in Despatch No.3, Governor Sir Lowry Cole to the Right Hon. Lord Viscount Goderich, Mauritius, twentieth October, 1827, BPP, 1828, XXVII.

Letter of Charles Anderson, Esq. to Lord John Russell, London, May 1st 1840, BPP, 1840, XXXVII (331).

Report of the Committee appointed to conduct and complete the census of the colony (1846): The Mauritius-Census of 1847, Enclosed in Despatch No.47 from Governor Sir William Gomm to Earl Grey, Mauritius, sixteenth September, 1848, BPP, 1849, XXXVII (280-II)

British Parliamentary Papers (BPP), Zanzibar

BPP. Vice Consul Mr. O' Sullivan to Foreign Office, May 13, 1901. Vol. 81. 1901. BPP.

Vice Consul O' Sullivan to Consul General Zanzibar, Zanzibar October, 26th 1897. Vol. LX, 1898. BPP.

O' Sullivan, Vice Consul Pemba to General Consul, December, 30, 1901. BPP.

O' Sullivan, Vice Consul Pemba. Received at Foreign Office, May, 1901. Vol. 81, 1901, BPP.

O' Sullivan, Vice Consul Pemba to General Consul. 30 December, 1901. BPP.

O' Sullivan, Vice Consul Pemba to General Consul. September 30, 1897. BBP.

Contemporary Sources and Accounts

Backhouse, James, 1844, *Narrative of a Visit to Mauritius and South Africa,* London: Hamilton Adams & Co.

'A Letter to Thomas Fowell Buxton, on the State of the Population of the Mauritius by James Backhouse, to which is appended a Letter from Edward Baker on the Apprenticeship System, Port Louis, May 1838', in *Extracts from the Letters of James Backhouse when Engaged in a Religious Visit on the Island of Mauritius: Sixth Part,* London:Harvey & Darton Press, 1839.

Baker, Edward, 1839, Observations on the Apprenticeship System in Mauritius, in Appendix to *Letters of James Backhouse when engaged in a Religious Visit on the island of Mauritius, Sixth Part,* London: Harvey & Darton.

Battie, Jean de la, 1842, Rapport sur les résultats de l'émancipation à Maurice, in *Abolition de l'esclavage dans les colonies britanniques: Rapports recueillis par le département de la marine et les colonies, Tome II,* Paris : Imprimerie Royal.

Beaton, Patrick, 1971, *Creoles and Coolies, or, Five Years in Mauritius* (Washington, New York, Kennikat Press, Reprint of the book which was first published in 1859.

Bernard, Eugene, 1890, 'Les Africains de L'Ile Maurice: Essai sur les Nouveaux Affranchis de l'Ile Maurice' in *Archives Coloniales, Vol II,* Port-Louis : Imprimerie de Maurice (Reprint).

Bolton, W. Draper, 1851, *Bolton's Mauritius Almanac & Official Directory for 1851,* Mauritius.

Douglass, Frederick, 1844/1955, *The Education of Frederick Douglass: Extract from Narrative of the Life of Frederick Douglass, an American Slave,* London, England: Clays Ltd/Penguin Books Ltd, 1995, Reprint of a section from the book which was first published in 1844.

Secondary Sources

Books

Allen, Richard B., 1999, *Slaves, Freedmen, and Indentured Laborers in Colonial Mauritius,* Cambridge, USA: Cambridge University Press.

Al-Maamiry, A. H., 1988, *Omani Sultans in Zanzibar 1832-1964,* New Delhi: S. Kumar.

Aptheker, Herbert., 1974), *American Negro Slave Revolts: Nat Turner, Denmark Vesey, Gabriel, and Others,* New York: International Publishers, Reprint of the 1943 Original Edition.

Ayany, S.G., 1983, *A History of Zanzibar: A Study in Constitutional Development 1934-1964,* Nairobi: Kenya Literature Bureau.

Bank, Andrew, 1991, *The Decline of Urban Slavery at the Cape, 1806 to 1843* (Cape Town: Centre for African Studies, University of Cape Town, Communications, No. 22

Barker, A J., 1996, *Slavery and Antislavery in Mauritius, 1810-33, The Conflict between Economic Expansion and Humanitarian Reform under British Rule,* London: MacMillan Press Ltd.

Barnwell, P.J., 1948, *Visits and Despatches (Mauritius 1598-1948)*, Port-Louis, Standard Printing.

Barnwell, P.J. and Toussaint, A., 1949, *A Short History of Mauritius (1598-1948)*, London: Longman Green & Co.

Bennett, N. R., 1978, *A History of the Arab State of Zanzibar*, Great Britain: Methuen and Co. Ltd.

Boswell, R., 2006, *Le Malaise Créole: Ethnic Identity in Mauritius*, Berghahn Books.

Campbell, G., ed., 2003, *The Structure of Slavery in Indian Ocean Africa and Asia, Studies in Slave and Post-Slave Societies and Cultures Series*, London: Routledge.

Campbell, G., ed.,2005, (co-ed. with Edward Alpers and Michael Salman), *Slavery, Forced Labour and Resistance in Indian Ocean Africa and Asia*. (London: Routledge.

Campbell, G., ed.,2005, ed., *Abolition and Its Aftermath in the Indian Ocean Africa and Asia*. Studies in Slave and Post-Slave Societies and Cultures Series, London: Routledge.

Campbell, G., ed.,2006, (co-ed. with Edward A. Alpers and Michael Salman), *Resisting Bondage in Indian Ocean Africa and Asia*, London: Routledge.

Campbell, G., ed.,2008, (co-ed.with Suzanne Miers and Joseph Miller), *Women in Slavery. Vol.1: Africa, the Indian Ocean World, and the Medieval North Atlantic*. Slave and Post-Slave Societies and Cultures Series, 2 vols, Athens, OH: Ohio University Press

Campbell, G., ed., 2007; (co-ed. with Suzanne Miers and Joseph Miller), *Women in Slavery*, 2 vols, Athens, OH: Ohio University Press.

Campbell, G., ed.,2009, (co-ed. with Suzanne Miers and Joseph Miller), *Children in Slavery through the Ages*, Athens, OH: Ohio University Press.

Cangy, J.C., Chan Low, J; Paroomal, M., 2002), *L'esclavage et ses séquelles: mémoire et vécu d'hier et d'aujourd'hui*, Actes du Colloque International, Municipalité de Port-Louis.

Carpooran, A., 2005, 'Le Creole a l'école a Maurice: historique et évolution du débat', Paris : L'Harmattan 1978 ; *Diksioner morisien* (Editions Bartholdi).

Carter, Marina, & d'Unienville, Raymond, 2002, *Shackling the Slaves: Liberation and Adaptation of Ex-Apprentices*, Pink Pigeon Press: London.

Clarence-Smith, W. G., ed., 1989, *The Economics of the Indian Ocean Slave Trade in the Nineteenth Century*, London: Cass.

Cooper, F., 1977, *Plantation Slavery on the East Coast of Africa*, New Haven: Yale. 1980, *From Slave to Squatters: The Plantation Labour and Agricultural in Zanzibar and Coastal Kenya 1890- 1925*, London: Yale University Press.

Cooper, F, Holt, T, and Scott, R., 2000, *Beyond Slavery: Explorations of Race, Labor, and Citizenship in Post emancipation Societies*, Chapel Hill: University of North Carolina Press.

Coupland, R., 1938, *East Africa and Its Invaders*, Oxford: Clarendon Press.

Crone, O., 1986, *Mecca Trade and the Rise of Islam*, Princeton: Princeton University Press.

Craton, Michael, 1982, *Testing the Chains: Resistance to Slavery in the British West Indies*, Ithaca, New York, Cornell University Press.

Curtin, P., 1969, *The Atlantic Slave Trade: A Census*, Madison, Wisconsin: University of Wisconsin Press.

E. van Donzel (Ed.) (Sayyida Salme /Emily Ruete), An *Arabian Princess Between Two Worlds*, (Leiden: Brill, 1993).

Draper, N., 2011, *The Price of Emancipation,* CUP.

Filliot, J.M. ,1974, *La traite des esclaves vers les Mascareignes au XVIIIème siècle,* Paris.

Foner, E., 1983, *Nothing But Freedom,* Baton Rouge: Louisiana University Press.

Fredrickson, G., 2000, *The comparative imagination: on the History of Racism, Nationalism, and Social Movements,* University of California Press.

Freeman-Grenville, G.S.P., 1965, *The French at Kilwa Island,* Clarendon Press,

Gordon, M., 1989, *Slavery in the Arab World,* New Amsterdam Books: New York, NY.

Haudrère, P and Le Bouëdec, G., 2001, *Les Compagnies des Indes,* Collection Ouest-France.

Hazareesingh, K., 1970, *History of Indians in Mauritius,* Revised Edition, London.

Herskovits, M., 1941, *The Myth of the Negro Past,* New York.

Hollingsworth L.W., 1953, *Zanzibar under the Foreign Office 1890-1913,* London: Macmillan & Co. Ltd.

Jackson-Haight, M., 1942, *European Powers and South-East Africa., 1796-1856,* London.

James, C.L.R., 1937, *The Black Jacobins: Toussaint L'Ouverture and the San Domingo Revolution,* London.

Kuczynski, R R., 1948-1949, *Demographic Survey of the British Colonial Empire, Vol 2, Part 4: Mauritius and Seychelles,* Oxford: Oxford University Press.

Larson, P.M., 2000, *History and memory in the age of enslavement: Becoming Merina in highland Madagascar, 1770-1822,* Heinemann.

Larson, P.M., 2009, *Ratsitatanina's gift: a tale of Malagasy ancestors and language in Mauritius,* Centre for Research on Slavery and Indenture, University of Mauritius.

Lewis, B., 1974, *Islam,* New York: Harper & Row, 2 vols 1990, *Race and Slavery in the Middle East,* Oxford: OUP.

Lodhi, A.Y.,1973, *Institution of Slavery in Zanzibar and Pemba (*Research Report No. 16.Uppsala; Scandinavian Institute of African Studies).

Lovejoy, P., 1983, *Transformations in Slavery,* Cambridge: CUP.

Maghaniyyah M. J., 1997, *Marriage: According to Five Schools of Islamic Law. Vol. V* (Tehran; Department of Translation and Publication Islamic Culture and Relations Organisation). 2011, *Mauritius Truth and Justice Commission Report,* Government Printing. Vols 1-6.

Miers, S. and Kopytoff, I. eds, *Slavery in Africa: Historical and Anthropological Perspectives,* Madison, University of Wisconsin.

Marx, K. *Capital, Vol III,* 1971, Moscow: Progress Publishers.

Mbotela, J., 1966, *Uhuru wa Watumwa,* London Nelson.

Nagapen, A., 1999, *Le marronnage à l'Isle de France-lle Maurice: rêve ou riposte de l'esclave?,* Port Louis, Mauritius, Centre Nelson Mandela pour la Culture Africaine.

Noël, K., 1953, *L'esclavage à l'Île de France pendant l'occupation française, 1715-1810,* Paris.

Northrup, D., 1995, *Indentured Labour in the Age of Imperialism, 1834-1922,* Cambridge, New York and Melbourne.

Nwulia, M. E., 1981, *The History of Slavery in Mauritius and the Seychelles, 1810-1875,* Farleigh Dickinson, New Jersey, Farleigh Dickinson Press.

Palmyre, D., 2007, *Culture créole et foi chrétienne,* Marye Pike.

Patterson, O., 1982, *Slavery and Social Death: A Comparative Study* (Cambridge, Harvard University Press.

Ly Tio Fane Pineo, H., 1984, *Lured Away: The Life History of Cane Workers in Mauritius*, MGI Press, MGI, Moka.

Prasad, K. K. & Angenot, J-P., 2008, *The African Diaspora in Asia*, Bangalore: Jana Jagrati Prakashana.

Popovic, A., 1999, *The Revolt of African Slaves in Iraq in the 3rd/9th Century*,Princeton: Marcus Wiener.

Romaine, A., 2003, *Religion populaire et pastorale créole à l'île Maurice*, Karthala Editions.

Scarano, F,, 1984, *Sugar and Slavery in Puerto Rico*.

Scarr, Deryck, 1998, *Slaving and Slavery in the Indian Ocean*, London: MacMillan Press.

Selvon, Sydney, 2001, *History of Mauritius: A Comprehensive History of Mauritius*, Mauritius Printing Specialists Ltd, Port Louis, Mauritius.

Shao, I., 1992, *The Political Economy of Zanzibar: Before and After Revolution* (Dar-es-Salaam: Dar- es- Salaam University Press.

Shell, Robert, 1994, *Children of Bondage: A Social History of the Slave Society at the Cape of Good Hope, 1652-1838* (Johannesburg, Witwatersrand University Press.

Sheriff, A., 1987, *Slaves, Spice and Ivory in Zanzibar: Integration of an East African Commercial Empire into the World Economy, 1770-1873*, London: James Currey.

Teelock, V., 1998, *Bitter Sugar – Sugar and slavery in nineteenth century Mauritius*, Moka: MGI.

Teelock, V.,1995, *A select guide to sources on slavery in Mauritius*, Bell Village, Mauritius.

Teelock, V., & Alpers E., eds, 2000, *History, memory and identity*, (NMCAC,

Teelock, V., & Alpers E., eds, 2006, *Mauritian History: from its Beginnings to Modern Times, Mahatma Gandhi Institute* (2nd edition).

Teelock, V. & Deerpalsingh, S. et al, 2001, *Labour Immigrants in Nineteenth Century Mauritius: A Pictorial Recollection*, MGI Press, Moka, Mauritius.

Tinker, H. . 1974, *A New System of Slavery: The Export of Indian Labour Overseas, 1830-1920*, Oxford University Press/Institute of Race Relations, Great Britain.

Vaughan, M., 2005, *Creating The Creole Island: Slavery In Eighteenth-century Mauritius* Duke University Press.

Walvin, J., 2001, *Black Ivory: Slavery in the British Empire*, Blackwell Publishers.

Williams, E., 1964, *Capitalism and Slavery*, London: Andre Deutsch Limited.

Chapters in Books, Journal Articles & Conference Papers

Akinola, G. A., 1972, 'Slavery and Slave Revolts in the Sultanate of Zanzibar in the nineteenth Century', *Journal of the History of Social Sciences of Nigeria*, VI/1

Allen, R.B., 1989, 'Economic Marginality and the Rise of the Free Population of Colour in Mauritius, 1767-1835' *Slavery and Abolition*, 10, 2.

Allen, R.B., 2001, 'Licentious and Unbridled Proceedings: The Illegal Slave Trade to Mauritius and the Seychelles during the early Nineteenth Century',*Journal of African History*, 42.

Allen, R.B., 2008, 'The constant demand of the French : the Mascarene slave trade and the worlds of the Indian Ocean and Atlantic during the eighteenth and nineteenth centuries', *Journal of African History*, 49(1).

Allen, R.B., 2010, 'Satisfying the "Want for Labouring People": European Slave Trading in the Indian Ocean, 1500–1850', *Journal of World History*, vol. 21, no. 1.

Alpers, E., 2003, 'Recollecting Africa: Diasporic Memory in the Indian Ocean world', in S. Jayasuriya, and R. Pankhurst, *The African diaspora in the Indian Ocean.*

Arafat, W., 1966, 'The attitude of Islam to slavery', *Islamic Quarterly* 10/1966.

Asgarally, I. ,1980, *L'Affaire Ratsitatane*, (Ed. Goutte d'eau dans l'océan

Austen, R. A. 'The Islamic slave trade out of Africa (Red Sea and Indian Ocean): an effort at quantification', paper presented at the Conference on Islamic Africa: Slavery and related institutions, Princeton.

Austen, R. A., 1979, 'The trans-Saharan slave trade: a tentative census', in H. A. Gemery & J. S. Hogendorn, eds, *The Uncommon Market: Essays in the Economic History of the Atlantic Slave Trade,* New York: Academic Press.

Austen, R. A., 1989, 'The nineteenth century Islamic Slave Trade from East Africa (Swahili and Red Sea Coasts): a tentative census', in Clarence-Smith, (ed.) *Indian Ocean Slave Trade,* 1989, pp. 21-44.

Bowser, F. P. ,1975, 'The Free Person of Color in Mexico City and Lima: Manumission and Opportunity, 1580-1650' in Stanley L. Engerman and Eugene D. Genovese, eds, *Race and Slavery in the Western Hemisphere: Quantitative Studies* (Stanford, California, Center for Advanced Study in the Behavioral Sciences.

Carter, M., 1998, 'Founding an Island Society: Inter-Ethnic Relationships in the Isle de France', in Marina Carter, ed, *Colouring the Rainbow: Mauritian Society in the Making* (Port Louis, Mauritius, Alfran Co. Ltd.

Chan Low, J., 2000,'Aux origines du malaise créole: Les ex-apprentis dans la société mauricienne (1839-1860)', in E. Maestri (dir.), *Esclavage et abolitions dans l'Océan Indien*, Paris, L'Harmattan ; Saint-Denis, Université de La Réunion : 2000.

Chan Low, J., 2002, 'Les ex-apprentis dans la société colonial: le recensement de 1846' in *Revi Kiltir Kreol*, No.1, February 2002 (Nelson Mandela Centre for African Culture, Port Louis.

Chan Low, J., 2004, 'Les enjeux actuels des débats sur la mémoire et la réparation pour l'esclavage à l'île Maurice', *Cahiers d'études Africaines*, 2004/1 n° 173-174.

Cohen, D. and Greene, J., 1972, 'Introduction', in W. Cohen, David and P. Greene, *Neither Slave Nor Free: The Freedman of African Descent in the Slave Societies of the New World,* Baltimore, John Hopkins University Press.

Freund, W., 2000, 'Introduction', in M.D North Coombes, Compiled and Edited by W. M Freund, *Studies in the Political Economy of Mauritius* (Moka, Mauritius, Mahatma Gandhi Press.

Gerbeau, H., 1979, 'The slave trade in the Indian Ocean: problem facing the historian and research to be undertaken', in Unesco, *The African Slave Trade,* Paris: Unesco.

'L'Océan Indien n'est pas L'Atlantique. La Traite illégale à Bourbon au XIXe siècle.' Un article publié dans *Outre-mer,* No 336-337, Décembre 2002, Paris, p. 79-108 par Olivier Pétré-Grenouilleau, pp.1-282).

Green, W., 1984, 'The Perils of Comparative History: Belize and the British Sugar Colonies after Slavery', *Comparative Studies in Society and History* Vol. 26, No. 1 (Jan., 1984), pp. 112-119.

Guérout, M., 2006, Le navire négrier 'Utile' et la traite Française aux Mascarignes', *Cahiers des Annales de la Mémoire*, no. 9, Nantes

Hunwick, J. O., 1992, 'Black Slaves in the Mediterranean world', in E. Savage, ed. *The Human Commodity,* London: Cass.

Klein, M. ,2007, 'Sex, Power and Family Life in the Harem; A Comparative study', in Gwyn Campbell, et al., ed., *Women and Slavery: Africa, the Indian Ocean World, and the Medieval North Atlantic,* Athens: Ohio University Press.

Lorimer, J.G. *Gazeteer of the Persian Gulf, Oman and Central Arabia, Calcutta, 1908-15*

Mason, J. E.,1995, 'Social Death and Resurrection: Conversion, Resistance, and the Ambiguities of Islam in Bahia and the Cape', Seminar Paper presented at the University of the Witwatersrand Institute for Advanced Social Research, 14th August.

Mazrui, A. A., 1997, 'Comparative slavery in Islam, Africa and the West', unpublished paper presented at the Conference on IslamicThought, Istanbul, 1997.

North-Coombes, M.D., 2000, 'From Slavery to Indenture: Forced Labour in the Political Economy of Mauritius, 1834-1867', in M.D. North-Coombes, Compiled and Edited by W. M Freund, *Studies in the Political Economy of Mauritius,* Moka, Mauritius, Mahatma Gandhi Press.

Peerthum, Satteeanund., 1989, 'Resistance against slavery', in Bissoondoyal, U & Servansing, SBC, eds, *Slavery in South West Indian Ocean* (Moka, Mauritius, MGI Press, 1999, 'Obsessed with Freedom', Paper presented at the 'Conference Commemorating the 160th Anniversary of the End of Apprenticeship, Post-Emancipation Mauritius, 1839-1911', at the Mahatma Gandhi Institute, 23-26 June, 1999, Moka, Mauritius.

Peerthum, Satteeanund., 2001, 'Napoleon Savy: Protecteur inofficiel des immigrants indiens', Unpublished research paper.

Peerthum, Satyendra, 2005, 'Forbidden freedom: Prison Life for Captured Maroons in Colonial Mauritius, 1766-1839', in E.K G. Agorsah, & T. Childs, *Africa and the African diaspora: cultural adaptation and resistance.*

Peerthum, Satteeanund., 2010, '"Forging an Identity of their Own": The Social and Economic Relations Between the Free Coloureds, Slaves, Maroons, Apprentices, Ex-Apprentices and Indentured Labourers in Early British Mauritius, c.1811-1844', Unpublished paper presented at the Mauritius 1810 International Conference in October 2010 in Port Louis, Mauritius.

Ly-Tio-Fane Pineo, H., 1989, 'Food Production and Plantation Economy of Mauritius', in U. Bissoondoyal & S.Servansingh, eds, *Slavery in the South West Indian Ocean* Moka, Mauritius, MGI Press.

Reddi, S.J. 'Aspects of Slavery during British Administration', in U. Bissoondoyal & S. Servansingh, eds, *Slavery in the South West Indian Ocean,* Moka, Mauritius, MGI Press, 1989.

Reddi, S.J., 1984, 'The Establishment of the Indian Indenture System, 1834-1842', in Bissoondoyal, ed., *Indians Overseas: The Mauritian Experience* (Moka, Mauritius, MGI Press, 1984)

Romero, P. ,1980, 'Where have all the Slaves Gone? Emancipation and Post Emancipation in Lamu, Kenya' *Journal of African History.* 27(1980).

Saunders, Christopher, 1994, '"Free Yet Slaves": Prize Negroes at the Cape Revisited', in Nigel Worden and Clifton Crais, eds, *Breaking the Chains: Slavery and its Legacy in the Nineteenth Century Cape Colony,* Johannesburg, Witwatersrand University Press, 1994.

Scott, R., 1987, 'Comparing Emancipations', *Journal of Social History,* 20 (Spring)

Sheriff, A.,1989, 'Localization and Social Composition of the East Africa Slave Trade, 1858- 1873', in William Gervase Clarence Smith, ed, *The Economics of the Indian Ocean Slave Trade in the Nineteenth Century,* London: Frank Cass.

Sheriff, A. '*Suria*: Concubine or Secondary Slave Wife? The case of Zanzibar in the nineteenth century', in Gwyn Campbell & Elizabeth Elbourne, eds., *Concubinage, Law, and the Family*, (Athens: Ohio University Press), 2014, pp. 99-120..

Southey, Nicolas, 1989, 'The Historiography of Cape Slavery: Some Reactions', Presented at Cape Slavery and After Conference, 10-11 August.

Teelock, Vijaya, 1990, 'Breaking the Wall of Silence: The History of Afro-Malagasy Mauritians in the Nineteenth Century', *Journal of Mauritian Studies*, 3, 2 (1990).

Vernet, T., 2010, 'La première traite française à Zanzibar : le journal de bord du vaisseau l'Espérance, 1774-1775', in Ramamonjisoa, S.N.L; Radimilahy, C. and Rajaonarimanana, N. et al (dir.), *Civilisations des mondes insulaires (Madagascar, canal de Mozambique, Mascareignes, Polynésie, Guyanes)*, (Paris, Karthala : 2010).

Villiers, P., 1998, 'Les établissements français et les débuts de la station navale française sur les côtes occidentales d'Afrique de 1755 à 1792' in *A la découverte de l'Afrique noire par les marins français (XVᵉ - XIXᵉ siècle), Rochefort et la mer*, Vol 12, Publications à l'Université Francophone d'Eté–Jonzac,1998.

Worden, N., 1992, 'Diverging histories: slavery and its aftermath in the Cape Colony and Mauritius', *South African Historical Journal*, 27 (1992).

Worden, N., 1994, 'Slavery and Emancipation in Mauritius and at the Cape: Towards a Regional Comparative Study', Paper presented at the Mahatma Gandhi Institute, 'Seminar on the Concept of Mauritian Studies', 27ᵗʰ-31ˢᵗ August 1994, Moka, Mauritius.

Worden, N., 1994, 'Between Slavery and Freedom: The Apprenticeship Period, 1834 to 1838', in Nigel Worden and Clifton Crais, eds, *Breaking the Chains: Slavery and its Legacy in the Nineteenth Century Cape Colony*, Johannesburg, Witwatersrand University Press, 1994.

Zimba, B. *The slave trade to Mauritius and the Mascarenes 1780s to the 1870s*, Truth and Justice Commission Report, Vol 4: Part VI Slave trade and Slavery.

Unpublished Dissertations

Allen, Richard B., 1983, 'Creoles, Indians Immigrants, and the Restructuring of Society and Economy in Mauritius, 1767-1885', Ph.D. thesis, University of Illinois, 1983.

Bundhooa, Karishma, 2010, 'Female Apprentices in Mauritius, 1835-1839' B.A Hons thesis, University of Mauritius, March 2010.

Gueyraud, Pierre, 1985, 'The Integration of the Ex-Apprentices into Mauritian Society, 1839-1860', M.A thesis, University of Sorbonne, Paris, 1985.

Howell, Brenda, 1950, 'Mauritius, 1832-1849: A Study of a Sugar Colony', Vols I & II Ph.D thesis, University of London, 1950.

Jumeer, Muslim, 1979, 'Les affranchissements et les libres à l'île de France à la fin de l'ancien régime (1768-1789)', MA thesis, Faculté des Sciences Humaines, Université de Poitiers, 1979.

Jumeer, M., 1981, 'Les Affranchis et les Indiens libres à l'île de France (1721-1803)' (Thèse de Doctorat de 3ème cycle. Université de Poitiers, 1981).

Mason, John E., 1992, '"Fit for Freedom": The Slaves, Slavery, and Emancipation in the Cape Colony, South Africa, 1806 to 1842' (Ph. D thesis, Yale University, 1992).

North-Coombes, M. D., 1978, 'Labour Problems in the Sugar Industry of Ile de France or Mauritius, 1790-1842', (M.A thesis, University of Cape Town, 1978).

Peerthum, Satyendra, 'Determined to be Free: A Comparative Study of Manumission, the Slaves and the Free Coloureds in the Slave Societies of Mauritius, the Cape

Colony and Jamaica, 1767-1848' (B.A (Hons) thesis, Historical Studies Department, University of Cape Town, South Africa).

Teelock, Vijaya, 'Bitter Sugar: Slavery and Emancipation in nineteenth Century Mauritius' (Ph.D. thesis, University of London, 1994).

Wahab, Saada, 1994, 'Nationalization and Re-Distribution of Land in Zanzibar: The Case Study of Western District, 1965-2008', M.A Thesis; University of Dar-es-Salaam, Tanzania, 2010.

On-line Sources

BBC Religion, Slavery in Islam. http://www.bbc.co.uk/religion/religions/islam/history/slavery_1.shtml

Yussuf Ali Trns. AL- Baqra http://www.harunyahya.com/Quran_translation/Quran_translation_index.php

Question and Answer in Islamic forum. http://www.Islamicforum.com

See Volume 4 of the Truth and Justice Commission Report, http.www. gov.mu/portal/pmosite

See the website of the Legacies of British Slave Ownership at http://www.ucl.ac.uk/lbs and proceedings of the Neale Colloquium in British History 2012: Emancipation, Slave-ownership and the Remaking of the British Imperial World, 30-31 March 2012.

Saugera, Eric. '*La traite des noirs en trente questions.*' Document downloaded from, http://hgc.ac-creteil.fr. Editions Geste. 2003. (75,030 words)

Printed in the United States
By Bookmasters